Philosophers Lead Sheltered Lives

By James K. Feibleman

DEATH OF THE GOD IN MEXICO
CHRISTIANITY, COMMUNISM AND THE IDEAL SOCIETY
IN PRAISE OF COMEDY
POSITIVE DEMOCRACY
THE MARGITIST
THE THEORY OF HUMAN CULTURE
JOURNEY TO THE COASTAL MARSH
THE REVIVAL OF REALISM
INTRODUCTION TO PEIRCE'S PHILOSOPHY
THE LONG HABIT
AESTHETICS

Co-Author of

SCIENCE AND THE SPIRIT OF MAN
THE UNLIMITED COMMUNITY
WHAT SCIENCE REALLY MEANS

JAMES K. FEIBLEMAN

Graduate Professor of Philosophy in the Tactim University
of Louisiana

Philosophers Lead Sheltered Lives

A FIRST VOLUME
OF MEMOIRS

London
GEORGE ALLEN & UNWIN LTD
RUSKIN HOUSE MUSEUM STREET

FIRST PUBLISHED IN 1952

PRINTED IN GREAT BRITAIN
in 12-point Garamond type
BY THE BLACKFRIARS PRESS LIMITED
SMITH-DORRIEN ROAD, LEICESTER

CONTENTS

*

CHAPTER ONE

To Answer a Simple Question

*

WHY write a book about myself? Believing as I do that concentration on the self is evil, how does it happen that when I am neither famous nor old, I should want to set down my personal story? There is a considerable logical distance between a man and his achievement; although he was originally responsible for what he has done, he is not so always; the achievement may merit survival and thus tends to lead a life of its own. A man's work should not be interpreted in terms of his life but rather his life in terms of his work. It is precisely this orientation which leads me to write my memoirs. I am convinced that my story contains a fable which needs telling. Briefly it is this. The existence and expression of philosophy is native to human beings, and to the world in which they live, so that in a country in which philosophy has never been assiduously pursued nor highly regarded, it yet tends to spring up of its own accord, out of the necessity for it hidden in ordinary occurrences.

Mine, then, is not entirely a personal story. It is a story about some events in the world which I can best explain by telling how I felt their effect or how I first heard about them. My life is not important; I am simply the only one I know so well. That is why I intend to make use of myself as a coign of vantage, as occupying momentarily a perspective, giving on certain aspects of the world which might otherwise be overlooked. These aspects are infinite aspects, and some of us always come along to occupy that kind of perspective even though each of us is uniquely dated. For instance, I was born into the middle of the first decade of the twentieth century in the United States, evidently, as I have since discovered, in order to seek an answer to the question which the English philosopher, Whitehead, has framed so simply, 'What is it all about?'

[1]

Let us be clear about one point. What I have experienced I have not created. I am in no way responsible for the existence of the things of which I have knowledge. Too many people confuse the world in which they live with themselves. But the world, I am humble enough to suppose, has its being quite independently of any preference of mine, a condition which might be inferred from the difference between what I should like to see happen and some of the things that go on.

What I am trying to say chiefly is that I do not deserve the credit for the account which I may happen to possess and endeavour in this place to transmit. I am writing not for credit but for the record. The writing concerns events that have happened to me or that I know do happen. That is why I intend to include some of my thoughts along with external and visible occasions ; for thoughts exert a powerful kind of compulsion upon thinkers, and come to us from outside just as much as do physical events. They are real experiences and must be reported, especially when, like physical events, they have some special illustrative value.

My object, therefore, will be to show through my own experience, to demonstrate with a few details from my own specific adventures, how by the logic of ordinary events I was brought to the recognition of the prime importance of philosophy. This book is in no sense a plain autobiography. In so far as I speak about myself, it is with an ulterior motive. For I have no proper place in these pages, and if I enter them at all it is only in the hope of leading others after me into the magical and fantastic realm of metaphysics.

Perhaps the most important fact of my childhood is that my father owned and operated a department store in New Orleans, which explains my being able later to devote myself to philosophy without, as they say, visible means of support. I was often ill as a child, which accounts for my interest in books for their own sake: what can a sick boy do except read? I read many books, lying on a sofa, usually in a semi-convalescent condition, in a comfortable home where, through prolonged gazing, the ordinary objects, the tables and chairs and lights and door knobs, almost revealed to me their essences; but what through mere reading could I learn about the life and times in which I lived?

A life apart from its ultimate purpose is an old wives' tale and the purpose is hidden from us. The sight of the wooden house on Harmony Street in New Orleans, with its dusty, grey-green coat of paint, the smell of the dirt road in front of the house, the fear of sudden stormy showers, the smell of honey-suckle on a hot night and of magnolia blossoms in the sunlight, the taste of raw acorns, the sympathy of friendship of the little boy across the street and the joy of delight in the little girl around the corner; what are these to anyone else who cannot feel them or to me now? The birth of an only son, the fright-ened mother, the hopeful father, the bearded doctor Czynowski who said gravely, 'He has come to you clean and whole. What happens to him now is your doing', the doctor who believed, then, so firmly in Locke's *tabula rasa* of which he had never heard. Were these real? Then came earliest childhood, dim and remote and later inconsequential; the voices of large authority, mostly forbidding, and the language spoken in the house, that language of adults, strange and condemning, which means absolutely nothing except the utmost boredom, a language which continued for æons, governing getting up and going to bed, drinking milk and eating food and taking medicine and bathing, a language and a set of commands foreign to the joys of life.

I turned away from myself as soon as maturation made this possible; our genuine aims lie in things beyond us, and we serve ourselves best only as instruments toward the gaining of ends.

Let me start back still earlier. My father was a German peasant farmer until the age of sixteen, when with his parents' consent he drove a cow to market and sold it for enough money to pay his passage to America. My mother was born in New Orleans, of the same German-Jewish, peasant-farmer stock. I went to Germany after the first world war, to the little village from which my grandparents had come. There existed records

[3]

going back some five hundred years, including that of a Feibleman (in American English pronounced to rhyme with "seize"
or "receive") who had been a court physician, and other more
or less successful people. But there was also the village tradition
of the young farmer boy who wished to be a poet but had had
the desire crushed out of him.

The Feibleman (or, as it was originally spelled, Feibelmann)
family has been traced back as far as 1250, when the German
Emperor, Sigismund, appointed a Court Jew named Feibelmann to some political council or other. Then there is a gap
until the seventeenth century due to the destruction of records
during the later French invasion. At this time the Feibelmanns
are disclosed making a living at Augsburg as traders and mer-
chants. They had been Germans continuously and they continued to be until the rise of the Nazis.

My own branch of the family stems from a group of farmers
in Ruelzheim, a small village near Mannheim in the Rhineland.
The family name has been traced for me alternately to *Phœbus*,
the sun-god, to *vivus*, the Latin word for living, and to the
Polish first name, *Feivel*, which means, so far as I can discover,
nothing at all. The last derivation is the cause of much distress,
since it is thought by some members of the family that the
Feibelmanns came from Poland; but others vigorously deny
this and give Spain as the point of origin of the German immi-
gration. It is a matter of indifference to me ; they could not
always have lived in Germany and must have come from somewhere. I have no tribal feelings except one of uncomfortable
confinement. I have always loved my father and my mother and
a brother of my father's named Max, who was almost a brother
to me, having been raised with me. I used to like rhyming his
name when I was very young: Max, tacks, backs, sacks, jacks.
But for my other and more distant relatives let me say that they
combine many of the shortcomings of both Germans and Jews.
In the interest of love I am obliged to pass them by.

As for my father and my mother, they have been extraordinarily loving and generous, and I owe everything to them. As
for their only child, well, they are both dead, and now his life

work lies elsewhere. I suppose that is how it has got to be; the stream of generations carries on. Is this what Jesus meant when he said that we should leave our mother and our father and cleave only unto him? Surely he was not recommending the denial of the parent-child relationship which is so precious to us. Yet he understood that somehow tribal loyalties which elevate the immediate family permanently above all other considerations militate against the brotherhood of man. The one who devotes himself solely to his family as to an ultimate end is not moving toward that greater entity which our classic American philosopher has described as the unlimited community. What has got to be saved is not only the immediate blood-relationship but all relations, including those which are more directly connected with the expansiveness of the universe. Mother and father meet again and are loved and even sacrificed for in the cosmic totality; their mission had been in vain should they themselves have become the final objects of it. Despite the failure of my parents to understand the nature of my work, their patience with it has led me to believe that in a fundamental way they comprehended the importance of its aim. That has been of immense assistance.

Certainly in return I have been an adequate son, not lacking in filial devotion. It is not that I have been unloving or disloyal. I simply mean that we must take off from the love of parents to a love of the world. We do not fulfil them if we stop with them. If we do not love our parents, of course we cannot take off to a larger love. If we love only our parents, then we can never take off at all. Hate is restricted to its object and is absolutely satisfied with the death or destruction of that object. Love is unrestricted and cannot be absolutely satisfied. All beloved objects in being loved for themselves also serve as the symbols of a greater love. Love is that which loves nothing concrete terminally but is always in motion toward a greater love.

My father started out in life as a poor man. It was as a poor man that, in 1882, he came to this country. He worked hard, and, as he told me about himself, leaned heavily on the faith of other men. He made enough money for us to live on, and when

[5]

he died I thought that I should never have to labour at anything except what interested me: poetry and philosophy. But the social structure has altered rapidly since that date and now I am not so sure. It is not that I am afraid of manual labour; I rather enjoy it. But in doing it I am left in some doubt as to whether I am doing the best that I can do; and no man can be happy unless he is doing his best.

I was born on July 13th, 1904, in a little frame half-house on Harmony Street in New Orleans. I can discover no singular astronomical occurrence which might be taken as a fitting mark for the occasion, and I have not yet dug back into the newspaper files to get the weather report for that day. I have no earliest recollections, or if I had any they are forgotten now. All that I can report is that the time was nearing the middle of the first decade of the twentieth century and that the place was deep in the southern part of the United States, but I was not to become aware of that until much later.

In a way, the century had more than five years start on me. For in the latter part of 1905 as well as in the years immediately following, I could hardly be said to have known what was going on. And plenty was going on; the western world was building up to a climax and preparing to decline. The greatest reaches of physical science were rapidly being approached. Philosophy, in the person of Whitehead, and history in the person of Toynbee, were getting ready to scale the heights, heights which had not been attained for centuries. Einstein was probably cooking up his discovery of the special and general theories of relativity, and Planck his quantum constant. Two gigantic world wars were being readied. But I was aware of none of these rather large-scale events. My environment was not the actual world but only a tiny part of it, consisting of breasts, cradle, sleep and the fear of being dropped.

I will pass over the unimportant details.

The development of children is a wonderful thing, but not to the developing child. The first experiences of life must be more of a shock than birth. I see them now as I see all primitive things: crude, ugly, full of potentiality, and at the same time a little gruesome. The mind of a child is like the belly of a pregnant woman; moving towards an eventual purpose but large in the meantime, ungainly and awkward in movement. All babies are in a sense monstrosities from which due proportions miraculously emerge: little old men, as yet undeveloped, with large heads and almost no bodies, like figures in the political cartoons. The young man of six months is not a beautiful thing except in terms of what he might become. His virtue is his helplessness, the pity he calls forth, the care he demands. But these, though beautiful, are excessive, and, as it seems to me, all on the side of selfishness. If that kind of development is the only possible one, then that is how it must be, though I cannot conceivably admit that a general satisfaction with the existing state of things is natural or even good for the future-bound human race.

All such speculation of course represents a backward glance from the present. What any baby has actually experienced, even though the baby be ourselves, is for us to know and the psychoanalyst to find out. What I definitely remember is of course my earliest conscious experiences, and these were of death and poetry.

A negro plasterer, working on a house across the street from where we were living, had a sunstroke and fell from his ladder. When they reached him he was dead. I had been playing alone in the yard and I had not seen him fall, but I did see his dead body. It was limp, and the face bore unmistakable signs of a secretly amused expression. The whole affair had been quite easy and noiseless. I did not understand the wailing of the relatives when they arrived on the scene, or the wailing of the siren on the ambulance which had been sent for in vain. The noises were frightening and the grief and despair of the women of the dead man sickened me. What had been so horrible? Nothing except their own loss, which could have meant nothing to him for he was dead.

From that day I was worried about the fact of death and what it held for me, since my parents appeared then to be ageless. From that day I can date my doubt. I had acquired good, reason, I thought, to question everything. I wanted to know however, only what appeared as ultimate questions. I had no interest in mechanics and did not care to learn what was under the hood of the Chalmers, the first automobile that my father purchased. But I did care about anything that seemed to be closely related to the final problem of what existence itself could mean. I questioned the earth on which I stood, the sky that lay over my head, the house in which I lived, the business upon which my father and uncle were engaged. The answers, and more often the impatience, of the adults in whose care I was placed by chance or design were to me most unsatisfactory. Doubt is only possible where there is reason to doubt, but equally there is belief only where there is reason for that, also. The explanations were too flimsy even for the mind of a child.

Almost as early as the witness of a death came the witness of poetry. Long before answers could be formulated, the meaning of existence suggested itself to me as the fact of rhythm, that heart of time which, rather than time in general, is what Plato must have meant by the moving image of eternity. I had always liked to make up rhymes; and I went from that pastime to the poetry of Shelley and Keats and Shakespeare. The strength of the rhythms was highly attractive but the antique language was distinctly repellent. The true experience of poetry was largely withheld, and I came to suppose that all formal poetry had to be written in an old-fashioned and out-dated language, a dogmatic slumber from which I was soon to be awakened. Poetry meanwhile gave way and came under the ban of scepticism which death had initiated.

Meanwhile, for lack of answers, I thought that I had good reasons for doubting everything fundamental, and my questionings began to take an unhappy subjective turn. The autonomic nervous system was the next victim of the terrific scrutiny which absorbed me day and night. One day, or rather, one night, I became aware of my own breathing. That was a serious challenge: why did I breathe? Theoretically, I knew the answer, but practically I was compelled to investigate. I tried to stop my breathing for a few seconds but soon gave that up. Next I tried irregular breathing, taking first breaths that were too long and then some that were too short. This also proved unsatisfactory. Only my heart-beats for some strange reason were overlooked in a survey that ranged over the whole body. One day, during the long-breath experiments, I became suddenly winded. I fancied that my breaths were beginning to grow shorter and shorter, and, extrapolating this into the immediate future, I could predict an end to my breathing that was not far distant. I told my mother and she called the doctor. He came late in the afternoon and after hearing my complaint casually advised me to continue my breathing. This put an end to the matter. Soon after, he went into the furniture business, which I have always considered a mistake.

It is amazing to think of the number of complex functions which have become automatic for us, amazing and almost a little frightening. Habit relieves consciousness of more than merely physiological functions, although these to be sure are complex enough. Only last year I had a spectacular experience of the way in which the most complicated behaviour patterns could be followed without deliberation or conscious attention of any sort. A mile from my house the main road branches out. One path leads to the business district of New Orleans where I leave my car in a parking garage every day about noon; the other leads to the principal residential section of the city. On this particular occasion, my wife, who is not only my best friend and severest critic but also something of a navigator, was out of town, and I had been invited to dinner by a friend. I had worked late and I left home a few minutes before the dinner hour, still thinking about my work. Suddenly I came to myself with a feeling of strangeness. Where was I? It was seven o'clock and I was on the street in front of the building in which was my office. I had been working at home, and I had evidently dressed, gotten into my car, started off, taken the wrong turn, driven to the business section, parked my car in the garage and walked toward my office, all without being conscious of a single step. Every one of my reactions, including, I suppose, stopping for red lights, and handing over my car to an attendant at the garage, had been conducted solely by the subconscious mind. The whole elaborate set of reactions had become so habitual that it was no longer necessary to think about them in a conscious way. I had to go back to my car and start out all over again; needless to say I was late for dinner. What heights could we not scale were we but able to make all our psychic functions subservient to subconscious habit! We should in that case, I imagine, leave the psychological level altogether for the next higher complexity of value.

Death must remain forever external, but in some curious fashion poetry issues from the subconscious level of the individual; for it is there that the mythological elements of society lurk. I must have been about ten years old when, one day, I was playing hide-and-seek with some friends in our paved back yard. I was, I remember, chasing another boy, when I slipped and fell. My head must have hit pretty hard. I know that I lost consciousness, and when I awoke, a little while later, I did not know the hour, the day, the month or the year. I had to go to the kitchen window to ask the cook. I had not been lying there half so long as I had thought. But, at any rate, since then I have been writing poetry.

It was a long time before poetry occupied more of my attention than thoughts of death. The young child is always preoccupied with the problem of mortality. Children play with more abandon than adults, but they can also be more serious. They play with more abandon because they are care-free; and they can be more serious because they have not yet given up the struggle to solve basic metaphysical problems, as have so many adults. From one aspect, coming of age seems to be merely a matter of deserting final causes for efficient ones. We turn away from our inquiry-into-being because we find ourselves compelled to engage in the struggle-for-existence; and we manage to substitute the manifold details of a daily career for the fundamental questions with which we had formerly wrestled. That is why it is possible to regard the philosopher, the poet, the artist and the pure scientist as men who have remained boys, or as boys who have never grown up. Certain very fortunate persons are able to unite the endless search for

[10]

meaning with some success in worldly affairs. Such a combination is rare and we must regard as a lucky accident the ability to pay grocery bills and taxes out of money made as an inquirer. In youth, at least, the search for reality would appear to be everyone's prerogative, and it takes the usual form of questioning life and death.

How old I was I cannot say, but I distinctly recall the occasion on which I tried to remember back before the time when I was born. I do not know that the effort exactly succeeded, either, but I do know that it was not altogether a failure. I can, or at least could then, think back to a time when I had had no thoughts. The energy and concentration required are immense, and logically they were doomed to failure, for the simple reason that it is not possible to think about nothing. What makes me suspect that I had succeeded a little is the fact that my 'nothing' was not quite nothing. This is very important. The diluting element may have come from a time when I had been in the womb; it may have come from later years read backward; or it may actually have preceded my existence. It is impossible to tell. But even now the retrospect comforts me.

From the period of preoccupation with thoughts of death I can remember two conclusions. I must have been between seven and ten years old. Something had happened: I had been interrupted in my serious thoughts by the trivial considerations of adults, I think it was. I can recall having made a mental note at the time that when I grew to manhood I would bear in mind the perspective of youth and try to have more sympathy for it. Not that my parents were not thoughtful, loving and considerate; they were all of these and more, yet like most adults they lived in a world remote from childhood. Perhaps the problem cannot be solved; but I remember deploring the fact that my parents wished to lead me as easily as possible into their world, which I suppose is called growing up, when what I chiefly wanted, and wanted very badly, was to have them come down and play with me. They never entered my world but always remained in character, as most adults do. I wanted them to

[11]

B

become again as little children. Not one adult, so far as I could discover as a child, was achieving this, and I was absolutely determined to keep always by me the thoughts and outlook of a child, so that when I had children of my own I could share their world.

Of course I never can. What adult is capable of such heroic continuity? I remember the occasion of my resolution; I remember quite clearly the resolve itself; yet where is the result? My son and I live in different worlds as surely as did my father and I. The tie is broken. It seems unfortunate that one condition of existence must succeed another without more constant remainders. Must we alter so much as we move from childhood to adulthood and again from adulthood to old age? What becomes of our feelings? Can we not arrange to be more cumulative in our emotional attitudes, as we are in our rational thoughts, for instance? Evidently not, but it is a pity. Development seems largely to consist in losing something in order to gain something else. We need to retain along with our increasing wisdom the flavour of the actual experience in which it was acquired.

The second childish conclusion which was broken by the interruption of adults was one that concerned the prospect of death. Perhaps I could not then have put my thoughts so clearly to myself as I can now; the actual considerations, however, have been carried over. They have been somewhat rounded and improved in recent years, so that I must offer them not as the pure reflections of a child but rather as the reflections of a child worked over by the rationality of an adult.

Life is an intermission between twin states of infinite non-existence which seem to have more in common with each other than either has with the tiny, half lucid interval which interrupts their continuity. We are tempted to wonder why. Deductions concerning the remote past, or inductions concerning the distant future, would appear to indicate that life is a disturbance in an otherwise orderly state. Let us say that I was dead, or rather unborn, for an indefinitely large number of years before my birth. When I die, it will mean to resume the state of death for another indefinitely large number of years. Between these two prevailing periods there will be an absurdly small period consisting at the most of not more than seventy-five years. Thus existence, so far as we can determine, is an extraordinary exception to the rule of being. The brevity of existence makes it an infinitely precious thing while we have it, perhaps, yet none the less an exception.

The argument leads to contradictory conclusions respecting the attitudes we are required to take toward life and death. The first conclusion is that we ought not to be afraid to die, since death is the return to a state to which we must be more accustomed than we are to the state of life—namely, to the state of being without existence. Why should we fear what must be the normal condition simply because we have fallen into the habit of enjoying ourselves more thoroughly in the abnormal? The second conclusion is that the rarity of existence makes existence immensely valuable and its loss the greatest of disasters. How could we be happy and at the same time willing to lose the precious thing that we have in our possession only once and then for so short a time? From this point of view we should quite naturally be afraid to die, and from the other we should almost welcome the coming of death. Can there be a resolution of this conflict? Rationally, there cannot; and yet the true balance of living consists in feeling the contradictions in a higher sublation of value.

Having been raised in a Christian society and early a friend of the New Testament I have the persistent conviction that everything matters. Surely if in solitude I think the thoughts I ought to think and do the things I ought to do, such faithfulness cannot go unrecorded. There has been abroad a firm prejudice to the effect that after death the books will be balanced and the rewards or perhaps even the punishments handed out. How can we know that this accords with the facts? The prophecy seems to be supported by no recent gains in knowledge. The blankest of blank walls stands between us and the grave, so that, despite the penetration of the sciences, thus far not a hint has come out as to what we might be justified in expecting. We are thrown back upon sheer surmise, surmise which in many cases has been raised to the status of fundamental belief by means of formal and organized religion. We know and accept the metaphysical arguments to prove the existence of God: obviously there is a supreme being, an Independent, in terms of which finite and dependent existence is possible. But this inference does not satisfy our curiosity; it does not answer the questions we ask about theological situations. We wish to know, logically enough, the future status of the human being both in this world and in the next. What is to be the fate of ourselves and our fellows in the brotherhood of man? We can see all too frankly what happens to the human body and we do not find it pleasant. It seems hardly a condition to dwell on. Yet what else is there? The immortality of the soul has been suggested, but this cannot be a conscious affair. The soul could not enjoy or be aware without the benefit of body, and the body is in its moribund state a hopeless mess, doomed before long to disappear altogether. What is the soul to do when left entirely to its own devices, except perhaps *be*? Actual existence is not only a value in itself but a very high one indeed. To give the soul a kind of tenuous existence by analogy to actual materials sounds incredible and dull.

If we cannot explain heaven in terms of the human desire for immortality, at least we can explain the human desire for immortality in terms of the many heavens which have been framed from time to time. Some day I hope to write a serious study of the heavens. It will be a survey of all the heavens that have been accepted by various peoples in various times and places, a kind of comparative mythology of the after-life. It has been observed that most heavens are expected to supply wants that were too little furnished by the life in this world. It may be for this reason that the rich man can never hope to enter into the kingdom of heaven. The heaven of those who have everything that they require on earth can be at best but poorly furnished. It is interesting to speculate upon the heaven of a people which had all its material requirements amply supplied. Let us suppose such a people, living in a wealthy land and with imaginative resources, who had invented tools requisite for developing their materials, so that a peaceful existence had been attained without too much hard work and with an abundance of necessities and even with some luxuries. What kind of heaven would these people imagine was awaiting them? Would it perhaps promise the same kind of life they had known on earth, only without the boredom? Thus far no social groups have ever devised a heaven consisting of a simple extrapolation of the present; heaven always corrects the shortcomings of existence: the evil drops out and only the good remains. If heaven is the same as a perfect world of possibility, then it may be that all peoples are correct in their knowledge of heaven, at least of the part of it that they happen to know.

These thoughts are not the thoughts of youth but a continuation of them. Not death but life is the proper concern of a vital person. We must learn, however, to think finally about life and efficiently about death. We must come to regard death as a limited and proximate affair and life as an unlimited one. In this way the meaning of death will be resolved in that of life, and both will emerge in the affirmation of the compulsion we already possess to live life to its fullest while not being at all afraid of death.

The compulsion of living consists in three basic human drives. Man can do nothing when he is hungry except search for food; the need to assuage hunger is certainly the first and most importunate of the commands he has to obey. Having been fed, he can still do nothing else until he has made arrangements for the satisfaction of his sexual appetite; the desire for sexual union or for children is the second most importunate thing in human life. Most authorities agree concerning the urgency of these drives toward feeding and breeding, but there they stop.

Yet there is a third drive which appears to be equally basic, and this is the drive toward the satisfaction of inquisitiveness. What does it mean, to *be*? Call it what you will: the hunger for significance, for value, for reality, it always appears as the activity of inquiry. As soon as we have taken the precautions necessary to keep ourselves alive (feeding) and to keep the race going (breeding), we are anxious to learn what it is all about and why we are here (inquiring). The first two may be the most importunate but the third is the most important. It is in a sense the justification for the others; we wish to remain alive in order to investigate the problems of living. We are certainly knowledge-seeking animals in a way the lower animals are not.

Among modern American philosophers, Peirce has pointed to the importance of inquiry, and Dewey has striven to show how inquiry creates the world in which we live. Peirce has done the most for our understanding of inquiry, having given a name, 'indagation', to that especially reliable kind of inquiry which consists of the interweaving of theory with fact, of the unity of reason and research as employed by science. It seems to Dewey that there is no world apart from inquiry, but surely this is going too far. Such exaggeration defeats the importance it strove to exhibit. To make any one thing everything is to rob it of the contrast in virtue of which its significance appears. Peirce had considered inquiry a central human activity among other human activities; Dewey elevated it into the creative God. But notwithstanding this absurdity, the fact remains that inquiry is a driving power. The human individual is like an arrow which has been catapulted forward toward the goal of inquiry; he is a moving spirit aimed at the achievement of knowledge, a machine cleverly contrived for the investigation of the nature of things.

With each of the three basic drives I had my agonizing private scruples. On the matter of feeding, for instance, I balked considerably. My extreme thinness was no doubt a function if not a direct result of the fact that food to some extent disgusted me. I did not like to touch dead things: quail, for instance, and little fish; how much worse it seemed to put bits of them into my mouth. Raw meat, or, what was the same to me, half-cooked meat, nauseated me not only when I ate it but even when I watched others do so. To walk through the kitchen while a meal was being prepared meant, for all practical purposes, that there was no use in my sitting down to it in the dining room.

Eventually I came to my senses about this business of feeding, but only after a struggle and a long period of adjustment. My attitude must have been occasioned by delicate health; becoming robust meant also becoming more ordinary about the matter of eating. Later it seemed to me that the vegetarians were the silliest people in the world. To refrain from eating meat in order to avoid the killing of animals is an attitude which ignores the gradations in the scale of life. It has been shown that plants are capable of feeling pain; surely they are alive when we cut them down or dig them up. The hierarchy of organisms evidently demands that some animals shall live on plants, some on other animals and still others on animals and plants. To refuse to fall in with this system by denying the eating of meat is to assume that higher values do not depend upon lower. We may think higher thoughts than a pig does, but we can only do so when our belly is full of pig or of some other form of organic life which may have felt the pain of death only a little less than a pig does.

It is equally silly to have scruples about hunting. There are not a few cases of men who claim that their sensibilities will not permit them to shoot a flying bird yet who will at the same time enjoy a dinner of duck. What is the difference between shooting game and having it shot for one's account? It seems immoral to kill for the sake of killing; there is little defence for the man who shoots more than he and his fellows are planning to eat. But to enjoy killing where there is an end in view which lies beyond killing, such as eating, can hardly be attacked. The nature of existence demands that no organizations shall thrive except at the expense of others. This principle has been seized on occasionally to justify fratricidal warfare. But the brotherhood of man has demands which are still higher. The point is that the killing of fellow human beings is *not* helpful to those who triumph, for man has what other creatures seem to lack:

[17]

a conscience which recognizes the objective validity of the moral law.

On the matter of breeding, also, I had scruples. The desire to engage with a female in the mutual operation of copulation for the purpose of psychic satisfaction or of perpetuating the race may be a necessary function. But that is not the way in which it presents itself to a young man. The young man is only interested in getting in as close physical contact as possible with a young girl. There was a time when the association of procreation with sex seemed to me an unnecessary way of spoiling a beautiful thing. I got over it. But I still feel that while both functions are tremendous events in the lives of people, they are also quite different. It is necessary to separate them. Not all intercourse is for the purpose of procreation; probably only a very small percentage of it is. And, conversely, not all procreation involves the pleasure of intercourse except indirectly.

At the beginning of my life I even had scruples about the business of inquiring. I assumed that the poets had all the wisdom and that wisdom was essentially irrational. From the very first the necessity for learning things in school went against the grain, and even later in life it was always necessary to dissociate topics from memories of academic curriculum in order to render them palatable and to make their retention in memory possible. This may have been the fault of my teachers, of the ideas which were current at that time, or of my own personal shortcomings. Inquiry was to become the chief self-conscious activity of my life. But from the very outset I fought it, and the basic materials for it which in another frame of mind I might have picked up early and easily had to be painfully acquired in later years.

It would be pleasant but untrue to say that I acquired any wisdom at an early age, particularly in my formal education. My mother had an idea that I should go to public school. It was an exceedingly intelligent idea, but, unhappily for my first few days, a painful one, for I was sent there dressed in navy blue knickers and white stockings, and with my hair cut in bangs. I have the picture yet, or rather she had. It was exactly the kind of costume which would insure getting kicked around; and I was. My clothes were nearly the death of me. At first I did not understand; I thought it must be some shortcoming in myself which attracted bullying, but as soon as I learned the real cause I took steps to correct it. I had made a bad start, however, and it took some while to live it down.

Mother was a very understanding woman. She did not want a bully but she definitely did not want a coward, either. A few years later, we moved to a new neighbourhood. Father had been promoted in the department store to the position of junior partner. He had magnificent moustaches which turned down around his mouth. He had a wonderfully clear face and great dignity. He really was a strong, silent man. We had moved because he had bought some ground and had ordered a house of our own to be built on it. In the new neighbourhood I acquired friends, but the old difficulty soon made itself evident. Across the street, in a half house, lived a boy of my own age with whom I played. I must have been about twelve. He became angry with me once and punched me in the chest. It hurt, and I began to cry and ran home to my mother. She was sympathetic until she found out what had happened. Then she gave me a whipping with a hair brush.

'The next time, maybe you will fight your own fights,' she said when it was over.

I had definite reservations about that—until the next time. It was the same boy again and we had gotten into an argument on his front porch which could not have been more than three steps from the ground. He hit me, and I hit him back, thinking mostly about that hair brush. I was surprised to notice how easy the whole thing became. But I had also noticed that I was fighting with my back to the steps. That was certainly a disadvantage, and we sparred around until I could work my way to the door. Then when I had him with *his* back to the steps, I gathered up all my strength and gave one hard jab. The boy went backward down the steps on to the grass. He was not hurt but he was very much surprised. The fighting stopped then and we got to be the best of friends. I liked him and I think he liked me, but it was a new sort of liking for him, based on respect. The entire situation changed and I was pleased with it.

My only other whipping, also administered by my mother, was occasioned by the theft of a nickel. Mother had left it out in the open for just such a test and I had fallen for it. I never took anything more because I had begun to realize the seriousness of my felony. I may add that these whippings were very good ways to emphasize lessons, and that they left no marks on my soul.

New Orleans is not a large city and neither is it a small town. But life in the neighbourhoods was close to what it must be in the small towns. The streets in which my friends and I played had not been paved. There were not many cars, and we ran everywhere chasing each other all day. The summers were the best. It was possible then to wear tennis shoes or to go barefoot. The street was dusty and had a good smell. The most fun was to run after the ice wagon and to steal a ride or eat the chips of ice that lay loose on the floor or fell off the back. The iceman did not seem to mind having us around. At night it was always light enough to continue our games, and we foregathered at the corner for baseball and football, to break street lamps, or simply to have a game of hide-and-go-seek.

We had our own gang, in which I was far from being the strongest member. Everything worked all right when we were together. We could do whatever we wished, from playing games to throwing stones at the large bugs that flew at night around the arc light. But divided we were extremely vulnerable. There were larger and tougher gangs wandering near us, gangs which never attacked other gangs but only engaged isolated members caught wandering at large. It was not very safe to be out night or day very far from base, when these gangs were abroad. This did not happen often, because our particular neighbourhood was somewhat off their beat, but it was something serious to watch out for when it did happen.

Most of the fun at that time was to be had out of doors. Inside life was dull unless Uncle Max was to be found. My father's brother, Max, a bachelor much younger than himself, who had lived in the house with us before I was born, filled a place in my life that might otherwise have been empty. He took me to the country on week-end trips and was probably very bad for me because he would let me do almost everything that I wanted to do, things that my parents would not have even considered seriously. I was taken to the movies at night, allowed to stay up late and eat as little as I wished.

I had never been away from home longer than week-ends until I was sent to a boys' summer camp, of the sort which are so popular nowadays. The one I went to was in Wisconsin. Like most other boys, I was in agony the first night at camp. I could think of nothing but going home. The veterans, those who had been at camp before, talked loudly of initiating the newcomers. I could not swim and they therefore proposed to each other, for my benefit, the possibility of throwing me into the lake. I was frightened and homesick. I knew no one and for that matter did not care to.

I wrote furious letters home begging to be released from my torture, but within two days the whole atmosphere changed. I did not write home any more, and began to enter into the new life with enthusiasm. The first thing I asked my parents when they called for me in Chicago on the way home was whether I could return the following summer. I did go back, but the next summer was my last.

I had been ill in the winter and was compelled to remain out of school for a whole year. I spent most of that time reading, and writing poetry. I was a bad pupil in any case, and it took me five years to get through four years of high school. The chief difficulty was algebra. I found that a stumbling block, but there were others of my own making. I did not see, for instance, why I should learn the rules of grammar. I had been writing poetry and having some of it accepted by the little magazines which abounded at that time. Since, I realized, the rules of English were made to be broken, why learn them? If someone had explained to me that rules such as those of grammar may be broken but that they must be broken judiciously, and, furthermore, that they cannot be broken judiciously by one who does not know them, it might have been different.

When I was fifteen I wrote my first poem. After that, I wrote poetry every day for years; there must have been rooms full of the stuff. Here are several poems written when I was seventeen but not printed until several years later in a preparatory school quarterly.

ON RECEIVING A LETTER

Word had not come from you for such a time
    That I had quite forgotten, could not trace,
    As once, the active outline of your face,
Or set a single syllable to rhyme.
For these two months a languorous solitude
    Near free from loneliness, had been my share;
    Comfort was found in beauty everywhere
To still the seldom ripples in my mood.

And then this letter, which has sorely shaken
    Content; troubled all sleep; against my will,
    Convinced me that I must remember still
And suffer more as wearying hungers waken . . .
    O pain I must endure, but I'll not let
    This sullen torture deepen to regret.

This, of course, is the conventional sentimental sonnet of the beginner. But the last two lines of the next one exhibit vague philosophical forebodings.

ADVICE TO ONE WITH TALENT

I don't see why you think that life is strange;
There's nothing near your guiding star to dim it
Because so few can even get that high.
O yes, you can be cheerful if you try:
Think of the things that never reach their limit,
And of the uncertainties that never change.

To me, the most important profession that any man could boast was and still is that of poet. It was a terrific shock when I discovered that everyone did not concur in this opinion. To some extent, it still is a shock; an inheritance, I suppose, from my youth. I am not at all sure now that the opinion is wrong: if we do not elevate the poet to his rightful place in society, that is society's fault and not the poet's.

In 1921, when I was seventeen, a literary magazine was started in New Orleans. Named *The Double Dealer*, it was edited by two men: Julius W. Friend and Basil Thompson. I was still in high school when, one Saturday afternoon, I put on my blue serge suit, and combed my hair, and climbed the two flights of stairs to the magazine's offices. Basil Thompson happened to be in at the time. He is dead now, a victim of the prohibition era, but I shall never forget him. He was the first human being to consider my poetry seriously; he talked with me for hours about it, and gave me helpful advice. He did not want to change me but only to show me the best way to do whatever it was *I* wanted to do, a superlative kind of guidance for a young literary man. Later I met Friend, and we became collaborators in philosophical work; but then it was Thompson who helped the most.

In February of the following year my first published work, a sonnet, appeared. It is hard to describe the elation of the poet when he obtains the use of a typewriter and sees his verses in print. It is as though they had suddenly appeared carved deep in stone by an immemorial hand which had then been held up to swear witness to their irrefrangible influence upon mankind everywhere and for all time. From poems in almost illegible and childish script to poems in eight-point type is a change that is almost too final to bear. Furthermore, a high school quarterly is one thing, a professional magazine something else. Nothing was ever calculated to transform the amateur into a professional half so quickly; as I gazed in admiration at the typed stanzas, I was firmly convinced that my mission in life had been decided, that it was a mission and nothing less, and that I was adequate to the responsibility which carrying it out imposed upon my shoulders.

The office of *The Double Dealer* was a strange place in those days. Itinerant literary men, restless painters, and all manner of odd fish drifted in and out, submitting manuscripts, borrowing money, and talking interminably about art. Here among second-rate men the æsthetics of the day was aired a thousand times, revealing itself behind and within the most casual as well as the most profound observations. The very excesses of theory entertained by those who do their thinking for themselves, plus the self-corrective nature of the artistic process, guides the best men to avoid the pitfalls to which their followers, who are watching the letter and moving wholly without the spirit, are so susceptible. Intense subjectivism reigned in the literary nineteen-twenties. It was truer of critics and of poetasters than of poets and novelists but of all to some extent, that they held the subject-matter of art to lie within the artist himself, and art to be an outpouring of the inner content of the febrile subject. Art was 'expression', not impression; or it was 'impression*ism*', which is to say, a gift of the peculiar eye of the artist. Each artist was presumed to be his own ivory tower, wholly indifferent to the surrounding countryside.

In this mephitic air I felt at home at first but later became very uncomfortable. I was happy to be among my own kind, men who were occupied with the arts; but I knew that all was not well by the narrowness of the field of interests with which the artists I had met were concerned. Writers seemed to know nothing at all about the business world in which they lived as outcasts. They had heard little of the great new development of physical science, and of what they *had* heard they were deeply resentful. The isolation of the artist was, I felt, a bad thing for art. Art should not, on the other hand, be merely reportorial. The artist ought to strive for eternal values—but only as an aftermath of subjection to the influences of his own date and place. Then, again, the ridiculous fear of science felt by the artists must be characteristic of weak men. The distinction, the sharp distinction, between art and science gives both enterprises many bonds: they are complementary as only different pursuits can be. There is no reason for the artist to fear that science is going to replace him just because the approach of science seems to be cold and unemotional. That would be as absurd as the fear of the replacement of science by art. The world is large, and philosophy, I believe, can show that both art and science have their very necessary places in a cultural whole.

All this did not occur to me as I sat about listening to the older men who based their artistic claims on their avowed lack of conformity to the customs of the day. The narrowness of outlook was not something I could at that time define even though I could feel it. And I have understood since that it sprang from the limitations not of art but of those particular artists. Art does not profit from the tendency of artists to hunt in packs. Unlike science, art does not gain a little from a little art. The achievement of science is made up of hosts of tiny discoveries which add up to the pyramid upon which the man of genius, the great theorizer, stands. But in art this is not the case. Each artist, thus far at least, starts from the very beginning. There being so few great artists in any one generation, it is not advisable for groups to forgather, since the principle of aggregation does not apply to art.

Much of education in later life consists in learning the reasons for sound feelings which may have expressed themselves earlier. It is good that when we are young we feel a great deal. We will be correct in some cases to feel as we do; and we will be wrong in others. In every case of course we do feel what we feel. The discovery that some of the things we feel are felt for the wrong reasons may cause us to react differently on future occasions. But the task is to acquire precisely those reasons which will dictate justifiable feelings in the future, reasons which, as it turns out, must rest upon truths. Thus only the dogmatist acts, or attempts to act, directly from reason, and his action as a result usually proves to be irrational simply because it is not reasonable to act directly from reason. The task of reason so far as action is concerned is the education of the feelings; a truly educated man is a man whose feelings are more reasonable. The importance of the arts in education is obvious, and the arts have been neglected in favour of the sciences. But the arts are highly strategic in the education of the feelings.

The opening up of a world of literature—a miniature world but a world nevertheless—and of art, right before my eyes in the city of my birth, was quite an experience. The situation has remained the same but I have changed. I know now that to some extent I must work alone. In philosophy, I know, too, that I must not seek for an audience among the artists of the *Vieux Carré*. Some of them are my personal friends and I love them. Roark Bradford and E. P. O'Donnell, for instance. But all of them have come somewhat under the influence of the implicit philosophy of recent decades: they are friends of mine but they are not to their own knowledge what Plato has described as 'friends of the ideas'. The anti-rationalism which reigned almost unchallenged throughout the days of my youth and young manhood has infected a generation, and few can see why a man who works with ideas, which are materials as stubborn as paint and canvas, or lives and sounds, might not be just as brilliantly original as themselves. They report and compress the lives of their contemporaries, and that seems to be the principal activity of the modern novelist. I erect architectonic blueprints of the world as it ought-to-be. Which of us is the most original? Who discovers the most? I agree that originality is not the only criterion; but I disagree with the opponents of evolutionism in holding that it is an important factor which cannot possibly be omitted in judging contemporary work. The fresh vision of the artist, the keen insight of the scientist, and the general scope of the philosopher's perspective, should give to the rising generation a wider angle of vision than was ever vouchsafed to their ancestors. Originality may not be the flour of the baking process but it certainly is the yeast, without which there can be no bread.

Originality is restless and art is a searching thing. It is less obvious in later years than in adolescence that life itself consists

in going somewhere. We never stand still: that much is obvious.
Where we are going is another question. It is not entirely for
us to know, but for the lives of one generation after another to
work out. First there is the struggle of the very young person
to learn what goes on in the world about him. At that time it
is important—or seems important—to taste everything once.
Then there is the struggle to find out what camp he is in. Is he
a musician? And if so, is he to be 'conservative' or 'modern',
'advanced' or 'neo-classic'? It is like this in every field. For
the philosopher must decide whether he is to express what
everyone else in his day is expressing by finding odd corners
of it which have not yet been uncovered, or whether he is to
seek his own way regardless of what is or is not being done.
There are even those to whom the mode of expression, whether
poetry, philosophy, music or whatever, is merely a mode, and
incidental to the main theme, which is the imperative need to
express whatever it is they feel ought to be said. Leonardo da
Vinci may have been such a man, and certainly there are others
today. The postulate of inquiry returns; we can feel it flowing
in our blood, hear it beating in our heart, and think about its
vast implications with our brain. For obviously we are mechanisms and as such intended for searching into the question
of what everything means.

Is philosophy in the widest sense anything more than an
extension of our childhood interest in things for their own
sake? When children first become aware of the world about
them, it is with an eager curiosity that knows no ulterior
motive. To come of age means to be tied down to the pursuit
of what is necessary for a preoccupation with feeding and
breeding; it also means to lose the kind of inquisitiveness
which is detached. Only a few manage to maintain this inquisitiveness intact and to work for it all their lives; they are the
true philosophers. They continue the inquiry which is conducted so naïvely by children into the nature of elemental
things; often they have improved tools, such as the terminology
of technical philosophy, but more often they do not advance
the research any further than the children have been able to

c

carry it. This is particularly true of so familiar—and so un-known—a domain as that of sleep.

It is with some anxiety still that I remember how puzzled I was as a child about the phenomenon of sleep. In those years when practically everything presented itself as a problem, the prospect of grave, serious and responsible adults exchanging their daily garments for special night ones, lying down on beds, falling asleep at regular periods and for fixed intervals, and afterwards resuming their activities as though there had been no serious interruption, always struck me as ludicrous in the extreme. For I had heard that death is like sleep. And, I thought, if this were so, well, to fall asleep midway in a closely-packed career when every moment counted and to get up for a fresh start where weariness and fatigue had rudely intervened, was to ignore the fact that the interruption was not only an event of some importance; it was (although I did not have the words to express what I thought then) a cosmic interruption. If it were true that in that sleep of death what dreams may come, and if we dream or might dream, during an ordinary routine sleep, then how could we afford to fall asleep so diffidently?

The answer, I suppose, is contained in the consideration of what would happen were all adults suddenly to become pre-occupied, as I was and occasionally still am, with the idea of sleep, and the attempt to analyze its meaning. The ordinary business of the world, including the normal care of wondering children, would suddenly stop, and a profound insomnia might even be the immediate result. We could not afford to have that. And yet the supreme aplomb with which members of the Chamber of Commerce take their sleep, as they take their food, their wives, their affairs, and everything else, is a source of constant wonder, and, in a way, of superb impudence.

The loss of consciousness deliberately and with malice afore-thought is no laughing matter, or anyway not entirely a laugh-ing matter. Is it possible to devote a third of one's lifetime to an activity whose meaning and purpose is not even to be questioned? Yet just that is what most of us do. Of course, several glib and true explanations of sleep have been put forth.

Sleep is to allow for the recuperation of the organism, says physiology; sleep betrays in dreams the subconscious libido, says psychology; and so on. But these lower levels do not explain what sleep is; only metaphysics can do that, and so far metaphysics has been baffled by it. The *fact* of sleep, not its analysis, is the thing with which philosophy has to cope. What does it mean ontologically to lose consciousness at regular intervals? To lie still with all activities reduced to the point where we no longer remain aware of them, is this not after all a premonition of death? Will we, when we die, simply cease to matter for all twenty-four hours as little as we matter now for eight out of every twenty-four? That may be the meaning which death has for life, but the meaning of death cannot be limited so strictly; there must be more to it, a positive side, perhaps.

But just as death means more than sleep, so sleep must mean more than death. The two categories are overlapping but not exhaustively inclusive of each other. Sleep is not simply the things that the physiologist says it is, although it is that, too, It is not simply a mythological ground for the Freudian psychologist, or a hunting ground for the illicit occultist. It must have some philosophical meaning.

Perhaps the best way to excite philosophical interest in sleep would be to propound some paradoxes concerning it. This seems to have worked for motion; perhaps it will do the same for sleep. How, then, is it possible to be and not to be conscious at one and the same time? Is there loss of consciousness entirely when we are experiencing dream images, when we remain dimly aware of the job that the striped muscles are doing, of the continued potentialities of the autonomic nervous system? On the other hand, is there consciousness when so much may go on in the immediate environment, sounds and activities, which the sleeper remains unaware of?

These may be worthwhile questions; they had their start but have remained unexpressed in the wonderings of a child. In extreme youth I returned to the problem of death as I have already in this story. I do not know whether every child returns to the question this often or not, but the fact of war makes death seem a burning issue. For me as for all my generation there was the remote though ominous presence of the first world war.

When the first world war began I was ten years old. I am afraid that then, and even for the next four years, it signified very little to me. I was dimly aware of the war through the newspapers, and I heard my parents talking about it in hushed and worried tones; but to me it meant only that the boys in my class in public school teased me for being of German descent. When I grew old enough to think for myself and to survey the social world about me, I found that I was in the middle of what has been described as the 'post-war generation'. The application of this phrase had some validity but not as much as it was ordinarily supposed to have. I for one felt no misgivings. It is true that I had not been in the war; but since most of my friends were older men, the atmosphere of my experience was that of the veterans. We had, as I can remember, no thought except for the future. We wanted to be free, but not simply for the pleasure of throwing over the traces; we were not merely concerned with anarchy and chaos. We had definitely positive and constructive reasons for wanting to be free: there were things we wanted to do. Most of all we wanted to tell the truth about something.

The modern vogue for historical studies and for the explanation of everything in terms of development has led us to wish to tie truth down to a social context. It is fashionable for the moment to believe that the explanation of anything is satisfactorily given if only we can outline its human milieu. Thus our ambitions and indeed our whole mental texture in those post-war years are usually explained in terms of the fact that we happened to be post-war products. But the social explanation, or the historical or evolutionary explanation, is compelled to leave much out of the account. There are elements in every period which do not depend upon the period for their meaning. In this group of elements belongs the search for truth. There are those who would seek the true, if allowed to, in any age.

The age governs them negatively by prohibitions, but cannot dictate the positive nature of their activities. To many men in the first world war, the sacrifice was a necessary duty of patriotism; one joined the army and one might be killed; that was a chance one took. But if one survived, it was to return to old activities in a manner calculated to ignore the interruption.

The spirit of inquiry is not furthered by anything but the allowance of inquiry which freedom makes possible. From time to time, it is necessary to fight in order to defend that freedom; but inquiry itself is indifferent to the fight. This is only another way of saying that we are condemned for our evil actions since they seem to belong wholly to us, but we are not endorsed for our good actions since these are expected of every human being. Part at least of the activities of artists, of scientists and of philosophers must be held to be independent of their date and place, even though such activity is to have a bearing upon the practical events of a later generation.

My adolescent years were an agony from any point of view. Poor health due in part to fast physical growth accentuated the period which is for most boys a trying time. I can recall, fortunately, only the steady composition of poetry, interrupted occasionally by doctors, tests, and enforced rest. There was one whole year which had to be taken out of school. Most of it was spent resting, lying on a sofa and watching a cigarette which I had lit and then stood on end burn down to the tray with a perfectly-formed ash. There was another year during which I wore a steel corset to correct a slight curvature of the spine. Doctors came and went and I came and went to doctors' offices. There was a poem a day composed through these years.

At the age of nineteen I was sent north to take my last year of preparatory education at Horace Mann School in New York. I had spent a year out of school for reasons of health, and four years in high school. I was distinctly not what is known as a brilliant pupil. I did rather better at Horace Mann, however; the difference in pace astonished me. I believe that I learned more in New York in a year than I had learned at home in four, more than I learned in the following year at the University of Virginia. Horace Mann had at the time exceedingly intelligent teachers. One in particular, a dour, grinning man named Dr. Martin, who taught us American history in those odd moments in the classroom when, as seniors, we were not learning from him about the world we would have to face in all its actual brutality when we left school, is especially vivid in my memory. At Horace Mann I saw snow for the first time and felt the exciting stimulus of cold, dry weather.

The slovenly pace of the south and its comparative lack of achievements since the Civil War is always blamed by southerners on the weather. Certainly the weather is partly responsible; the six months of solid heat which lies like an enervating blanket on all activity is not exactly calculated to make the southerner an enterprising fellow. But then it is also partly his fault for letting the north set the pace. What we need in the south in summer is a summer way of life: a different kind of ambition, to be attained by a late start in the morning, or a midday siesta, perhaps with work until seven o'clock in the evening. I cannot forget that the great civilizations of the Mediterranean world, the civilizations of Egypt, of Mesopotamia, of Greece, were developed in tropical climes.

The brisk pace of the north stirred me a little, and I did better. This fact in turn put in my head the idea of competition in studies, although I have never liked the idea. Perhaps the way in which we look at competition is wrong; it should not be necessary for everyone else to do worse in order for us to do better. Then, too, the standards of judgment are far from absolute. What happens later in life to the brightest boys in school and the dullest? It is the ones we never hear of from our classmates, not the ones who are voted the most, or the least, likely to succeed, who make the greatest splash in the world. We ought to learn how to substitute for the urge to rise above our fellows the urge to be distinguished among them for lifting them up the highest; this would be a truly social kind of struggle. But that is not the way things are. Competition reduces friends and enemies to a common level but it is not the level of love. I had high hopes for friendship.

My friends at Horace Mann were nothing extraordinary. The boy I liked best was expelled after the first week. My roommate, on the other hand, had evidently been designed by God to devote his entire life to doing only what seemed expected of him. One friend, a younger boy with musical gifts for whom I entertained some respect, became a dance-band leader by preference. I was one of the boarding students, and on one occasion the musician's mother invited me to spend Saturday night with the family in New York City. She asked me that evening what I thought of her son's musical gifts. The family was one of means, and I suggested that since this was fortunately the situation, he ought to devote his wonderful talent to serious music, either as a composer or as a conductor, which he would be able with his leisure to do. I was never asked to return for dinner. Evidently his mother was right and I was wrong: the man's present level of success is pretty good evidence that he could never have been more than he is: a highly-paid player of popular music.

It is a tragedy, I suppose, to feel too intensely about anything. But look at the fun the insensitive people miss! I have always disliked being lukewarm about friendship, and I cannot understand the relationship known as acquaintance. Those I have welcomed to friendship are those I love; the others are people to whom I am united by the bonds of the brotherhood of man. What can it mean to be half-friends? I do not know, but I know this; that to put everything in friendship and to hold nothing back is eventually to be hurt very badly. I believe that this has happened to me several times. Some of those, and one in particular with whom I was very close and from whom I learned a lot, I have believed to be my friends, have proved sooner or later that I could be used to their advantage when it was expedient to do so. Such experiences are saddening, but the only proper revenge is not to let them be embittering. We must be sure to leave ourselves wide open after disillusioning experiences, so that if necessary they may happen again. There is nothing better than to be that kind of fool.

Perhaps my early physical weakness united with my feeling

of the brotherhood of man in my fondness for large cities and for large hotels, and the feeling of security both gave me in my adolescent years. Being at Horace Mann School meant being near New York, and New York contained large hotels, doctors, people in droves. I had the feeling that soldiers are reported to have when they go into battle as members of an army division: what harm could come to me among so many of my fellows? I have this feeling now about non-human nature, the world of the swamps between New Orleans and the Gulf of Mexico, the solitary openness of the ocean and other lonely places: what harm could come to me as a part, however·infinitesimal, of the infinite nature of things? But then I had the feeling only in cities and among people; I had not quite grown up. That is why I preferred the theatre then to the motion pictures; the theatre was full of large and friendly people, or so it seemed to a boy who often attended alone.

Week-ends in New York meant wonderful opportunities for going to the theatre. I knew little about the theatre; I liked the revues and the serious plays but nothing else. The revues were a combination of comedy and sex, classical since Aristophanes; the plays were tragedies; both filled me with emotion. But musical comedies seemed to be merely sentimental; and sentiment, I held then and still hold, is the direct opposite of emotion; it is false emotion. Emotion is biologically enervating but psychically elevating; sentiment is merely demoralizing. The sickly sweet songs, the painful plot, and the general scheme of the musical comedy are dreadful concoctions; the best that can be said for them is that they may be harmless: those who like them are usually confirmed in their viewpoint sufficiently to be beyond the reach of education.

It is about here that I should begin to talk about my experiences with sex and women, because I was often alone in New York, but I have chosen to leave both topics out of my personal account altogether. This omission, I suppose, calls for some tall explanation. All I can say is that it would be necessary in any case to leave out names but that, even so, certain women might be recognized by description since they are still alive—

very much so. Furthermore, the morals of the day being what they are, it seems to me obligatory that "frank" journals be scorned. I do not wish this book to be read for sensational reasons. We respect the man who 'gets by' with whatever he does; those who under these circumstances write about their adventures are credited with having wished to shock their readers. I desire neither to be scorned nor to shock; hence I shall confine my remarks to abstract considerations.

A painter of my acquaintance considers everything touching upon sex to be extremely funny. He will laugh heartily at the mere thought of human copulation, although this does not seem to hinder his own activities in that direction. We are slow in separating the progenitive from the purely sexual functions. There are bachelors who retain their acute interest in sexual activities undiminished. Others I know who were quite animal in their regard for sex before marriage, have changed. They now regard sex not as something casual but as something taboo; it is not considered a 'decent' topic. This I am sure is an attitude assumed out of deference to wives, but it seems to me to be the most savage kind of indictment. Has their experience with their wives taught them that sex is something unmentionable?

For myself I have continued to entertain the most complete curiosity upon all matters touching upon the sexual. I always want to know about everything that goes on. The next best thing to sexual activity is sexual speculation; and next to speculation in interest is conversation. I am not trying to imply that I am a sexual athlete (although this seems to me to be still one of the best gifts that the gods have in store for mortals) but only that my interest in the subject knows no bounds.

We are limited in our activities to our immediate environment; beyond that, any topic we touch upon turns abstract. There is something wonderful and at the same time discouraging, however, in thinking about the temporal cross-section of human activity all over the world. There are a great number of persons alive today: several hundred millions in Europe, four hundred millions in China, three hundred and

[35]

fifty millions in India, and so on. Now of this vast population, think how many women all over the surface of the earth will have to have their sexual desires gratified this very evening! It is a vast male undertaking, involving an amount of energy probably sufficient to win a world war or build a new heaven on earth.

The multiple image is most fascinating when put in terms of sexual activity, but it will work in much the same way for any other ordinary human practice. Think of the number of meals which will have to be prepared tonight everywhere; think of the dishes that will have to be washed, of the books that will have to be read, the faces washed, the lights turned out; think of the diapers which will have to be washed, the sleep obtained; think of all the dressing and undressing that will have to go on; think of all the muscle there will have to be in all the arms just to keep the wheels of human enterprise turning and turning. It makes a man very proud but also quite humble to think about his own tiny contribution to the world's endeavour.

There are qualitative as well as quantitative social issues raised by the fact of the sheer immensity of the human mass in a large city in the north. Living in New York eventually must include one thing for a southerner: a reconsideration of the status of the negro. One of my earliest recollections is of a negro nurse who took care of me and who was regarded by me as by a son. There is no patronizing in this. I can see as little to discuss in the negro 'question' as in the Jewish 'question': the statement raises a difficulty which does not necessarily exist. There is no negro question, only a white question of why there is prejudice against the negro. I know that I grew up at first without prejudices against the negro, and that they were developed in me later as a careful though unplanned part of my education. By the time I had gone north to school for a couple of years and then crossed to Europe, I was a full-fledged professional southerner. I was prepared to explain that northerners did not understand the negro question and ought not to presume to interfere. I was prepared to declare, and freely did, that the problem was insoluble. My acquaintance with

William Alexander Percy did not help to dispel the attitude. Percy was proud of his tolerance, but it was tolerance just the same. Here, I said to myself, is an educated man, a poet and a southerner, who feels pretty much as I do about the thing; therefore I must be right. I ceased thinking about the issue altogether, which is often an indication of the profoundest kind of belief. It is difficult indeed to alter those beliefs which are so strong that we no longer feel the necessity to consider them.

One night I was dining with a friend in a Soho restaurant in London. She suddenly remembered that she had to see a well-known American negro singer for a few minutes on business. I had heard the gossip: it was rumoured that she had been his mistress for some time, and she quieted the rumour by admitting its truth. She wanted me to go backstage with her to see him at his theatre. I declined, categorically, on the grounds that as a southerner I could not possibly afford to meet a negro through his white mistress. Back in America, many years later, I refused to go with my sister-in-law and her husband to a negro night-club in Harlem, simply because I had heard that there negro and white were treated as equals. The literary negroes I met at teas in New York pleased me no better; I was sure that I disliked the whole approach.

Then one day I awoke to the truth. I cannot possibly remember what did the trick, my recollection fails on this point But I do know that I changed and that the change consisted in dropping a little of my education. Fundamentally, I am sure that the patronizing of a Percy, who was willing to lay down his life for the coloured people so long as they kept their place, was never an attitude in which I could have felt comfortable; I must have only thought that I shared it. For I have always been faithful to the notion of the brotherhood of man, and the brotherhood of man does not distinguish between men on the basis of their colour.

The school test was always to put the query, How would you like a negro to marry your sister? Unfortunately for me I had no sister and so the test was meaningless. But I have seen many sisters, white as well as black, that I myself would not particularly like to marry. Of course, there are true racial differences but I am not sure that they can be proved to be anything more than skin-deep. The white, the yellow and the black races are distinguishable at their most pronounced. We know night from day yet it is difficult to tell where they shade off into one another, and the same is true of the races of mankind. It is not possible to make restrictive judgments concerning miscegenation. Evidence shows that the only recognizable evil in social mixtures is inbreeding and even this not always. But cross-breeding between the races is the opposite of inbreeding, and therefore most likely to prove advantageous to both groups. Somehow the barrier must be bridged and the distinction eliminated, at least so long as the latter rests on its present grounds.

There is a deep resentment toward the negro in the south, based partly on the necessity for a scapegoat but partly also on the negro's strength in numbers. The birthrate of the negro in the south is much higher than that of the white. In many counties in southern states, the negro outnumbers the white. Now, as the white knows, there is no love lost on either side. The negro has a justifiable grievance for the way he has been ill-treated, and probably looks for a chance to even the score. On this basis, no problem can be settled; for scores are never evened to the satisfaction of both sides. One side has got to ease the restrictions, stop the injustices, and hold out the hand of equality. Why can it not be we?

Now and then something concrete happens which crystallizes the situation of the negro and shows clearly what its abstract values are. Some time during the early years of the third decade of the twentieth century, there arrived in New Orleans an English novelist who was intent upon seeing, and as far as possible participating in, the Carnival celebrations. He had two letters of introduction from friends in England. One letter was to a prominent negro family; the other, to a prominent white family which had for years been in the forefront of society. After some careful thought, the novelist presented the letter to the negro family first. He was invited to become a house guest, and he accepted with alacrity. From this coign of vantage, he then proceeded to present the other letter. The white family was in a terrible predicament. Here was a literary lion who was eager to drop in at the most auspicious time, namely when he could be exhibited before the townspeople to the greatest advantage. However, one could not possibly invite a house guest to parties without extending an invitation also to his host and hostess. The dilemma was terrific. The white family finally informed the English novelist that if he would move to a hotel, the invitations would come pouring in upon him and the festivities could then begin.

This is a funny story, yet it is not so funny as it seems at first glance. The point is that the novelist really did act in a way perfectly conformable with the brotherhood of man. There seemed to be no reason why he should stay with one family rather than with another—that is, if his actions really represented his state of opinion. From the outside, and to southerners, it appeared to be only one more example of the decadence of the British. The southerners, as it turned out, were right. I am not of course suggesting out of patriotism that southerners are always right. But they must have been at least partly right in this case, because, faced with the alternative that was presented to him, the novelist moved to a hotel.

One more illustration of the situation is worth telling. For some years, a few of us in New Orleans had a small discussion club which met twice a month. At each meeting a member read a paper, usually on some philosophical or scientific topic, after which the rest of the members engaged in a controversy over it. The club was quite friendly, and although the conversation frequently got warm, personalities were never called into question. The members consisted of teachers from the two neighbouring institutions of higher learning: assorted professors from Tulane University, and doctors from Louisiana State University which maintains its Medical School in the city. Then there were always a few odd professional men: doctors or lawyers. Most of the members were originally northerners; I do not know why this was so, it just happened to be.

At one meeting, a member was scheduled to read a paper on anthropology. He suggested that there was a good anthropologist, a negro, teaching at Dillard University, the negro institution, and that it might be a good idea to have him as a guest at the meeting. We agreed and he was accordingly invited. He came and conducted himself in splendid fashion, being neither too forward nor too backward. He talked neither too much nor too little, and seemed perfectly at ease, much to the surprise of some of our members who hardly felt the same way about it. At the next meeting it was suggested that perhaps we might make the anthropologist a permanent member. We had a ruling that anyone could be kept out of the group by a single dissenting vote; the club had been so friendly and the meetings so congenial we wished to keep it that way. It had worked out well, too, because no one had ever availed himself of the blackball privilege. When the negro's name came up, however, a northern professor spoke up vigorously against him. No prejudices were involved, he said, but would not mixed meetings be more embarrassing for the negro than for us? If we put the matter to a vote, he went on, he for one would not vote against the candidate, but he strongly advised us against forcing the issue in that way. He was supported in his stand by all the northern members of the group. The southern members, wishing to seem without prejudice, or perhaps actually being without it, leaned over backward in the negro's favour. But the matter was dropped, out of deference to the northern members. Now I am not suggesting that anybody acted from false feelings; I simply believe that a change must occur in the morals of the country (and this involves a belief in what is real), before the genuine equality of persons can be attained. The difficulty is that most Americans are warm-hearted and generous, but that prejudices get inherited or arise from one quarter or another, in terms of which people think or feel that they have got to act. And the actions which result, the opinions which are held, do not correspond to what is really felt and, deep down, believed. I hold the best about Americans and know that they have only to be shown that what they really and truly want is not anybody's derogation but only the improvement of all, in order to do what is right.

Many times—too often—the individual feeling for what is fit and right runs counter to the prevailing mores and after a subconscious struggle is overlaid by it without, however, disappearing altogether. The result is an irreconcilable difference and the parading of a false front of conformity which tends eventually to break down and allow the individual feeling to assert itself. There is more to the atmosphere of opinion than most persons suppose. I grew up in the so-called post-war generation of the nineteen-twenties. I did not feel its influence at all in some ways, but I believe that I felt it in other ways much more than I was able to understand at the time. Long before I recognized the effects of the recent war, I held the whole business of formal education in great contempt. As soon as I acquired an interest in poetry, I knew why. I disliked everything about school, and when I first heard Shaw's dictum, that 'those who can, do; those who can't, teach', I knew that was how I felt about it. I really believed that everyone who had written a fine poem hated the professors; that no professor had ever written a poem with any merit; and that as a consequence, I, who had determined to write poetry, had nothing to learn from the professors. This was not altogether a profoundly felt conviction but largely a socially-imposed attitude, and hence it was not destined to last, at least in the extreme form in which I then held it.

Meanwhile poetry preëmpted the field. Before I was fifteen I had read most of the 'standard' British poets, and thought them stuffy. I did not understand why it was so necessary to write in an antique language. I was a purist who hated the use of apostrophes and omitted letters. Then one day I found a copy of Rupert Brooke's *Collected Poems* in the library; someone had sent it to my mother. Immediately my whole life was changed. I was lost in admiration, and immediately resolved to become a poet: my first choice of a career. Brooke's writings seemed to me to be the exemplar of classical poetry in my own time. It was true that he had been breathing the same air I breathed, doing the same things I wanted to do, liking the same things I liked. He used the familiar language of the morning newspaper, without frills or unnecessary striving for effects; and yet the effects were there, the lightning could always strike. Brooke was the first poet I had read whose works were written in the contemporary style. It seemed to me not only fresh but also very close and comforting. I began to write poetry of my own at once, volume after volume of it, strongly influenced at first by all the contemporaries I then began to discover. I was in my own eyes a poet; I had found a place in the world. I began to wear large knots in my ties and Byronic collars, and developed a great scorn for those who were not either members of my profession or in possession of a great respect for it.

Brooke (for some convenient reason I forgot that he had graduated from Oxford) had gone to Tahiti. This only served to increase my pagan contempt for the professors. I added Yeats to my list of admirations and always recalled his picture of Don Juan in Hell, frightening the timid with his 'sinewy thighs'. I thought of Brooke bathing in the waters around Papeete, and of the little girl around the corner from my house on Valence Street, and I resolved never to be concerned with those who had been born dead. To *épater le professeur*—what more relaxation could anyone ask when the day's work of writing poetry was done?

Since this was the mood I took with me to preparatory school and the university, the effect can be well imagined. I thought that if the professors had had any sense they would not be professors, and that if the students had any sense they would not be wasting their time. I resolved not to waste mine.

The result was disastrous. At the University of Virginia, my first act was to drop logic in favour of something called music appreciation. The young instructor, in whose tender care was entrusted the duty of making us acquainted with formal logic, maintained a curious view of his mission. He was dreadfully bored with philosophy, and he managed to communicate his mood very successfully, after the manner of a good teacher. He rather resented us and would have as little to do with us as possible; for he knew that we knew less philosophy than he did, and having been a student longer than he had been a teacher, he had retained the conventional contempt of the upper-classman for those below him. And so he would walk into the room and endeavour feebly to instruct us at long distance in order not to soil his hands with our ignorance. He would write some syllogisms on the blackboard, and then, half turning, would observe to us that we were obliged to learn them. When once I had the temerity to ask why, the reply —frank enough—was that otherwise we would not be allowed to pass the course.

This answer only put the problem back one remove. Why did I have to 'pass the course'? I answered this one for myself: I didn't. I failed the mid-term examinations, and changed to music appreciation.

The move was wise. Music appreciation was held in a moderately small room with an immoderately large piano. The class filed in and sat down. The instructor entered and went straight to the piano. There were usually no windows open and the heating system was on full force. The piano keys began to sound, music that we could not recognize except that we knew it was not for our kind of dancing. The class was bored by classical music; I resented it. I resented it because the composers had got almost no credit at home in the Auditorium or in New York at the Philharmonic Symphony concerts to which I had been taken. The applause from the audience and the bows from the performers were all intended to acknowledge the brilliance of the performance. Composers seemed to be only the by-products of a necessary evil most of whom had fortunately happened long ago. I knew that contemporary composers were receiving little or no credit. And so I behaved just the same in the presence of classical music as did my classmates who were bored by anything not performed by Paul Whiteman.

[43]

D

And so the piano playing of the teacher dragged on. It always stopped with a question, how did we like what we had been hearing? I do not know yet whether it was the cessation of the music or the timidly asked question which awoke us, but in all events we came to ourselves long enough to reply that we not only liked the music but that we especially liked the way in which it had been played. This called for more music by the teacher and more sleep by the class. It was very successful. I left that course, too, before the end of the term, because I also left the University; but I was told later that nobody had failed music appreciation.

Something else happened which also helped to dampen my ardour for a formal education. The something else was my course in English. I had for some time been contributing poetry to the little magazines about the country, and so fancied myself an Established Author. The professor in my English class, I felt I could see at a glance, would have given his eye-teeth to have written what he himself would have referred to as a creative contribution to contemporary literature. He was a failure; I was on my way toward being a brilliant success: I was twenty, and I wondered how then could *he* be teaching Me? Clearly it ought to have been the other way round; only, if it had been, I would not have bothered. If he wished to bother in his situation, with things as they were, well, that was his business, but I would not be a party to it.

One day in place of a written examination he had asked us to bring in an original literary effort. I went back to my room and looked over what I had in stock. There was plenty because I had been writing about a poem a day for years. Some were rather good, but not all. Many of the best had already appeared in print. I selected very carefully a sonnet which had been the most often rejected by editors and which, to tell the truth, was slowly becoming suspect to me also, despite the endorsement of repeated rejections (for were not editors, too, people who could not *do*?). I retyped it and handed it in as my assignment, expecting to be properly reprimanded by an indignant teacher who, of course, would have seen clearly through the whole ruse and understood perfectly well the intended affront.

Much to my surprise, the sonnet received a mark of one hundred and honourable mention before the class. The teacher beamed at me as one of the pupils who had learned his lesson well. So that was it, I thought. I was to be one of his star products and he was to point to me with pride, was he? Well, I would be damned if he was! My contempt for the institutions of higher education immediately increased a thousandfold. I say this now with no vanity, since it is obvious that I was holding the university responsible for an inherent weakness in one of the departments of the college of arts and sciences.

This weakness is a common one. There is a claim made by every department within a university that it is in charge of the study of a certain subject-matter, and therefore the authority best qualified to speak about it. In certain instances this is justified. The task of a department is theoretically twofold; it is supposed to conduct the education of the young and to promote knowledge through discovery. But the two functions are quite distinct. In most physics departments, for instance, both endeavours are carried on. In the larger universities, different sets of men specialize in these separate functions. There are men who do not have to teach but who conduct researches into physics in an effort to extend the boundaries of human knowledge in that field. There are, of course, other men whose task it is to make the students familiar with the knowledge already available in text-books. In other words, there are teachers of physics and there are experimental physicists working side by side. This is in general a fair example of what goes on in the physical science departments of universities.

But now let us consider topics in some other departments. Let us consider the languages. The Romance languages are taught, and the only research consists in what is known as scholarship. That this is authentic research of a sort there can be no doubt, but it is still fairly remote from the daring and imaginative work that is done by the best of the experimental physicists, despite the comparison which is often claimed by the scholars themselves. It is, however, necessary work. We want to know, for instance, about the origin of languages, and we want to know about their development. Efforts in these directions are greatly dwarfed by the wholesale task of teaching the fundamentals of grammar and syntax to undergraduate students.

In the English department, the claims are greater and their justification somehow even more lacking. Here language becomes confused with literature. The English teachers have never been able to decide whether they are teaching language as a tool or language as an art-form. The English language is more than illustrated by its greatest writers; it is almost identified with them. This may have literary justification; but the logical structure of language has its legitimate claims, too. More important, however, since more spurious, are the claims of the English professors to be in charge of their fields. In addition to teaching, they wish to hold themselves before the students as authorities on their subject, as somehow critics before whom the professional writers must cringe. Their justification having to be so small, their pretensions are correspondingly large. Of the two functions exercised by the physics department, the English department exercises only one: namely, that of teaching. The original work conducted in English literature, the work of poets and novelists and playwrights, is all done outside the university walls, frequently even by men with no formal education. I am not of course attempting to justify this curious anomaly. I am simply asserting that so long as the "creators" in English labour outside the academic circle, while the "creators" of physics labour inside, the claims of the English department to authority cannot equal those of the physics department with anything resembling justice. The picture I am painting of the English professors is not, of course, without exception; but that it is a true one is borne out by the abject attitude of inferiority assumed by every English professor in the presence of a novelist of reputation.

At the University of Virginia, the name of Cabell, who lived not far away, was a name to conjure with. He was heard of but never seen. But the aura which surrounded the mere mention of his name suggested that it was too much for students even to contemplate him at a distance. The English professor had met him; what could we poor miserable freshmen expect? Now this did not exactly tally with my own outlook. I had a poor opinion of the English professor, and only a fair opinion of Cabell, an opinion which, by the way, has not improved in recent years. *Jurgen* almost succeeded in being something; it makes a very good first impression on a young man, but it does not wear well. It is hardly mature. And the rest of the books contain only occasional flashes which are as good as *Jurgen*. What Cabell can do is to describe conversations which are amusing because of baffled cross-purposes: the glaum who wishes to brag about women, the Jurgen who bores the king with his respectful attitude toward the princess, the Jehovah who boasts of his social success. But he cannot raise these stories to any symbolic importance, and the rest is merely elaborate talk. But at least Cabell got his books written, published and read, which was more than the professors could do. Theirs remained merely unattained ambitions in the back of their pompous manner. It was disheartening to the boys and very impressive to the girls. An English professor who is under forty has only to leave his collar open to convince undergraduate girls to whom he reads poetry in and out of the classroom that to have an affair with him would be just like hearkening back to Shelley.

The University of Virginia, and cultural Virginia in general, suffer very badly from one fault which has allowed leadership to slip away from them altogether. Virginia is one of the English snobbisms in America. Actually, three spots in the United States vie with each other in the desperate effort to claim to be the transfer of cultural England to the New World. These are: Massachusetts, Virginia, and South Carolina. Each severally supposes the other two to be pretenders and itself the true inheritor of the English cultural tradition in these United States. Each can name names, and each has its special claim. Each supposes that it has much in common with an England that is living, whereas it only faintly resembles, in its contractions of puritanism and prudery, its carefulness and self-consciousness, an England that is dead. For the England of the nineteenth century, religious and moral scruples notwithstanding, was still something of a boisterous and joyful place. At least it was so for the extreme upper and lower classes. The lower middle class managed to develop a caution that was something new in the world. But Boston, Richmond, and Charleston actually manage to delude themselves that they are imitating aristocratic England. This unfortunate pretension has been fostered and played upon by itinerant lecturing Englishmen who find it quite flattering, but it is very far from the truth. The fact is that these states, in so far as they remember England, are living in the past. Nobody, not even living Englishmen, are wholly interested in what is dead.

The consequence is that the cultural life of this country has moved to New York, and, in an academic way, to the West. If anything comes out of our universities it will be from the University of Chicago, the University of Iowa, of Ohio, of California: vast institutions, raw, green, and abounding in energy, and with no traditions of stiff restrictions to hold them back. An original and vital culture will not come from Harvard and it will not come from the University of Virginia. It is possible that the United States is not destined to develop a culture of her own, that hers like Soviet Russia's is a moonlight culture which lives in the reflected light of Europe, just as the Romans developed a civilization but lived in the reflected light of Greek achievement; but this is a depressing prospect to which we have no right to abandon ourselves. Life belongs to the future, not to the past. Tradition follows those who perform worthy accomplishments; whoever writes an important novel, a distinguished symphony, develops a wide philosophy or finds a principle of science, will be seen by those who come after to have belonged to the great tradition. For what makes tradition if not those whose work deserves to live after them? The guardians of the past, the watch-dogs of culture, do not recognize a living member of their family when they see one.

The guardians will not admit to the sacred precincts the work of anyone who has not been endorsed by their heirs. The necrophiliac instincts of the guardians is one thing which compels culture occasionally to migrate.

The problem of a living culture and its reconciliation with the preservation of the cultural past is not entirely divorced from the general problem of education. The teacher is obliged both to convey the knowledge discovered in the past and to instil a desire to discover new knowledge in the future. All teachers are not equally suited temperamentally to meet the demands of both types of instruction. It was while I was attending college that I first began to think about the problems of teaching. The business of teaching is a practical application to the formal principles of education, and teachers are further determined by whatever philosophy of education they happen to accept. The psychological effects of the various philosophies of education also have to be taken into account. Later I learned that all teachers are divided into three groups: the drones, the pioneers, and the natural teachers.

The drones are just what their name implies: men who have good memories but no imagination, and who can be taught to carry on the same routine, year in and year out, until the end of their life-expectancy. They had come to college as bright young men whose retentive memories had fooled the authorities in charge of them into supposing that what they were dealing with was marked with genius. They had remained in college, taking course after course, garnering degree after degree, until they had finally passed from a part-time instructor's career, conducted during the writing of their thesis and the pursuit of their graduate studies, to a full-time teaching position. By virtue of never breaking either written or unwritten rules, by faithful and conscientious if not hard work, and by remaining at the same task for several decades, they find themselves finally full professors and perhaps even heads of departments. They manage to get students through their work, although they have been known to discourage study by making it dull without showing its depth. They become recognized authorities, especially if they have been extreme specialists, and they are some of the most boring people on earth. They constitute, let me add, about ninety per cent. of the teaching staff of most universities.

The remaining ten per cent. is divided between the pioneers and the natural teachers. By pioneers I mean what is ordinarily meant by the term 'creators', the men who carry their fields forward by making discoveries and widening the boundaries of knowledge. The men in this classification may or may not be good teachers; they are great men and their value is not in proportion to their number. However few they may be, it is *their* work without which there need be neither teachers nor students. They live on the inside of their subject-matter and know it with great familiarity. However, their ability to teach is dependent upon many other factors, such as their memories, which may be bad as well as good, and their personalities, which may be crotchety as well as likeable. In the larger universities, particularly in the science departments, it is possible to find men engaged in research who do not have any required teaching burden. They occasionally do have classes but it is not demanded of them. This kind of opportunity for fresh work should be possible in all fields, in philosophy, for instance, as well as in science.

Finally, the last five per cent. are what I have called the natural teachers. The natural teachers are men, usually incapable of creative work, who have an innate feeling for the communication of knowledge. They do nothing original, nothing which will last beyond their own lifetimes. They are in a sense, therefore, lesser in value than the pioneers; yet their value is very high indeed. They are on fire with interest in their field, and they have the faculty of being able to communicate not only the factual knowledge of their subject but also their own enthusiasm for it. They are usually possessed of an attractive personality, with charm and understanding of the problems of others. They seem to exist only for the purpose of conveying knowledge to students, in all of whose problems they manifest a genuine interest and concern.

Unfortunately for the whole business of education, the youth in his career as a student is lucky if he meets one or perhaps two teachers of the natural teacher type. He is even luckier if he meets a pioneer. But either type of personal contact must be little more than an accident. The usual experience of the student is with the drones. The drones have only a neutral or a mildly negative effect upon him. But often the drones may be more dangerous. They manage to work themselves into positions of power and authority; they lean heavily on institutional connections. Having no ability of their own, they also have no confidence in themselves. This makes them resentful of anyone with marked ability in the field, and they become spiteful and suspicious. They will go out of their way to stop the activities of someone whose achievements may be able by comparison to throw a slur upon their own lack. They nullify the whole business of education and of inquiry in which presumably the educators are leading. The thwarting of genius is an old occupation, and for centuries it has been largely in the hands of men with titles, academic positions and institutional connections.

Apart from the persons involved, however, something is basically wrong with modern education. The education of university graduates and of skilled labourers is equally incomplete. I can speak impartially on this score, since I had the advantage of neither kind of training; I am as completely prepared to do nothing as anyone I know: the perfect equipment for the poet and the philosopher. Still, I feel that if I had had the education of the one and not of the other, I should consider myself unprepared for life. For the combination must be nothing less than superb.

The university graduate does not think himself unprepared for existence if only he has a degree, if he is a Bachelor of Arts, say. But can he be said to be educated when he lacks manual skill? Certainly the converse is true, and the skilled labourer misses the advantages of four years spent in a liberal arts college.

Many thinkers have offered emendations to the present

scheme of education. Hutchins of Chicago, if I understand him aright, has suggested dividing the colleges into trade schools and institutions of higher learning. This would breed snobbish scholars on the one hand and skilled labourers on the other, both woefully underinformed and unprepared wholly to participate in the culture in which they happen to live. Dewey has suggested a plan which consists in learning by doing; he wishes to abolish the knowledge of principles in favour of their practical application. But what do principles exist for if not for practice; and on the other hand what is practice if not the practice of principles? It seems to me that a formal education ought to consist in a study of principles together with a manual skill at some craft—for everybody. This would be a truly democratic education.

Some years ago the *New Yorker* magazine published a cartoon showing two labourers carving a motto on a newly-erected building. 'Does *ex* take the dative or the ablative?' one workman asks the other. Now, I submit, this is funny only to a society which considers it ludicrous for a stonemason to be familiar with Latin syntax. Yet why should not a stonemason have just as much right to know Latin as anyone else? Would the reverse cartoon, for instance one of two Yale professors in cap and gown repairing a motor, in which one asks the other, 'Does the r.p.m. depend upon the firing order?', be considered equally funny?

There certainly are four kinds of learning, and these are distinct even though they are closely interrelated. The four kinds are: philosophy, the sciences, the arts, and the practical techniques. Some knowledge of ontology is essential to a true education, and so is some knowledge of how to bake a cake. The empirical sciences and the fine arts are equally dependent upon the theories of philosophy, and this is no less so because it is a fact which is ignored by some scientists and artists. How to fit these subjects into a curriculum of formal studies is a difficult problem, but certainly the university student should never face commencement exercises without a fair familiarity with the whole picture of formal studies and a considerable amount of sampling.

But when we have finished providing for formal studies, we have by no means done. All formal education overlooks the unofficial but powerful educative influences which have their effect indirectly. I learned to shoot dice from the chauffeurs of neighbours after school. I learned about sex and how to swear from my grammar-schoolmates. I learned a lot more through my sense of smell, quite inadvertently. The smell of dusty roads, of moss in summer, the sweaty hair of little girls, the smell of books and newspapers. I learned a lot more from a kind of large-scale wonder which always went out beyond the actual things with which I was confronted at the moment.

I learned what I did not want to be from the friends of my family. They were dull people for the most part. Their comings and goings in the house made it seem peculiar for me to have an interest in books. I might have learned earlier than I did, however, that art and science and philosophy are not absolutely exceptional things in our American life, were it not for a few of these people. But I can thank them for an early independence which made me feel the necessity for carving myself out of timber that they had never seen growing. In a culture in which the philosopher is not considered very important, it goes without saying that there are additional difficulties confronting him. Fame, however hard to come by, is cheap at the price demanded by the movies and the audiences for popular novels. I am often reminded of the mathematicians of the nineteenth and twentieth centuries, into whose work the most daring imagination has gone, without any sort of general recognition for their achievement being counted in the reward. Fortunately for society, however, the general public is not the judge of what is of social benefit. The mathematician is certainly a man whose work has wide social reverberations and may continue to have even after the particular society which has ignored him no longer exists.

The philosopher is a public man whether the public takes cognizance of the fact or not. How is he to keep this sense of contact? That, I take it, is a personal problem. Certainly there are philosophers who can console themselves in their solitude; others must seek the crowd in one way or another. I have friends, but I have always felt especially gregarious in the presence of street crowds and street music. Not only the formal celebration which is Mardi Gras in New Orleans, in which almost everyone takes part, gave me this feeling, but also more informal celebrations. In the Carnival spirit there is no contrast except against other days in the year. The feeling of publicity is to be obtained in purer fashion from small parades in the middle of business days. Street music makes life a dance and heightens the intensity of the most trivial of occurrences that happen out of doors. The old circus parades on Saturday afternoons, military contingents, any small affairs which interrupt ordinary routine only a little and that momentarily; these are the occasions which stand out the sharpest.

The essential part of such a parade is a band. Even sitting in a chair I have always had the impression that we are all on our way somewhere, and music in the street heightens this impression formidably. After seeing my first Russian Ballet, I had a name for the kind of thing I still feel. Life in the street is life at its baldest, and life in the street is a ballet; it is always better when accompanied by music. People on the stage sometimes step out of character; people in ordinary life, never. The doctor is perfectly willing to be always a doctor; the lawyer always a lawyer. And the policeman on the corner never comes out of it to put on his ordinary suit and go home. Do such people know that life and more generally all existence stretches beyond them to infinity? Do they realize that they are always standing on the edge of an abyss; that they are frail but glorious creatures; that their solemnity makes them somehow precious, like a baby which should suddenly express serious concern on its wizened and much-loved little face?

Of such realizations, too, as well as of more formal elements, is an education composed. In later years the acquisition of a terminology, to learn how to sing or to inquire, requires a knowledge of words which can but painfully express what the

heart has long felt. How are we to crowd this kind of information into the adolescent years? Some of it is always present but
not enough. Who has ever had enough of sensing life and its
manifold activities? Who can appreciate all the confusion or
all the order which could be? Certainly, no single study can do
as much. And yet my prejudices tell me that philosophy, well
taught, can make a start. Which of us with all our precon-
ceptions and routines, can teach it so?

The importance of events in any life is more directly pro-
portionate to their intensity than to their extensity. It may take
a man a year to travel around the world—and leave absolutely
no impression on him. Then again it may take him only a second
to see the face of a woman—and change his entire future. The
example is an extreme one though far from uncommon. Our
lives are made up of the alternate rhythm of accepting premises
hastily and drawing conclusions at leisure. But more of that
elsewhere. I am thinking now particularly of how much I
learned, or rather unlearned, while at college, although my
attendance lasted less than six months.

Consider the problem of money, for example. I was an only
child, and my father was well off. When I left for the university
in the fall, he paid my tuition by mail and gave me an amount
for current expenses, to be deposited in the bank when I
arrived and drawn against by cheque. I took the cheapest room
I could find; one without bath, situated next to and overlooking a railroad trestle, where the noise and smoke of the
passing trains had rendered the building undesirable. I spent
almost nothing, because I could not imagine asking for more
when the money I had been given was gone. At home I had
bought many books, charging them at the local store without
noticing the price. At college, although the local bookstore
offered many temptations, I bought almost nothing. The
money had been earned by my father, not by me. All my life
I have felt that there is something morally wrong about money;
it is wrong to have money when so many people are in need,
and equally wrong to have to depend on others. Why? I do
not know, for here we enter the region of feelings. I have a

feeling that it is so, and I know that it would be the same for me under any economic system, even under one in which property was never said to represent theft. Capitalists will blame this feeling upon my socialist leanings; communists will ascribe it to my middle-class upbringing. I only record it as a fact, and moreover one which seems to be fairly prevalent.

After a month or two my funds ran low; I continued to write home to give an account of myself, but I never mentioned money. Things had reached the stage where I was beginning to worry. The following week I would be obliged to borrow or do without and that meant, so far as I was concerned—doing without. Then, unexpectedly, a cheque from my father turned up in the mail. I was free to continue my life, for I had no scruples about spending money so openly given, even though I did not feel quite right about the whole situation.

Money has always seemed to me to be laughing at all of us from behind the dim curtain of chance. One night I won ten dollars in a poker game. The boy who lost it gave me a cheque. After the Christmas vacation I had returned to the University in a second-hand Chevrolet. When I got in my car I noticed on the wheel a summons for parking beyond the allowed hour. The following day, the traffic judge asked me why I had parked illegally. I told him the truth; I had been in a poker game and forgotten the time, having won ten dollars. 'The fine will be ten dollars', he said without smiling. Somehow I regarded this as justice. I was grave about it, until the cheque for my winnings was returned by the bank marked 'Insufficient Funds'. Then I saw the point.

The only way in which it is possible to be free of the money problem is to have some, but not too much. Those with too little money are plagued with the problems of subsistence; they must concern themselves with making money, else they cannot hope to survive. Those with too much money are plagued with the problems of investment, and of maintaining a high standard of living. Both groups are definitely preoccupied with the problem of money. It is only those who have enough for subsistence but not enough for display who are free. To them money is a means to some other end; to me, for instance, it represents freedom for inquiry. In the words of Ecclesiastes, 'Wisdom is good with an inheritance: and by it there is profit to them that see the sun'. This seems to fit my case somewhat. I had the inheritance; and I sought not wisdom but the truth.

The proper amount of money to have, then, is just enough. Of course the background requisite for such an adjustment in the case of all individuals would be a stable economy. Too much money, like too little, breeds preoccupation. For all but the banker and the economist, money ought not to be an end. It is what enables us to *do* what we wish to do but it ought not to *be* what we wish to do. Sherwood Anderson once said that $500 was his proper amount. When he had less he began to worry about eating; when he had more he began to worry about investments. Certainly it is a fact that when we have a great deal of money we are confronted with all the problems it entails, and when we have none we are preoccupied with the necessity of having to earn some in order to meet the primary requirements of food and shelter. The comedian who observed that although money will not bring you happiness it will enable you to select the kind of misery you prefer, was not far from at least one aspect of the true situation.

It is not difficult to understand the fascination of the mathematician for gambling, a fascination often shared by the artist. Reason may work from knowledge gained in the past, but it can only affect the future. And the future is after all not so far away. It is just around the corner; it is only the next roll of the dice, the card about to be upturned. To the extent to which we are able to know about the future, we are agents and not patients, powers and not victims. Prediction bestows the tremulous illusion of control. We are masters at one level of analysis, and that is such an absorbing business that we forget how we ourselves are mastered by other levels. We may cleverly design a mechanism in such a way that it will fly, while our heart is developing an aneurism at the same rate. We may gamble successfully one evening only to deposit our winnings the next morning in a bank that will fail in the afternoon.

Nevertheless, the effort to encroach ever so little upon the next moment has brought men like Dostoevski and Peirce back, again and again, to the problems of the gaming-table.

Perhaps the reason why I am not a good gambler even in this sense is that my tendency to think abstractly about concretions carries with it the disabling tendency to think too concretely about abstractions. Money to the gambler is an abstraction; he gains or loses, just as the indicator on some pointer-reading shows increase or decrease, say the miles-per-hour dial of a motor car. Money to me is exhausted by the things it can purchase. I know detachedly the fallacy of this, and I am also familiar with the functional nature of exchange-value. But when dealing with money, I find the knowledge of no use. I can be extravagant in the purchase of clothes, gramophone records, books. But if I lose five dollars at bridge when I can very well afford to do so, I return home to think about the shirts, albums and volumes which the money might have been better spent on. The weakness points to a reverse viewpoint in me, but also to something perverse in the very existence of money. We think about the future in terms of what it ought to be, fear for what it might be, and shudder at the prospect of what it probably will be.

Money and the exchange of goods in the world of business affairs must go on, somehow, everywhere. Yet the poet does not function very well in the world of business affairs. It is evidently not possible for the same man to discharge equally well his lyrical and pecuniary functions. When the songs of the world and the exchange of products make their separate demands upon him, he finds that, while they do not conflict necessarily among themselves, they do in him, for the talents they call forth are somehow at odds. Since feeding takes precedence over inquiring, it is the economic aspect of existence which temporarily prevails. That was well recognized when I was a young man.

Now that the world is a chaos and the field of social relations has been almost entirely torn apart, I remember affectionately the days when a business man could look down upon a poet with genuine righteous indignation. The poet was a loafer, a pretender, and probably immoral as well; whereas the business man was the incarnation of all the virtues. At least in those days the poet knew exactly where he stood; he could recognize who the enemy was and where were the weak points in his armour. He could press against the firm wall of commercial disapproval and find it solid enough; and he understood, too, that the business man had moments: in front of the shaving mirror, before sleep, driving downtown in the car, when he was not so awfully sure that the poet did not have something which he himself had missed. Now that the old scheme of things seems to be disappearing under the impact of economic change and total war, the poet and the business man can almost shake hands and share together their rueful loss of the past. For both of them feel abandoned and both know that a new thing has come into the world which was not there before, in the presence of which they do not feel at home.

Fortunately for our self-respect, most of us are more than one thing. We are in the same person at once poet and peasant, father and husband, tax-payer and fisherman. In the moments when our chosen interest is under a cloud, we fall back for solace upon our other functions. But this is temporary at best. For the poet is first and foremost a poet. The outbursts of pure lyricism are more than expressions of moods; they are also mythological presentations of truth. They are not the nuances of ineffable vapourings but the apprehension of some essential values. For the poet, then, there is no relevant, as there is no irrelevant, event. Like all artists, he seeks the eternal through the temporal, but through that aspect of the temporal which remains unaffected by social upheaval. This is not to say that he is anti-social; not at all. He does not work for himself or for society but for the values of which he and society are the most appreciative. Thus he does not keep his eye on human beings as such, or on social organizations as such, but on values; and such values are of meaning to his fellows in the long run.

The poet has his eye fixed upon the beauty of the world. He goes on to the realm of pure value and has a glimpse of what

E

perfection all by itself can mean. He comes back to us with homesickness for eternity in communicable form, and lays it before our admiration with no charge. Shall we expect this to survive the disruption of printing and the shortage of rubber which wars bring about, or the presence in the actual world of the murderous intent of other peoples? The answer is that it can survive, yes, but not in the way that we have come to understand. For the modern evolutionist, to survive means to remain in existence, to present a continuity of effect which is uninterrupted. In this sense, poetry does not survive, for nothing does. But that which is intermittent may be the most persistent; what survives the longest is that which cannot be destroyed but which returns again and again in the periods after its dismissal. I firmly believe that poetry is a thing which human beings cannot do without. They may give it up for a while, but they are always compelled to return to it. In a sense it is possible to say that poetry can do without them but they cannot do without it.

For the poet has an insight into the essential values of the world, as though he had been allowed to penetrate the veil of conflict to the realm of pure essence behind it. There he is blinded and forced to withdraw, not without memory, however, fortunately for the rest of us. He tries to get on paper what he has seen but he cannot describe it; he can only speak the language of religion, the analogue; but we somehow know what he means, although we have not had the benefit of his experience.

Once upon a time I came into the living-room and sank into a chair as though I were utterly exhausted. When my mother wanted to know what had tired me so, I said that I had spent the whole afternoon writing a sonnet. I had. The poor lady thought my explanation indicated that I did not have the slightest idea of what real work was. It was true, of course, that I had never done any work in her sense of the term, but I have since, and I can honestly affirm that the occasion upon which I spent the entire day composing a sonnet, the entire day, mind you, not just an hour or an afternoon, was the one which produced the hardest day's work of my whole life.

How many times have I heard prosaic people exclaim that they too wished they had had the time to write poetry? Their assumption always is that anyone could do it, but that they have undertaken more serious and adult tasks. This is the kind of hard background against which the true poet (who is quite hard, too, in his way) needs to sharpen his teeth. Oh for the days when the business man, scorning literature and the arts as soft, went into commerce in order to accumulate a fortune, and, having done so, spent some of the money sending his son to a college which featured for undergraduates a full semester course on Shelley and Keats! We knew where we were, then. But now that the standards have been upset, and a poet is considered as good as his neighbour, the news in the paper is all about war, and the books in the stores are all by reporters, with an occasional novel concerned with current events. The poetry has been eclipsed; but, let us hope, only momentarily. In any case, we have the consolation of knowing that it can never remain for long out of the world.

So much is a product of chance—half the actual world, in fact: money, poetry, position in society; these are the mere trifles of chance so far as their historical ordering is concerned. The accidents of life are more often unpleasant than pleasant. The inheritance of sufficient money to make me free to write is pleasant; the fact that I have been born of Jewish stock is unpleasant; neither is me. For I shall no doubt come upon days when the money has evaporated and when I may be penalized by some fascist government for being Jewish. That will be too bad, since I do not believe in these superficial distinctions. After the ascension of Hitler, I investigated the Jewish tradition and found nothing in it to attract me. I am essentially Greek.

In my family, there was almost no religion in the sense of an organized affair. We were reformed Jews and my mother made me go to Sunday School and often to Saturday morning services, but only so long as it took her to appreciate the fact that it meant nothing spiritual to me. Every philosopher is a theologian in disguise; but religion has deserted the organized religions of our day, and a new one is needed. In a way, I envy the orthodox believers of any persuasion; they are so sure. Blessed are they when what they die for is their faith. So far as organized religion is concerned, this privilege will be denied me. For me, living in the period of reaction against political liberalism, the Jewish question has become both a critical problem and a boring subject. It hardly arose in my life until college days, and even then was not a problem for me. I do not believe that thus far in my life (I am now thirty-seven) I have ever been the victim of racial prejudice. In high school I had been persecuted for a short period, but only because my father had been born a German and we were at war with Germany. But these attacks were relatively short and unimportant; they made almost no impression.

Once while I was a boarding student at Horace Mann School in New York a student asked me to his home for dinner on a week-end. During dinner his younger sister, who must have been then about thirteen, suddenly said that her gloves had been stolen in school. 'Oh, I wouldn't say that unless I were sure', her mother cautioned, 'after all they may have been lost'.

'No, mother', she replied, 'at school we think that one of the Jews must have stolen them'.

The silence at the table was awful, but I can honestly say that I did not feel sorry for myself but for the family.

The feeling against Jews is based to some extent upon the assumption of their strangeness, and also upon a belief in their feeling of superiority. Since I have no sympathy with the Jewish tradition when it extends beyond the days of Jesus, my own conviction has always been that complete assimilation is the proper solution. Certainly the Jewish question is an awkward one, as embarrassing for some Gentiles as for all Jews, and the solution is aided somewhat by refusing to admit its existence whenever this is possible. I suppose that this is a difficult task for those Jews who have been brought up exclusively among Jews. But for Jews raised in small towns where the Jewish population is a small one, the question hardly exists.

At the University of Virginia, the question of anti-semitism was raised for me by the Jews. Members of the more orthodox Jewish Greek-letter fraternity thought that I ought to join the reformed Jewish Greek-letter fraternity. Members of the reformed Jewish Greek-letter fraternity thought that I ought to join the Christian one into which I had been invited. I thought that Greek-letter fraternities with their deliberate cultivation of snobbishness ought to have been abolished altogether, and this was an attitude which was not calculated to make my stay more pleasant. Those serious undergraduates who must reconcile their own researches into ultimate questions with the fact of the veneration accorded athletes and gentlemen may appear just as insulting as the athletes and gentlemen are to truly democratic students. One set is perhaps as bad as the other, viewed objectively. What saves the situation is that there are few truly democratic students and therefore almost nobody to assume an objective view. College is a very trying time of life.

There are only two anti-semitic groups: the Jews and the Gentiles. It would not be fair to guess which came first, the chicken or the egg. But certainly the vexed difficulty is aided and abetted by insisting upon its existence. Of course, there are extremes which must be taken into account; nobody in Nazi Germany could will away what has been described as the cold *pogrom*. Yet there are lesser degrees which will disappear if we refuse to take notice of them. I am a man who has to be insulted twice before he takes cognizance. I would much rather be mistaken about a wrong than anticipate it. Objectively, this does not always work, of course, even though I know that it is love and not hate which moves the world. Hate can destroy the thing whose limitations have outgrown its usefulness but it cannot construct. All constructive enterprise is founded upon love. The workman who does not love his tools and the plans upon which he is labouring will not do anything worthwhile. I want to contribute something to the common lot of my

[63]

brothers all over the world, and I know I can only do this through love.

My own preference in the matter of solutions for the so-called Jewish problem is, as I have already said, complete assimilation. If there are good things in the Jewish tradition that have not yet been assimilated by others, let them be contributed to the common pot. The disappearance of the Jews as such, not by wholesale murder and extermination or emigration, as the Nazis so inhumanly preferred, but by love and intermarriage, contains the only possible solution. If the Jews became indistinguishable from the general populations, there would not be any to hate. In one town in the west which I once visited, there were few Jews and consequently no prejudice. I had the fancy that presently some more Jews might arrive from the crowded areas of New York, set up their social barriers (for they, too, have their prejudices) and then spend time trying to break through them to a status of equality. The prejudice must be eliminated on both sides. Tolerance and the democracy of fellow-feeling are the only rational attributes of a good society which can eliminate the friction. The problem of anti-semitism is a Gentile problem provided the Jews do not return hate with hate—provided, that is, they behave in an ideally Christian manner, in which the Christians themselves have been so lax. If the Jews wish to distinguish themselves in a religious fashion, let them be the best Christians. Why is it considered so un-Jewish to follow Jesus who had himself been a Jew? Even though this will not solve the Jewish problem so long as there are those who make the erroneous racial distinction, it ought to be done because it is the right thing to do. In the last analysis, Jesus stood for love and the brotherhood of man, and that position cannot successfully be controverted.

Jacob Epstein, the sculptor, once told me that he only became conscious of being Jewish when some damned fool indiscriminately attacked the Jews. This best expresses my own feelings. I can find nothing sympathetic in the Jewish tradition. It seems to me to be essentially anti-rational, and so I feel much more at home in the Greek tradition. Spiritually I belong among the *epigoni* of the Greek philosophers who have produced modern philosophy and science. This leads me to embrace original Christianity, the Christianity of Jesus and the Fourth Gospel. With the essentially moralistic tradition of Judaism I can feel much admiration but no intimacy. I may have been born of parents who held to the Jewish faith, yet I know that I have always belonged to the Greek *epigoni*. This irritates the professional Jews who regard me as they would regard a rat deserting a sinking ship. I cannot take my departure under these circumstances, but on the other hand I cannot acknowledge allegiance where I do not truly feel it. So I remain vulnerable upon both counts, yet, I hope, faithful to reason.

All the same, I shall someday do a book which I have long had in mind: the philosophy of Christianity. It shall be called *The Logic of Jesus*. The neo-Platonism of Christianity is a story as old as Christianity, and, in a systematic way, at least as old as Origen and Plotinus; but the Platonism (as opposed to the neo-Platonism) of Christianity has to my knowledge never been brought out. Neo-Platonism is exaggeratedly mystical and irrational, whereas Platonism is metaphysically realistic and rational. The ontology of the metaphysical realism of Christianity is what remains to be shown. Perhaps I will be able to show it.

A young medical student who comes of good Baptist folk once asked me how he could solve the question of the divinity of Jesus which continued to trouble him. In the light of modern scientific knowledge, he asked, how can Jesus be regarded as a human being and also divine? He saw through the hollow mockery of most contemporary religious leaders and the politicalizing of the churches; yet while his own teacher had been a simple and sincere country minister whose days were spent in practising what he preached, in improving the conditions of the poor and otherwise in assisting those who could not help themselves, his laboratory work had convinced him that humanity is something irreconcilable with divinity.

My solution consisted in asking whether there is any essential difference between the greatest of men and the lowest of gods. If we admit that all things by their very being partake to some extent of divinity, since to be at all is somehow a major miracle, then the wisest and best of men is the most divine. On the other side, if Jesus is conceived to be the most human of the Trinity, the distinction between man and god seems to be partly obliterated. In the language of that branch of mathematics known as vector analysis, the lowest god may be understood by analogy with the 'Least Upper Bound' and the highest man with the 'Greatest Lower Bound' of something that we can feel but cannot sense. The whole conception of Jesus may be a myth, but it is a viable one. We must all get over the idea that to call a belief a myth is to condemn it. That was Frazer's original intention in *The Golden Bough*. He came to mock but remained to pray when the prevalence of certain myths convinced him of their fundamental importance. Among the most prevalent is the myth of the dying god. We seem as human beings to need it, or something very much like it.

The medical student thought I had resolved his difficulties for him when actually he had helped me to resolve mine. For in posing the problem in a particular way he did, he had suggested the solution to me. This is always the way of the seeker after knowledge. I cannot write a book with any success unless it is on a topic about which I know nothing. I learn as I investigate as I write.

A last episode of college days. While I was living in Charlottesville, Anatole France died. It created quite a stir in English department circles. The editor of the college paper, a fraternity brother of mine, asked me to contribute an editorial in the form of an obituary. This student was the idol of the campus, a senior law student and member of the honorary fraternity. I had never written for his paper and was surprised at the request. Being deeply moved myself by the first death of a great contemporary, I consented eagerly. The editorials were all unsigned, and I was with the editor the next day walking down the campus when he was congratulated on his excellent editorial. He accepted the laudatory remarks with becoming modesty and never blinked an eye. It was something of a revelation. The brazenness of the *idola fori* is a proper subject for comedy.

The end of my college career of six months left me with the question which I had asked in childhood and tried to express in poetry: what does it mean to be? For decades, centuries, æons perhaps, I had not been; and now, suddenly and for no accountable reason, I was. The increase of self-consciousness and of the awareness of the world around me through the process of education only served to intensify and to objectify the question; from the necessity for explaining my own being, I was to turn to the infinitely larger and more important necessity for explaining all being. At the University I had learned at least that there are avenues of inquiry other than those of which I had already taken cognizance. But I was to range far afield and be very much surprised before settling down to the kind of inquiry which I had not chosen but which came to choose me. The history of a man may be almost totally explained as the attempt to answer a question which he had asked as soon as he was old enough to wonder.

CHAPTER TWO

The Self Beyond the Hills of Home

THE third decade of the twentieth century had begun, but I was only half aware of the fact. That is to say, I knew what was going on but I could not view it from any broad perspective; therefore I took it to be the usual kind of thing. Most of the talk in my home concerned the operation of a department store. It seemed to me that to beat last year in sales had always been both the slogan and the aim of mankind. Since business had always been progressing, the effort to help it to progress was the natural outlet for man's interests and energies. I knew in a general way that men lived by the production, the distribution, and the exchange of goods, and that to do so was the natural and absorbing passion of the vast majority of persons, but there my own interests ceased. I wanted no part of it. Business seemed to me just what it was: necessary, crude, demoralizing, ugly, and powerful. I was afraid of it, for like all artists of the day I conceived it to be inimical to art.

The business man, his life and ambitions, convinced me that I was correct in my conclusions. America was being developed at a pace almost unheard of anywhere else. Materially, the country was growing up very fast and ready to come of age. The grim spirit of competition took possession of everyone, and things were estimated at their survival value only. The test for everything was that which had been reported rather than discovered by William James: does it work, can you make it function, can you get away with it? Everyone took a moral holiday, except James who had recommended it. The decks were stripped for action.

This kind of situation put art and all cultural concerns very much in the shade. To judge art by its exchange-value made artists very self-conscious, and a patronizing tone crept into the attitude of everyone who took the artist and his work seriously. If women wished to undertake cultural activities, provided such women were too old to attract men or to have children, why then let them. Charity became confused with forum lectures, art with philanthropy, beauty with a certain reserve, culture with puritanism, all in the hands of elderly women. Even religion assumed a kind of sour expression, and became limited to moral obligation. Cultural activities in the care of over-age females lost their joy and their abandon. The business man took his energies to his business, his relaxation to his young stenographer. For the artist, it was a hard choice to make. Cultural activities under such circumstances were nothing for the virile to undertake.

The artist who wished to be neither patronized by women nor looked down on by business men had but one choice remaining provided he remained in America. He could build an ivory tower and retire into it. This is exactly what most of the artists did. Fortunately for them, Freud happened to become known widely in America about that time. The vogue for psychology had begun. Freud was interpreted by the artistic brotherhood as meaning that everything worth while was internal to the human individual, and thus both singular and arbitrary. The external world was an indifferent affair; all that it gave to the individual was a set of problems for adjustment. It was conceived of as something with which we had to cope, not an aid in any way. Of course, Freud was not responsible for this view of the indifferent external world; the view was as old as Newton, but it was perfectly suited to the purposes of Freudian psychology. In art, Freud meant first of all freedom of expression, and freedom of expression meant first of all freedom of sexual expression and only secondarily freedom of artistic expression. Self-expression became the motto not only for artists but also for advanced education. What was to be expressed was never supposed to have come to the individual from the external world. All issued from within him and was assumed to have originated there. Everyone was held to be in possession of something which he wished to say.

This period, it should be remembered, was the "post-war" period; and its premises explain the attitude which was taken toward the first world war. The conflict had been a ghastly mistake; nothing had been accomplished by it; this was now generally understood, hence all wars were considered a thing of the past. The democratic fashion in government spread to countries which did not understand anything about democracy except in its crudest external forms. That the world actually had been saved for democracy for twenty years was not credited to the victory over Germany and her allies. Rather was it regarded as part of the nature of things, the natural course which events were bound to follow.

Those who were just a little older than we regarded themselves as members of the lost generation. The war had done them in, they claimed. By this they meant that they had no morals and no aims. But they certainly could not have meant that they had no ambitions. They wished to shock people and to make themselves known as great artists, and they succeeded somewhat in doing both. Prohibition helped them, for it made drinking something at least legally exceptional. They had fun, of course; we of the younger group envied them and set about to emulate them as closely as possible. But they fooled us, and we went farther in their original direction than they did. At the first signs of public welcome they abdicated from their old pretensions, while we took their original direction seriously. Gertrude Stein, for instance, became a popular lecturer and writer; Hemingway grew into a popular novelist; T. S. Eliot, whom we had regarded as an artistic revolutionary, turned out to be a political and artistic conservative, even in some ways a reactionary. But at the time we could not suspect that this was to happen. We still thought that the adherents of custom and tradition and puritanism were to be opposed, and we struggled against them. It made life an exciting adventure.

Fortunately for my education—I had been getting very little from the formal side of my college experiences—a combination of influenza and measles put me in the hospital for two months. The doctors forbade me to make up my work during the summer, and I was unwilling to be a freshman again in the fall, so I left college never to return as a student.

I went to Europe instead. It was not my first trip but my second. I had been taken on the first trip by an uncle. We had gone to Paris, where I did not see anything but the inside of cabarets for a month, and then to Germany where I did not see anything but the outside of relatives for a week. My German grandparents were still alive and quite old. They were peasants and lived in a tiny farming village in the Rhine country, Ruëlzheim, near Dusseldorf, a village of some five hundred families. We did not remain long there but spent most of our time in Mannheim and Dusseldorf where my uncles and aunts lived. I thought them impossible: lower-middle-class Germans, the class upon which Hitler drew, unctuous, superior, and ignorant. They could not understand my love for Paris when I was free to go to Berlin; and they could not understand why I refused to take their word for it that Longfellow was the greatest American poet. When I feebly mentioned Whitman and Poe, their answer was that if these fellows were important would not the Germans have been the first to know about them? The younger members of the family spent their time with friends in the town, stealing for fun and excitement; and, as is now clear, planting the seeds of Nazism.

But, by and large, travelling in Germany between wars and before the rise of the Nazi party was certainly a pleasure for the foreigner. The Germans in general were polite and helpful and did everything they could to make things pleasant. All the same, I felt uneasy and did not enjoy being in their country.

The French were quite another story. On casual acquaintance I found them just the opposite: rude, quick and on the whole impolite, yet in the end fairer to strangers and better to be around. Paris was certainly where all good Americans could plan to go when they died, if they could not remain there when alive. It is the only place I have ever cried at leaving, and still remember with much longing.

It was in Paris that I came of age. The event which precipitated my initiation into adult life had nothing to do with women. I had been writing poetry for years and contributing to the little magazines; that was the sentiment which I managed to convey to an impoverished and unsuccessful belletrist I happened to meet at a literary party. He seemed very sympathetic and invited me to come to his house one afternoon later in the week to read my poetry to him. I had the impression that if he liked my poems, the book was as good as published. He lived in a remote environ, and sustained himself, his peaked wife and even more peaked baby by writing one book review each week for an American paper, for which he received the sum of fifteen dollars. This occupied the whole of one afternoon; the remainder of the week he rested, chiefly in *cafés* with second-rate French writers, with whom the talk was about first-rate writers, who were, incidentally, too busy to sit about all day in *cafés*.

At the appointed hour, I hied me to his house with the manuscript tucked under my arm. I rode to within hailing distance of the address and then walked. As I approached the house, I noticed dimly that other young men were converging upon the same spot, all with similar manuscripts carried in much the same fashion. My egotism protected me at this point. I was only a little irritated at my host for inviting so many other people to hear me read my poetry when I had intended that it should be not a formal reading but rather an avenue to publication in book form. We reached the door where each one rang the bell for himself, none of us accepting other rings as official Soon a maid answered and ushered us into the living-room as though we had been expected. We sat there very stiffly, glaring at one another, each wondering indignantly, I suppose, when our host was going to enter and single him out as the star of the occasion, thus putting the others properly in their place.

Some time passed, though probably not as much as it seemed, before the antagonistic silence was broken. And then it was not broken by us but by our hostess. She came in very cheerfully and spoke to the following effect.

'Boys, I am very sorry that my husband cannot be here as he had planned. He has gone on a bicycle trip with a young girl he met recently. He had hoped to be present when you read your poetry to each other, but circumstances willed it otherwise. Perhaps some other time'.

My anger was nearly uncontrollable. On the way back to my hotel, I could hardly breathe because of the emotion. To me then it was a sell-out on a gigantic scale; a preposterous, a cosmic, joke, made out of the worldly ambition for publication of a great though naturally somewhat childish genius. It was cheap and low and something for which not only the perpetrator but perhaps the whole world ought to be made to pay a terrible price.

By the time I reached my room I was almost ready to cry. Then suddenly, how I do not know, I saw the episode in its proper perspective and myself as a highly ridiculous figure. I was almost grateful to my quondam host for having aided my development so rapidly. I was now ready to face the world without illusions.

The world itself came back to me in a funny way. Youth is a period in which we feel that events never quite measure up to what we think their critical character will demand of us. We are always ready to meet crises but we are confronted only with the commonplace. It is not until later years that we understand how commonplace events were actually critical without having been recognized by us as such. After Paris I was ready for almost anything. I would imagine that I was in the rank and file of a great army which would melt away when danger came, leaving me to confront the enemy single-handed, a task at which, of course, I would be successful and the deserters eternally grateful. Or again many beautiful women were in love with me, all at the same time, a rather awkward situation from which I would manage to emerge triumphant. I was tense, bracing myself for the expected onslaught. 'Keep cool', I kept reminding myself, 'remember that this action will be something upon which you may have to stand or fall for centuries, perhaps for ever'.

What actually did happen then was that I spent two weeks of complete relaxation on the beach at the Lido. Such is the recuperative power of youth that I managed to enjoy it. What

I particularly liked there was the fashion in clothes: all day on the beach in bathing trunks, then suddenly in the evening white tie and tails for dinner and dancing. It was a wonderful transition, one which I have remembered with pleasure. To be a beachcomber and a night-club habitué in quick succession is my idea of sartorial heaven. I have always liked clothes but pay attention to them only at times and then only in extremes. And I have always liked dancing and I have always liked beaches.

The Lido dance-floor was nothing like the best that Paris had to offer. I sometimes wonder if anything ever was as good. The cabaret 'Florida', with its two orchestras: American jazz and Argentine tango, its close hot atmosphere, almost suffocating with Guerlain perfume, its beautiful women, its easy intimacy combined with formal manners, was something unequalled anywhere then or since. But the Lido at night also meant a beach in the daytime.

Beaches indicate to me something faintly redolent of sex: epicene and ultimately attractive. It is a feeling which I have found to be shared only by Proust and certain of the French Impressionists. Proust's hero first saw Albertine on the beach, I believe, and associated her with it for some time. But it has to be an American or a French beach; an English or Dutch beach would never do. In America, it is the smell of shell-fish rotting, perhaps, or the seaweed and salt-water; some combination which is reminiscent of infinite yearnings and evasive feline values.

These were the days in which it was possible to be amused and diverted by what one of my friends has called the C.I.S., the Cheap International Set. Englishmen fresh with enormous wealth made in the far east consoled themselves for not being anything more in England than contemptible colonials by remaining in Paris and spending money on broken-down Hollywood actresses who had reached just that stage of ripeness which struck the Englishmen as juicy. Hysterical, soft East Indians of doubtful ambition mingled with pock-marked Cockney vaudeville managers. French women from the half-world whose refusal to bathe made their lavish use of perfume even more necessary, bowed to the superior bank accounts of American men in a hurry. American women on leave from their working husbands picked and chose. It was certainly a spectacle lush in its profusion and quite dazzling to a young American fresh from the University of Virginia.

Only for a brief second did the shadow of academic Virginia appear over the wonderful life of Americans in Paris. Early one morning I recovered consciousness, or so it seemed, and found myself at a *café* table with three young Americans I had never seen before. I was still in evening clothes at six in the morning; perhaps the former contents of the two empty coffee pots in front of me had done the sobering trick. One of my companions proved to be a tall young instructor in philosophy whose name was familiar to me. At Virginia he had aspired to the greatest aloofness of all on the campus. Now he was a little bedraggled and most astonishingly carefree and clever, and I liked him.

An old woman passed us on the street, and the philosophy instructor tipped his hat to her politely. With an impeccable accent he said, '*Et votre tante! ça marche?*'

I had the most trouble with a middle-aged, fat ex-movie actress from the States who had fallen in love with a Frenchman. She wrote to him in English and he answered her in French. Since she could not read his letters she always brought them to me to be translated. It was obvious that he was trying gracefully to sever the relationship without hurting her feelings. She wanted to know not only what he said but also what he meant, and this was a source of considerable embarrassment. I did not have the courage to tell her the truth and thought it better to let her find out for herself. With an Englishman from the Malay Peninsula who was very wealthy she had better luck, but he was only an income to her. After lunching with him she always walked him a little way, as far, that is, as Tiffany's shop in the Rue de la Paix. There before calling a taxi she would see the darlingest diamond bracelet in the window. That night she would receive it in the middle of a box of flowers. I do not think she ever slept with him.

The Englishman was a pathetic case in a way, though hardly

[75]

evocative of righteous sympathy. He was a bachelor and came to Paris three months out of every year for his vacation, while his partners took care of the business in Singapore. Then he returned home to allow them to do the same. He was immensely wealthy, and terribly bored with himself and everything. At Singapore it was impossible to spend even part of his income, so in Paris he did what he could. During the summer months I knew him he had purchased a complete racing stable at Deauville but had gone there only one week-end to watch the horses run. The remaining weeks he stayed in Paris, and I was with him often when the telegrams arrived from his manager informing him of the races his horses had won or lost that day. After a few weeks he did not even open the telegrams. Every night we dined together, some ten or twelve of us. Caviar and champagne, *caneton pressé*, the finest wines, everything. The British subject, as we came to call him, paid the bill. It was expected by him as well as by the others that he would do so. He would have been surprised at anything else.

He was in fact very much surprised. One night we happened quite by accident to find ourselves alone. All the other parasites were somewhere else, through some misdirection, no doubt. I dined as usual with the British subject. It was rather nice and he proved to be a charming man; I had almost not met him before. After dinner the waiter brought him the bill, of course, but I reached for it and quickly paid it before there could be any argument. He was surprised and a little hurt.

'Why did you do that?' he asked with some bafflement.

'Simply because I am tired of being a parasite,' I said. 'Every night I have eaten your dinner because I could not get a separate check and because I could not afford to pay for all the others. But now that there is a chance, I most earnestly do want to buy you at least one dinner'.

The gratitude was astonishing. Evidently nobody had ever thought about him before; at least so he said. He offered me a position in his business in Singapore, and promised me an attractive salary and rapid advancement. Poor man: he meant well but always based his boredom of other people on a failure to read them correctly. At the moment, business was the worst thing I could imagine, and I was very busy trying to discover how I could get out of one at home.

Paris, the Paris of Americans who were escaping from the success of American business, was a city that never has existed; the French would be amazed if they could learn about it, and those of us who were there in the nineteen-twenties remember it now with extreme incredulity, like the details of a fantastic dream. Not that Paris was so odd or unbelievable; what was strange was the Paris that we thought existed. The French were a sober and hardworking people. It was the imagination of Americans which fostered the Paris we lived in then.

I can remember that I did not admire the French. Not because they were rude to Americans: they were, and indeed much of their manner was deserved. I saw an American enter a theatre late one evening and in a very loud voice object to the *strapontin* seats in the middle of the aisle through which it was not possible for him to pass.

'We would never allow a thing like that in America', he exclaimed in a shout, as though what was and what was not allowed in America must be the criterion for the rest of the world throughout the ages. But I did not admire the French especially because of their rudeness to each other. Probably this did not apply to the working class. But it did apply to the white-collar workers: each regarded the other as the enemy, and not once did I hear a civil word spoken or see a polite action pass between them. All was gruff, ill-done, grudging and against the grain: as though every man's hand was set against every man and each one knew his brother for his adversary. Why this was, I could not understand at the time.

But all the same Paris was a wonderful place. The French contributed a low cost of living, and an absolute indifference, to our gaiety. The first thing I did the summer I spent in Paris on my own was to purchase the following articles: a cane, gloves, spats, a chequered vest of white flannel, and a black monocle. Better than that: I wore them—for a while. When I began to inhabit the left bank I naturally discarded this finery.

[77]

I wanted to wear old clothes but that would not permit me to return to my hotel in the evening. I had to compromise somewhere between the extremes. Quite unwittingly, the compromise took the form of wearing just what I would have been wearing back in the States: an ordinary suit. Although I did not know it, the American cut made me conspicuously a foreigner in both places: the left and the right bank.

On the left bank, there were three *cafés* situated very close together: The Dome, the Rotond and the Select. Every summer when I returned to Paris, I would always begin at the *café* which had been fashionable the summer before, and it would always be necessary for me to become reoriented. My friends would look at me with a most supercilious smile, and say, 'Well, you could not find us because you looked for us at the Dome (or Select or Rotond); *nobody* goes *there* anymore. We're all at the Select (or Dome or Rotond) now'. We would sit and pile up the dishes and talk about art. Hemingway's *Torrents of Spring* contains a very amusing and true account of this life. It never occurred to any of us that the artists whose work we were discussing so critically and admiringly were in Paris but were not to be found at the *cafés* except very occasionally, and then only in the evenings. During the day, while we were boasting to each other about them, they were home working like dogs to get something done.

By 'them', I mean of course James Joyce. Joyce owes the speed of his reputation as a writer to the little coterie of left-bank enthusiasts. They were worthless and lazy pretenders, but so far as Joyce was concerned they served their turn admirably, for they blew his horn for him. It did not matter that they failed to understand in the slightest what he was doing. They thought him a Freud-man, a leading cultist of the unconscious, the mantic, the irrational, and the chaotic. They ignored the warning against such an interpretation issued by Stuart Gilbert in his book on Joyce, wherein he showed the enormous complexity and self-consistency of *Ulysses*, and they used his name to justify their enthusiasm for automatic writing, surrealism, and all the thousand revolts against reason. The chthonic

[78]

deities played their role in the work of Joyce as they had played it in the tragedy and comedy of the Greeks, but it was not a leading role nor the protagonist of the play ever. However, the members of the little group which centred about the magazine, *transition*, never found this out and Joyce evidently did not tell them.

Why is it that the revolt against the omission of value by the reign of reason must always come in the name of disvalue? The orderliness of the physical universe as presented by science seemed to leave no corner for human value. Very well, then, the artist would retaliate by worshipping all the human disvalues. He would turn against the kind of society which had produced such a monstrous science and would seek refuge in the oldest of human things: unreason, ancient myth, primitive art, impulse. The painters would try to paint like savages, the musicians would leave the melodic line and seek a haven in assonance and atonality, the philosophers would devote their work to an attack upon the whole enterprise of philosophy itself, and the poets would take their departure from a denial of all that had been done in the poetry of the past. Guided by the unhealthy hand of Freud, whose insight into the importance of sex and its enormous capabilities in everyone had led him to suppose that all is sexual, the artists saw an identity between the art of adult primitives and that of their own civilized children, and attempted to copy it themselves with a naïveté that is still amazing. They did not know it then and they would not admit it now, but activity of this nature on the part of the artists proves once more that, wittingly or unwittingly, such leadership really is leadership: we were being led by our advance guard back into war and disintegration. Hitler was a product of the same forces that produced the subjective idealism of Dali. I am not suggesting, of course, that Dali has the same kind of evil intent that Hitler represented. Of course not. Dali is an ephemeral comedian whose temporary vogue has caused him to take himself quite seriously. I am simply suggesting that a kind of philosophy is loose in the world which is apt to throw off all sorts of irrationalisms. The artists and intellectuals being more sensitive than other persons, feel it and express it first.

Consider, for example, the case of Edmund Wilson. I have followed the writings of Wilson with interest for some years. He is, I feel sure, a desperately hard worker and a very sincere man. He is also a very bright one, and so he cannot help being in the realm of letters what the French would call a *chic type*. So far as the trend of ideas goes, he is better than Bulova watch time. Culturally speaking, it is always possible by watching Wilson's latest slant to tell what time it is. In the nineteen-twenties he was a Freudian and interpreted everything in terms of sex. In the nineteen-thirties he was a Marxist and interpreted everything in terms of economic determinism. Since nineteen-forty he has been a disciple of cultural Russia; he has studied the language and writes articles about classic Russian literary figures. What will the next decade bring? He has, it is obvious, no protection against the impact of current intellectual forces; in all probability he lacks the requisite philosophical background. Were he to study the history of ontology and epistemology with the same assiduity that has marked his study of the Russian language, he might well become a great critic. But he will probably leave metaphysics alone because, for reasons he feels rather than knows, the *zeitgeist* is set against it, and he is more of a leading follower than a leader. Meanwhile, since there are no other contenders for honours in literary criticism in the United States, we are the losers.

That is why I interpret the presence of such thinkers as Whitehead, and the spread of such influences as that of Peirce, as good omens: the return to reason is just around the corner: the future is bright though the present be dark enough. Our novelists, if not our painters, are beginning to affirm rather than deny, to love rather than hate, to aspire rather than despair. There is hope loose in the world now, and it will have its effect as surely as it is an external thing independent of us and living a life of its own.

But in those days when we sat around the Dome, and tried

to be tough, we were like the originals of Hemingway's *The Sun Also Rises*. If you were tough enough, you qualified as a writer, and anything you wrote thenceforth would be viewed with respect. I was not considered hard enough, but one boy from the middle-western States actually entered his claim on the basis of the fact that before running off to Paris to write, he had quit school and also had violated a young girl, and abandoned her when she fell in love with him. It was in the circles of the expatriates that the mutual admiration societies were formed which came home to dominate New York's literary and intellectual life.

This seems to be as good a place as any to take a fling at that particular phenomenon. Most of the genuine writers of America, the novelists and poets and short-story writers, come to New York to visit but seldom work there. They work in California or New Orleans, or in the heart of the country. They only sell their wares in New York. But in New York, as seems quite appropriate, live the critics and the publishers. I may treat these gentlemen in that order.

First the lesser critics. Since unreason has taken the place of reason in our modern society, most of the critics have resorted to impressionism in criticism. That is to say, they wish to analyze nothing in criticizing a book, they feel obliged only to state their own impressions. If the critic were a super-sensitive man, as indeed he purports to be, then the mere statement by him of what feeling a work of art gives him would be enough to explain the feeling the same work of art ought to give others. The critic is using himself as exemplary, sensitive, recording mechanism whose reactions offer a reliable pointer-reading of what the value of any work under examination actually is. This is, obviously, quite a pretension, and the only justification offered for it by the critic is something that may be referred to as literary style. If the critic can write in such a way that even school children would throw his sentences out as non-syntactical, why then he has a style. Assuredly, rules of grammar, as of anything else, are made to be broken judiciously. But not all breaking of rules is justifiable. Great writers may write in such a way that their writings would not be approved by the authority of the departments of English; yet not all the writing that would qualify to meet with such disapproval is great writing.

I offer as exhibit A of the kind of horror I am speaking about, the theatrical criticisms of Stark Young. In the files of the *New Republic* exist example after example of how *not* to write. There are pages in which exquisite innuendos are suggested, and where nothing forthright is said. The line of Shakespeare applies to such critics perfectly: ' 'Twere to consider too curiously to consider so.' The whole attempt to convey feeling in rational terms, to make another feel what you have felt by conveying that *feeling* in prose is an error. All that may be conveyed is a rational description of what such feeling implies, or else recourse must be had to metaphor. The Stark Young school is attempting to use rational language metaphorically, an obvious impossibility. Young's abject disciple with regard to style, Otis Ferguson, has betrayed the master in attempting to reconcile super-sensitivity with the imitation of the hard-boiled school. The result is frequently more amusing than Young's profundities, but hardly more illuminating.

There are only two ways of expressing philosophical observations in such a way that they will be accepted and appreciated by the reading, which is to say the 'literary', public. One is to utter profound statements lightly. This is the way of the French professional philosopher and often of the French literary man. The other is to utter trivial statements profoundly. This is the way of the American critic and popular sage. Only too often, the American literary man will drag in the name of a classic philosopher in order to deepen the water and show his learning. A few examples of this practice might be to the point.

A political columnist once referred to the fact that time was of the essence of the contract. The word, time, to him seemed the height of this proposition, so he went on with it. We owe this enlightenment to Bergson, he added, meaning, of course, nothing more than that Bergson had written about the importance of time. Another man, a literary critic, referred to someone who had been positive about something or other. 'This kind of positivism', he began, obviously in total ignorance of the fact that positivism is a negative rather than a positive doctrine.

Style to me is something pretty bad. I have liked only two stylists. One was named Sparrow Robertson (or Robinson?), the sports reporter on the Paris edition of one of the two American newspapers. Sparrow, who got very drunk with my uncle, could always get all the first person pronouns into his opening paragraph. 'Your reporter went to the fight last night,' he would write, 'and one enjoyed it very much. I had a very good time because the manager had given us ringside seats despite the sellout.' Sparrow is dead; too bad. My other stylist was the theatrical reporter for a New Orleans newspaper, who has since been discharged. His accomplishment was to mix the categories by considering everything inside the physical boundaries of a theatre as on the same level of analysis as the play. In his daily column, he would refer with admiration to the performance of some play he had seen the night before. 'The acting and ticket sale were extremely good.' Or he would not like it. 'The leading lady turned in a poor performance and the lighting was bad.'

It would not be fair to leave the notion that an obvious prose style is an inappropriate one without devoting a few words to the philosophy of Santayana. There is some doubt whether any recognized philosopher ever succeeded in devising a worse vehicle for his ideas. While it may be permissible for the literary man to allow his ideas to be diverted by his words, it is surely not so for the philosopher. 'Intellectual anarchy,' we learn from the first sentence of *Platonism and the Spiritual Life*, 'is full of lights; its blindness is made up of dazzling survivals, revivals, and fresh beginnings.' What on earth, if anything, does this mean? Philosophy has difficulties enough expressing its abstractions without striving for effects which can only serve to show through examples how difficult it is. Does Santayana mean that he *really* thinks he is 'an ignorant man, almost a poet', as he tells us in the Preface to *Scepticism and Animal*

Faith? Either he is not saying what he means or what he means can only be expressed in purple prose; in both alternatives he must stand equally condemned.

The pretensions of the publishers are a little more hollow and do not do quite as much damage to public sensibilities as do those of the critics. First of all, the publishers themselves do not reach personally nearly so many people, and then again the books they publish are written by others. The harm accomplished by the publishers is not serious, even though their pretensions are. Briefly, their offence is this: they pose to authors as business men and to business men as artists. They are business men, it is true, but they are not *big* business men, they are only little ones. On the other hand, they are not artists at all. Their contact with authors does not make them authors, and the side of authors they do come into contact with is the very worst side. Authors are notoriously bad business men, and so they hate and distrust their publishers, often, though not always, with good reason. Hence, the publishers cannot really be said to know their authors on any kind of personal basis; each is trying too hard to get something out of the other. A little honesty and pride of enterprise, shorn of pretence, would reduce the status of publishers in their own estimation but improve their situation immensely. Needless to add, this criticism of publishers is not without exceptions. Everyone respects those who respect themselves.

There is no doubt something very wrong with the commercial side of art. The artist must eat, he must sell his wares to the public somehow. This requires middle men: art galleries, publishers, theatrical producers, and literary agents. All the same, there is something unclean and panderish about the whole affair of making a living on men who make a living on works of art. I cannot explain this altogether, because I do not altogether understand it. I only know that the man who sells shirts is more honest than the man who sells paintings, regardless of whether both are honest or dishonest. I mean that it is a more honest thing, let us say, for a dishonest man to sell shirts than for him to sell paintings. Molière observed it;

'*c'ést une étrange enterprise, celle de faire rire les honnêtes gens*'. He was speaking as a play producer, not as a playwright, voicing the cry of the artist who must live by pleasing the public.

Perhaps what I feel about the profession of entrepreneur of the arts can best be explained by what Sherwood Anderson once told me about the relations between men and women and money. I had been objecting to a friend of ours who had married a woman for her money. Sherwood disagreed; we did not know enough about their relationship to talk about it, he explained. It is all right to take money from a woman if you love her, he said; otherwise not. We are altogether too careless about taking and we should do so only where there is love; that was his point. Something of that explanation enters into what I feel about publishers and operators of art galleries; there is no love to make it all right.

In those years between world wars, when along with other Americans I went to Europe in search of a friendly feeling toward the arts, there took place what almost amounted to an organized raid on continental culture. There must have been something like 200,000 Americans flocking to Europe every summer. Not all of them wished to go; they went for many trivial reasons: for instance out of curiosity, because of the change of scene, for amusement or to have been where the neighbours could not afford to go. But most of them went for serious reasons: in general to worship the culture of the old world which, as Dostoevski once remarked, is a grave-yard but a precious one. I met many pathetic instances of the search for culture, and a number of them unwilling victims.

There was the lawyer from San Francisco, for example. I met him at the house of an American in Paris. When the evening was over we walked part of the way home together and stopped for a beer. He was a bachelor and had done very well: good university, *summa cum laude*, lived at his club, faithful retainers, largely corporation work. This was not only his first trip since graduating from Harvard, it was also his first vacation since he had begun to practise some ten years before. He had gone all through Italy and was now on his way home. He breathed a sigh of relief. Soon he would be within sight of the gymnasium, the nightly bridge game, the office, the drug store lunch. I ventured to investigate.

'What did you do in Italy?' I asked.

He looked pained. 'I went through all the art galleries.' There were art galleries in America but he had never been inside them. 'I believe,' he said meditatively, 'I believe that I have seen Christ in every position: hanging from the cross, folded in his mother's arms, lying in the tomb, standing by the sea of Galilee.'

He was happy to be going home.

Then there were the college boys in the hotel lobby in Genoa. They had just been to see Da Vinci's *Last Supper*. They were engaged in a violent argument as to the number at the table.

'There's twelve.'

'No, thirteen!'

'No, twelve.'

'Aw, you guys, you just didn't count Jesus because he had passed out, that's all.'

There were the tired mothers leading their children through whole countries full of culture; there were the school teachers amazed to learn that there were such things as street cars in Paris, a city which they had thought would be more primitive.

It was not pleasant for me to remember that I, too, was an American travelling in Europe. I was arrogant enough to forget it most of the time because I was also young; and I was also humble enough to remember it sometimes because I had a deep respect for literature and the arts. John McClure, a poet and an older man who was helpful to me (but who was unfortunately to drop his interest in the writing of poetry at an early date) gave me good advice before I sailed. 'Do not look up famous people', he said. 'The second-raters are apt to be much nicer.'

He certainly was right about that. There is something very hurtful about success. The famous writers and artists all wear masks. It is not possible to get to know them, which is often unfortunate for them. They are lonely people and very difficult to help, isolated as they are in their pride and prominence. But it is equally true that the good qualities of men emerge in adversity; the second-raters are very human.

I had been annoying the owners of big names in my field for some time in England and on the Continent, but when I reached Ireland, I stopped. William Butler Yeats was one of my large admirations. I understood then my extreme shortcomings: I knew what he had to give me, but what could I possibly offer him? I had a good letter of introduction to him from friends in England, and an Irish friend also offered to introduce me; but I declined, wisely as I have thought since; no matter how much I regret that he is dead and that now I shall never even see him.

Among all those I met in Paris none were so wonderful as the Norwegian poet, Hermann Wildenvey, and his wife, Gisken. Through them I met many members of the Norwegian literary colony in Paris, which forgathered for a while at a *café* entitled Chez les Vikings. I heard many tales about the Wildenveys, superb tales, and had myself many experiences with them. I shall not tell them all nor in the proper order.

What more wonderful fate can befall a poet than to be born in a little country? Wildenvey has probably had a drink with every contemporary adult male in his land at one time or another, and everybody knows him and his poetry. Before world war second, whenever he gave a formal reading of his poems, the king and queen would take a box, the royal box; where else does this happen to a poet? Wildenvey was the typical nineteenth-century type of poet; dreamy, impractical and a little mischievous. I met him once in Paris on a particular mission; he had telephoned me to help him obtain an American visa. He was coming to the United States to lecture before some of the mid-western universities in those states having large populations of Scandinavian origin. An official at the American consulate inquired into Hermann's business in America and upon learning its nature suggested that if Hermann could obtain a letter from the Ministry of his government in Paris he could be given a diplomatic visa which would cost him nothing.

'Can you get such a letter?' we asked him.

Hermann thought about this for a moment, then quite naïvely said, 'Yes, I can get a letter from the King.'

We decided for him that it would be unnecessary to appeal to such high authority, and I accordingly took him over to the Norwegian Minister's house after he had made an appointment by telephone. I was formally entertained in an outer office by the First Secretary while Hermann went into the Inner Sanctum of the Minister. The First Secretary was a youngish man who laughed a great deal and had no mean fund of dirty stories; I liked him very much and we got along famously. Time passed; but the thing that worried me was that I knew I had to get Hermann back to the American Consulate before it closed, because he wanted to sail for America the next day. I ventured to suggest the nature of my difficulties to the Secretary. He understood and sympathized. Wiping the smile from his face and assuming the requisite dignity, he tiptoed over and knocked gently on the door of the Minister's office, then entered.

He emerged a few minutes later, and, closing the door behind him, burst into full though stifled laughter.

'I forgot to tell you,' he explained, 'the Minister broke his leg horseback riding a few days ago. He has it in a plaster cast, resting on a chair. He is fond of Hermann's poetry and always keeps a few volumes in his office bookshelf. Just at the moment, they are drinking highballs. The Minister is seated before a big fire, and Hermann is standing next to the fireplace, reading his poems aloud. Hermann always does that to everybody's working day,' he added.

Hermann, like his fellow countryman, Knut Hamsun, had come to the United States as a boy, and worked at manual labour in the middle west; he had driven street cars, too. On his lecture tour, many years later, he received a letter from an old boyhood friend.

'What kind of a country is that United States of yours?' he asked me over a beer in a sidewalk *café*.

The letter read in effect as follows. I was glad to see your name again after so long, and happy to learn that you have now become famous. Do you remember when we used to play together in G——? Well, that town is not there any more. There's a sawmill there now, and the town has been moved across the river and several miles down. I should perhaps tell you that the river isn't there now, either; it's been dammed up and makes a lake as quiet as you please, with scum on the surface around the edges. And you remember my sister that I once caught you kissing behind the barn? Well, she's moved to California and married a camera man and has three children of her own. You wouldn't recognize me, either, Hermann. I have changed my name and grown a moustache, and I live in Weehawken.

'What kind of a country is that?' Hermann wanted to know.

About 1925, all the school children in Norway put their pennies together, and the money was spent to buy Hermann and Gisken a little house in Friedericksvern, the summer resort of Oslo. The house was on a hill overlooking a fjord or deep inlet which the sea had cut into the mountains. Mind you, the school children bought a house with their pennies, not voluntarily for a movie star or compulsorily for a politician, but actually for a poet. It was truly wonderful. The little things that happened in that house make up the beautiful story of Hermann and Gisken.

I must add that Hermann is short and stocky and that all the vagueness is in his body and all the mischief in his eyes. Gisken is somewhat younger but tall and stately, delicate and strong, with all the power and majesty of the people of the north countries. She was in fact born in the northern part of Norway, the land of the midnight sun where sleep at night in darkness is impossible except by pulling shades and shutting blinds. Gisken's youthful interest in poetry led to a correspondence with Hermann, and a correspondence with Hermann led to an exchange of pictures. She had seen him in a photograph before, but she was seventeen and he had never seen anything like that. The marriage took place shortly afterwards.

[89]

When I knew the Wildenveys they had a habit of wandering off to Paris separately or together. Upon one occasion, Hermann had been away and was welcomed home by Gisken. He brought her as a present from the city a horrible little commercial china figurine of an elephant. Hermann presented it with the appropriate remarks and Gisken received it with uncontrollable distaste and recoil.

'Hermann,' she said, 'whatever made you buy that frightful thing?'

'You don't like it?' he asked.

'I think it's awful!'

Hermann was both shocked and angry. He had prepared his speech and gift for some time, and had expected better than he got. He picked up the elephant and dropped it out of the window; while his emotion overcame him they could both hear the little elephant clatter down over the rocks of the hillside below. Gisken then expressed her remorse. The elephant was out of sight, and so she thought she could comfort Hermann.

'I'm sorry, Hermann, I didn't mean you to do that. After all, it wasn't *that* bad.'

'You don't think so?' he asked hopefully.

'No, I don't. I was really glad to have it after you had gone to the trouble to bring it all the way here from Paris.'

'You really mean that?'

'Of course I do.'

Hermann rushed out of the house and down the hill as fast as his years of drinking and lack of exercise would let him. Unfortunate miracle of miracles, the elephant was intact and unbroken. He brought it back to the house with joy and great care, and Gisken this time was compelled to receive it with a resignation veiled by the appearance of gratitude and delight.

Upon another occasion, Gisken had been away and was welcomed home by Hermann. As usual he had wished to prepare some kind of special welcome for her arrival. He planned to bring their best friends to the railroad station, but that was not enough; he wished also to have a special suit to wear for the celebration which was to follow. He went to his tailor in Oslo and together they concocted something which proved to be a grey tweed cutaway. How they worked that out or what it was supposed to be, other than a costume for a gala occasion, was more than anyone could say. But anyhow it was worn, and Gisken, who could never overcome her surprise and astonishment at the actions of Hermann despite the length and intimacy of their acquaintance, exclaimed before she left the steps of the coach:

'Hermann, where *did* you get that *awful* suit?'

Hermann again was crestfallen, but the rest of the party managed to laugh it off, and the celebration was continued at the Wildenvey home. Among the guests was a very good friend of the Wildenveys, a man who was the professional comedian at the National Theatre in Oslo. Hermann refused to join the fun until the offending suit had been changed to one of his old ones. When the comedian left, it was with the suit; he had seen in it great stage possibilities. For years thereafter, any role which called very obviously for comedy was filled by the comedian in Hermann's grey tweed cutaway.

Was I wrong to pity the writers in small countries because the potential circulation of their books was sure to be small? Evidently so, for circulation is after all not everything. Norway is a small country, but everyone could read and everyone who could read had read some of Hermann's poems. In Havana on my wedding trip, my wife and I sat at a bar next to a young Norwegian sailor who had been working on a freighter. We began talking and buying each other beers. Just on an off-chance, I asked him if he had ever heard of Hermann Wildenvey, and then suddenly it seemed he had his arms around me and we were brothers. When he had left home, quite young, to make a living on the sea, he said, his mother had given him two books with instructions to read them and never to part with them. They were the Bible and a copy of Hermann's poems. Can mass circulation in great countries ever compare with that?

In sharp contrast with the spectacle of the popular poet in a

G

small country was that of the intellectual poet in the great English-speaking world. If Rupert Brooke's poetry had been my first shock, T. S. Eliot's *The Waste Land* was my second.

Eliot taught me that it is possible to make poetry carry a great deal of denotative meaning—far more than prose has ever been able to carry in a similar amount of space. He accomplished this by using combinations of familiar phrases rather than combinations of familiar words, as in ordinary speech and literature. His idiom is simply in larger units; and while his use of the new method is itself greatly limited, it *is* a new method. Perhaps Eliot has done all that can be done with it; it may be a blind alley with some very attractive houses on it but only one square long. Or it may open up vistas of literature greater than any we have yet seen. It is hard to tell so early. Eliot himself has simply employed the method to juxtapose classic bits from the past with sordid bits from the present—to the obvious detriment of the present. He has accomplished this of course only by leaving out what was bad of the past, its wars and commonplaces, and by leaving out what is good of the present, its sacrifices and pure science. But the effect is telling, and the mood is a sure one. I wrote a long poem heavily derived from *The Waste Land*, entitled *Department Store Fantasia*. Then my poetry began to take a tack of its own, in the direction of abstract metaphysical conceptions.

Eliot is the most significant example of the necessity for making a distinction between a man and his work. I had a profound respect for Eliot's poetry, and I still have that. But there is little to admire about the man. He has posed as the aristocrat who is hurt by the common things of life: the morning newspaper, the cheap popular novel, the slang of common talk, the advertisements. The solemnness of the professional literary man who is self-conscious all of the time, has become incorporated into his very being.

I was once invited to attend a monthly dinner given by the *Criterion* staff, in a little Italian restaurant. The dinner was held in a private dining room upstairs, and only one outsider was invited each month. The regulars included Humbert Wolfe,

F. S. Flint, and many others. The dinner resembled the Lord's Last Supper to the smallest detail. Eliot sat at one end of the table, nobody at the other. The disciples ranged themselves on the two sides, talking in whispers only when Eliot did not talk, and allowing themselves to be interrupted whenever he did. They inclined toward him and hung on his every word, and one looked about instinctively for Judas. After dinner, the men retired to someone's chambers, and Eliot lingered on the steps conversing with a disciple but leaving almost immediately, so that the general talk after he left could be an exegesis of the remarks he had made earlier.

I heard about a later dinner, attended by various groups of literary Englishmen, and given for some benefit or other. One side of the large table was occupied by beef-and-bully Englishmen drinking beer out of large tankards and toasting the U.S.S.R. not because they were communists but just for the hell of it, probably because they knew it would make Eliot shiver. Eliot, he said, sent out for a bottle of port, poured a little into each of the glasses of those who sat about him, then rose, followed by them, and said, 'Gentlemen, I give you the King,' holding his glass on high. They drank, and then Eliot smashed his glass on the floor. Looking around slowly, with wonderful timing, he said, 'Gentlemen . . . you may sit down,' then later, after a pause, 'Gentlemen . . . you may smoke.'

Once he asked Henry Miller for a story. Miller says he sent the story, but Eliot returned it with a note explaining why he had not liked it, and asked for something else. Miller wrote back a very long explanation of the reasons why he thought Eliot should have taken the story.' Eliot's reply was contained in a single line, 'You forgot to date your letter.' There is something fundamentally false and wrong about living out a life entirely in terms of a future 'autobiography with letters. Something ought to be left to chance.

T. S. Eliot, like most of us, was dissatisfied with the spiritual attitude of life in the post-war western world. To those who were malcontents so far as the present was concerned, there appeared to be two alternatives. In terms of the time-categories, it is always possible to escape into the past or into the future. In either case the actual world can be avoided in favour of a world of the imagination. But the mind is like an empty room; it must be furnished with materials from the external world, and the external world exists either in the past, the present, or the future. Those who are brave and who wish a new world which will have the virtues lacking in the old and will lack the vices common to the old, may use their imagination, together with the values and the logical relations learned in the past, to set up an ideal toward which the actual world may be brought. Others, however, wish to return the actual world to an old condition which they have idealized as having been better than it actually was. The latter choice is Eliot's. His golden age lies entirely in the past and not at all in the future. A rebirth for him must come from the hollow men, from the grave.

Eliot's interest in the Church and in the English way of life is occasioned by the fact that his sense of order, which is great, could not be satisfied with anything else in the present. It might be said of Eliot that he has too high a sense of personal order and too little a sense of the cosmos. Generally speaking, those who, like Santayana, Cabell and Eliot, are preoccupied with problems of style, end up with the wrong philosophy. Santayana's private realms, Cabell's mediaeval France, and Eliot's ideal England no longer exist, nor do we necessarily want them in the future. It ought to be possible to devise a future better than anything wholly in our past.

A familiarity with philosophical principles ought to teach that actuality by its nature can never be perfect; it ought to show that while progress exists, certain periods in the past have been better than the present, and that to return is to seal advance irrevocably within a certain definite point. For history does not repeat itself and a return to the past is impossible. The golden age must be placed, then, at some infinite point in the remote future. This requires some belief in the present, some hope for the future, and great self-abnegation. Such demands are exactly the ones which Eliot seems to lack. He has, however, represented something, and his ability as a poet is undeniable. Let us remember him for what he did well. People, like books and philosophical systems, must be remembered for what is good about them; and to this end it is necessary to view them in a favourable light.

One of the things I had definitely planned to omit from this book was personal letters. Like all firm resolutions by frail people, this cannot fairly be carried out I now find. For an inextricable part of my youth is the meeting with Bernard Gilbert. He is dead and nearly forgotten; it would be all right for me but quite bad for him not to quote something from what he wrote to me. For he had dreams of what America could be and how I could express this, and he wrote to me about it.

In the middle nineteen-twenties I sent a letter to Gilbert from London asking for a meeting. Gilbert had been one of the few foreign contributors whose work appeared in the pages of *The Double Dealer* and the only one whose few pages had made a strong impression upon me. Gilbert was living in Grantham, and he replied cordially. We had several meetings in London, and I began to read more of his work. He had published a number of volumes: plays, poems, novels, everything; and his master plan called for a number more. What he wanted to do was to put England between covers. He had similar hopes for America and for some American writer, and mistakenly thought that I might be the one. He wrote a volume of *Letters to America*, and died not long after. The *Letters to America* is not his best work; he seems to have written it under a cloud. I prefer his ventures in his own field, particularly the volume entitled *Bly Market*. But perhaps I had better let him speak for himself.

STOKE ROCHFORD
GRANTHAM LINCS
2/9/25

DEAR MR. FEIBLEMAN,

It was a pleasure to meet you and I shall look forward to your next visit. Also I feel that I owe you an apology but what can I do? You're aiming after Pound and Eliot and I've told you that I think them of less significance than two gnats! But that isn't to say you won't presently develop a line of your own. One of the pleasures of the future is that it can't be forecast. The wind blows where it listeth. But America's art can't come by copying the art of Europe which has been decaying for some centuries. I'd rather have O. Henry and the Saturday Evening Post than Pound and Eliot. Much rather!

I sent Gilbert the manuscript of the long poem about my father's department store. Gilbert replied as follows:

AUTHORS CLUB
WHITEHALL COURT
December 26, 1926

Now about the *Fantasia* and Literary America. By this I hope you have got my *Letters* the *Letters to America* and you will understand pretty well—tho through a glass darkly—what I feel about literature in particular and art in general. I've no use for either. If it were feasible I'd never write another line but march the countryside with a stick and wallet and preach to the people: but it aint feasible in the 20th century and so I must use the vehicle of art to put forth what it is I want to express. Besides—curse it—I cant express that otherwise than through a work of art. But when I've done that I'll never write more. This sounds strange from a gent what's engaged on the most extensive work of art that anyone has ever contemplated in the world's history—so far as I can learn—but I feel that. Well: the *Fantasia*: it's damn clever. I couldn't have done that at your age. You bid well to outdo Pound and Eliot at their own game and I raise my hat to you for it. Of course if you press me I say it's the wrong tree you're barking up but that's a matter for you and not me. Anything may happen to you in the next ten years. If you were writing this *Fantasia* at 35 I'd tell you I despised such work from you *then*: that it wasn't worth the doing and so on. And oh, my dear fellow, what a chance stares you in the face. You have the Store under your thumb, by God, and you might in a year or two turn out a work that would knock everything stiff. Wouldn't I, just! I'd do for a store what I did for a village: present it as a blooming WHOLE: with the owner and staff and customers: I'd present the goods and the routine and the bargains and oh—a million things. You could, in fact, present America through one good fat work and take the place that Masters made a bid for but failed so miserably to fulfill. Oh, James, why dont you do it? Well . . . why not?

Evidently, the advice didn't work. Neither did the desire to walk the countryside, for a year later Gilbert wrote me:

My Dear JKF for gods sake dont talk about literary virtuosity or I shant recognize you as a friend any more. Your job and mine is to be like Bach: a craftsman: live: work: be a member of our tribe: eat drink smoke rear a family live a very full complete life and in the meantime use our overflow to what purpose we are intended. The doing of these didnt stop Bach turning out more music than three men can copy in their lives, and as for myself I've had a pretty full and certainly chequered career already and so must you.

Gilbert of course was quite right. He saw that my early poetry was clever but far too precious. He saw the problem in terms of reflecting the cosmos in a single English village. But is not the problem a question of the ideal selected? The poet, even the precious poet, has a definite place which can be filled no other way. So has the chronicler of the English village. I chose to see the task as wider even than the culture as a whole. I wanted to mirror the universe so far as it lies within our power, and for that task the proper method is by means of metaphysics.

As soon as I went home, I tried to take Gilbert's advice. I wrote several bad novels which, fortunately for me, were not accepted for publication, although I mailed them around to many of the big firms. One of the novels was based on a good idea; I still have the manuscript. The title is *A Saviour in New York*, and the story relates the adventures of a mechanical saviour who gets out of hand and tries to lead the world back to the values which have been overlooked in our industrial life. But the novels were evidently not the correct answer for me. I went back to Europe, still writing poetry, while continuing occasionally to try my hand at prose in the form of short stories

Once more in Europe, I oscillated between Paris and London. It was in London that I met Jacob Epstein. The woman who took me to meet him had been writing articles about European artists for an American magazine. Epstein was to be her next victim. He received us with a friendly welcome, gave us tea, and took us on a trip around his studio. He makes a significant first impression because of his quickness, the warmth and sympathy he exudes, and his sheer physical size; he is large and somehow rather comical. I liked him at once and was happy when he invited me to return. I learned later that he is very sensitive and suspicious, and has a quick temper. He has managed to antagonize many people, but for his work has earned the respect of all. I once thought of doing a book about Epstein, for he seemed to me to be a Whistler kind of wit, quite apart from the merit of his sculpture. When his own autobiography was announced, I became very eager, because I know the kind of thing he can say; but nothing of the sort was said in his book. It is a staid and rather dull factual account—one which leaves out most of the significant facts.

Every time I returned to Europe I saw a great deal of Epstein and, together with a friend, I had on one occasion made arrangements for the sculptor to have a one-man show in New York. I was in Southern France, and Epstein had written asking me to let him know when I was coming to London. For various reasons I had flown from Paris to London on a Sunday. I telephoned a friend and together we went in the evening to the Café Royale. It was not the place for me but it was where my friend wanted to go, and I was so glad to have company on that dreary day, of all days to be in London in the summer, that I offered no objections. I knew it was a favourite haunt of Epstein's, so when I saw him at another table with a girl I was not surprised. I excused myself for a moment and went over to his table.

'Good evening, Epstein', said I.

Epstein looked up with an amused expression and so did the girl, but there was no reply. They looked at each other and burst out laughing. I was furious. I thought that it was Epstein not wanting to be disturbed with his guest of the evening. I turned on my heel and walked back to my table determined never to see him again.

A little while later I saw him rise to leave. He and the girl started for my table although the way out was in the opposite direction. I looked down at my glass deliberately.

'Everyone mistakes me for Epstein', a voice said to the back of my neck, 'although I really am not. They say that Welchmen and Jews look alike, so I won't hold you responsible. Please forgive my rudeness.'

It was my turn to be embarrassed. I stood up and apologized also.

'My name is Henry Nevinson, and I am a painter,' he said. 'I hope that you will come to see me some time.'

He was very cordial and understanding, much more so than Epstein was the next morning.

'The trouble with Nevinson is that people always mistake him for me and never mistake me for him,' was his comment.

I was to sit for a head to Epstein, an ordeal that usually lasts a week but took ten days. The sittings were supposed to be every morning from ten to one; but since I frequently remained for lunch, if the afternoon light was good the sittings might be resumed. I found it agonizing work for the sitter. To keep perfectly still for an hour, sometimes for two hours, is no easy task. There were several moments when I felt faint, and others when tiredness took charge.

Most of the time I enjoyed myself thoroughly, chiefly because Epstein did not mind talking while he worked. He was most entertaining on the subject of contemporary sculptors, for most of whom he had a vigorous contempt. The procedure became amusing. I would mention a name and Epstein would then announce the epigrammatic phrase which in his mind went with it.

'What do you think of Maillol's work?' I asked him.

'O Maillol,' he said contemptuously. Then, after a pause, 'He throws masses about. But he doesn't fool *me*!'

'Manship,' I suggested.

'Let me tell you about Manship,' he said, after a pause. All the while he was talking he was at work on the first covering of the armature, or on the more fully-developed bone structure with terrific concentration. The words were part of old decisions and required no immediate thought. 'Manship keeps a book of photographs of archaic Greek sculpture on his bed table. In the morning when he wakes up, before he opens his eyes he yawns and as he stretches he turns a page in the book. Sitting up in bed, he puts his finger on the photograph and says, "Today I'll do this one".'

Other sculptors fared no better. The only man who managed to come off with any credit at all was Despiau; and he proved to be 'conventional but sound'.

Epstein himself gave the clue to the criterion upon which his judgments were based when he told me that he had been invited to go to Palestine, on the promise that there he would be 'the world's greatest living Jewish sculptor'. I thought I sensed his objection, but asked anyhow.

'Well,' I said, 'what's the matter with that?'

Epstein snorted. 'The sentence would be improved if the word Jewish were left out.'

Nevertheless Epstein is not a conceited man; he is rather humble, a hard worker who lives almost entirely for his work. If he recognizes his own eminence in sculpture, can that be helped? Ambition and great effort, together with the awareness of a certain profundity of insight and facility of manipulation, would be almost certain to make themselves known to the man who possessed them. To fail to admit the recognition of gifts in oneself is false modesty, sometimes more overweening than frank confession.

It was interesting to watch him work. The clay and the stand were kept close to the model, and Epstein danced from one foot to another in an effort to alternate his vision between them as quickly and as often as possible. I am sure that he has never studied a sitter's psychological peculiarities; he has never attempted to analyze character or personality. He simply concerns himself with modelling: with form, with bone structure and with flesh dimensions. A sitter for Epstein is a certain peculiar spatio-temporal physical configuration presenting specific problems of transmission to clay, and involving certain other general qualities, all of which, however, present themselves to him as surface light and shadow, shape and line. He is objective in the sense that he deals only with phenomenal properties, on the assumption that whatever those properties represent will reveal themselves clearly when they have been indicated in the head or bust that is being done.

Epstein starts with a bare armature, usually a straight perpendicular iron rod, some clay, and a model who has been unmercifully stared at for some while over tea when the sittings are being arranged. He then rolls little pellets of clay the size of matches and places them around the armature and, later, over each other. These pellets build up not to a head but to a skull. It is a little frightening to see one's own skull staring at one not more than four feet away. This skull is later filled out as though real flesh were being put on. The process is continued until the head is finished. The rough surface so characteristic of Epstein's bronzes does not have to be added; indeed the surface has to be smoothed out where roughness is not wanted, since roughness is the first effect in the finished product.

The head of myself at the age of twenty-three was cast; and when Epstein had chosen and applied the proper patina, he stood back and inquired what I thought of it.

'You know,' I said, 'that I think it is a fine work. Of course I am not concerned with likeness but with good sculpture, but it certainly does not look like me.'

'No,' replied Epstein, 'but it will.'

It is fair to say that this quip carried a deeper meaning. Like all great artists, and indeed like all rationalists, Epstein is more concerned with the future than with the past. It is not the faithful reproduction of what-is that concerns him as an artist, but rather the delineation of what-ought-to-be. He is preoccupied not with a world that ever was but with one that could take place.

Among the influences upon him, he has told me that the Roman portrait busts in the British Museum, the Renaissance sculpture and primitive African wood carvings, have had the greatest effect. He has an active and keen interest in æsthetic theory, and I have heard him display considerable knowledge of the history of his art in conversations with the late Bernard van Dieren at the Café Royale.

The nature of Epstein's mind has always been a fascinating topic for speculation so far as I am concerned. He combines a retentive memory with the knowledge gained through avid but disorderly reading. What he has read he remembers, but his reading is as unsystematic as it could possibly be. Mrs. Epstein would return home from a visit to their friend's second-hand book shop with an armful of books. These were placed by Epstein's bed, and he would pick them up one after another. The books might be almost anything: novels by D. H. Lawrence, textbooks on entomology, histories of the Chinese people—whatever had been on the counter where Mrs. Epstein had gathered them. Epstein read and retained knowledge; and if the conversation turned to something he did not know he was silent and listened; but it was always possible that it might turn to something he had learned and then he would talk. He generally understood what he was talking about regardless of the reconditeness of the subject.

The various public controversies which used to rage over his work are hard to analyze. Were they, as some persons suspected, the result of a shrewd talent for publicity, or were they accidents? It is difficult to say. Epstein has a sharp tongue and can generally contribute something amusing. What militates against the charge of publicity-seeking is his talent for suspicion: Epstein had no confidence in the good faith of his defenders any more than he had in the motives of his detractors. When Bernard Shaw defended some recent work over which a storm had burst, Epstein was always sure that Shaw was himself in search of publicity, 'simply trying to get his name in the papers'. Those who failed to come to his aid, however, were labelled cowards and weaklings. He seemed to have a great respect for Cunningham Grahame, but for few others.

Epstein's house, whether by design or accident, was always the typical madhouse of the famous Bohemian artist. It was a confusion of eccentrics, hero-worshippers, models, critics, and buyers. And through this tempest Epstein always walked calmly, as though the madness were none of his own making, the people none of his own seeking, and himself the most conventional of men.

I recall especially a family of East Indians who were intimates of the Epstein household. There were a young brother and his sister, an older sister and her young son. The latter two were the models for the mother and child group. The youngest of the sisters was a dancer, and the brother attended Oxford. But the oldest sister was the most amazing member of the family. She was rather large and had great beauty and personal dignity. I have often wondered what happened to them. The older sister, I have since heard, died under mysterious circumstances, but I do not know. The brother drank a great deal at the time, and the dancer, rather incongruously, was interested in jazz and would strike poses half-way between those of Siva and the Charleston.

Several brief pictures stay in my memory.

Epstein is talking with me. Over the dining-room table, his wife can be seen, a large woman with many skirts, making a supreme effort to estimate their income for the past ten years (they have kept no records) in order to satisfy the income tax inspectors who have suddenly taken cognizance of their existence.

Epstein is called to the telephone. A controversy has been raging in the *Daily Mail* over the question of whether it is moral to wear a nightgown on the stage, as was being done at the time in some bedroom farce. Epstein is asked to give his opinion. He leaves the telephone in a fury.

Again, we are having drinks at the Café Royale. A once-beautiful but now very dissipated model passes by and slaps Epstein on the back, a little too hard so that it hurts.

'Hello, Epstein,' she says gaily.

'Who was that?' one of the men at our table asks.

'O that,' says Epstein angrily, his back still stinging. 'That is the Virgin of Soho.'

Epstein has always said that he would like to come to New Orleans to do the heads of negroes. Shortly after he told me this, he signed the lease to a house in London for thirteen years. He himself could not understand why he had chosen exactly that length of time. But the fact is that he does like England. He has never been appreciated in France where he studied for so long, or in the United States where he was born. Despite his attitude, the English have not failed to appreciate the wonder which is his work and to reward him accordingly.

What was it that really drove us all abroad in the nineteen-twenties? Why did the American artist seek in Europe in that decade what he could not find at home? The questions can share a single answer. The uniformity of mass-production together with the success of American trade led everyone to suppose that the only decent occupation for a grown man was to be in business. To this end, conformity in a high degree was required, since our efficiency and similarity must resemble the interchangeable parts of a product of the power tool. The first naïve impact of the technology of industrialism was to have its meaning applied, without the proper intermediation, to everything. The two functions of industrialist and artist are opposed in this respect; the artist could not exactly resemble his fellow artist and be an artist worthy of the name. Moreover, he could not work in peace with any understanding and encouragement. Hence he went to Europe. That it might have been a braver thing to stay at home and endeavour to convince Americans that they were wrong in derogating the artist, did not occur to us until later; it was an after-thought. We know now that as Americans we should have felt that our first duty was to show America what an artist is like by remaining and going quietly about our work. But we did not stop to think about such things in those days. We went across to Europe where life could be lived in gentler surroundings, and where the peace of old age reconciled us somewhat to our chosen field; for we were new to it. You see, *we* were Americans, too.

The problem of living in a country other than one's own throws an interesting light upon the whole question of cultural and environmental relations. I never spent enough time in Europe to feel detached from my home base in New Orleans.

Despite a sympathy with life in Latin countries and the suspicion that I might even like to live abroad semi-permanently, I knew that I would be returning to 'the States' soon. Some of my friends, however, had lived in Europe for many years and had no intention of returning for more than a visit. They were, or thought they were, thoroughly Europeanized.

Each of them had the problem of his own adjustment to face, and the solution differed not only from individual to individual, but also from country to country.

The American in Europe had in general two choices. He could either remain as self-consciously American as possible, or he could attempt to assimilate to the people among whom he now spent his days. In either case, he was sure to meet with some failure. He could not become as French as the French, as Italian as the Italian. But on the other hand, neither could he remain quite at his ease concerning the land of his birth while staying so long away from it. The result was a pose in the first case and a strain in the second.

I knew an American who had resided in England for some fifteen years. He had decided to remain American, and so had with some effort remembered and continued to use American slang. But American slang changes every six months or so. His use in 1928 of the slang of an earlier decade did not sound like anything natural. 'Twenty-three skiddoo' echoed in my ears like a voice from the grave. Then again, he was eager for news from home. What was 'our President' doing, 'our Congress'? I do not believe that any two Americans in America ever used the term, 'our', in this connection. The example is trivial, but it is in such trifles that the colour and atmosphere of a way of life reveals itself.

In general, Americans in England usually decided on the policy of retaining their identity with the home country. Just the opposite was true of those in France. Americans in France always deluded themselves that they could become French, simply by exaggerating the characteristics of the French in a superficial manner. Americans living in France—I do not mean the summer tourists but those intending to remain—wore their hair longer and more pompadour, especially behind the ears, than Frenchmen. Their trousers were higher and shorter, their moustaches (or beards) smaller and crisper. At lunch every day they drank more wine; they went to work later in the morning and worked longer at night. In every possible way they parodied the French while meaning only to become indistinguishable from them.

In Italy, the problem was somewhat different. The press of Italian culture was less hard to bear, and Americans were able to go about their business with a greater feeling of ease than anywhere else. This of course was at the time peculiar to them and was not true of the Italians, a difference which they did not observe. The effect of Italy upon Americans was that of a general laxity and lassitude, an excess of the same effect that all European living had upon them.

For every case of Americans living in Europe, the emphasis necessarily devoted to adjustment seemed to be out of proportion to the general problems of living and inquiring. The men I have had in mind in all three countries were literary men, artists, philosophers, and sensitive persons generally, engaged upon the tasks of the arts and the sciences. Their viewpoint was warped by the amount of rearrangement of circumstances which ought to have been for them old problems long ago resolved. The average artist and scientist has his living to make, his hair to get cut, his income tax to pay, his relaxation with his friends to depend upon, all ancillary to his main career. Why, then, should he devote more time and energy to side issues than is ordinarily necessary? Yet just this is what living abroad means. It means settling down in a strange land and pretending that it is your own. It means keeping in touch with the American consul and keeping up connections with the home country. It means making friends in a strange tongue and pretending that they care as much about you as they do about themselves. It means all sorts of minor adjustments and insuperable minor difficulties; it means, finally, all sorts of little pretences in which the foreigner is required to delude first himself and then others that all is well.

The joker in the situation is that almost all Americans living abroad retained their American citizenship.

I am by no means suggesting that it is not possible for a man to live anywhere so long as he lives among human beings. Cultural differences may be enormous but they will never exceed the sheer fact of the brotherhood of all mankind. What I am trying to say is that against the theory of the universal human situation there is always the particular predicament, and no general description can ever tell us about the singular difficulties which must be encountered and overcome. Living abroad with one's body, I decided, somehow paradoxically militates against ranging abroad with one's mind. The perfect functioning of the mechanism which makes awareness possible, like all powerful results from complicated mechanisms, requires some very fine adjustments of part to part. It may have been otherwise with Kant had he ever been required to leave Koenigsberg, and Plato might have discovered a different Syracuse had he not taken Athens with him.

So the American in Paris who moves from exquisite cuisine to exquisite cuisine, dreaming the while of soda-fountains and hot-dog stands, may be a bad judge of the culinary art yet sound in his innermost being. The wine of the country may be Chablis or Coca Cola, but its geography is somehow as important as its year, and the thoughts of home are long, long thoughts. The artist, the philosopher, the scientist, is an accident anywhere, and must have his home-longing for the world; yet he is not a disembodied spirit but a man of flesh-and-blood with all of the nostalgia that the soft parts entail. He must begin from somewhere so long as he cannot be without a centre; he must, in other words, have a home which is more than a place to hang his hat. If he can do it in a foreign land with ease, then more power to him, for he is on his way toward demonstrating the brotherhood of man in an important fashion. I am not suggesting that home is the only place; I am merely asking whether it is not the easiest. The timid will answer affirmatively and for the wrong reasons. But there is another reason for the same reply. For we have more than the surface of the earth to

H

care about; we have its occupancy in endless time. There are those who have been and those who will be, as well as those who are. We must share with them the direction of all human life, and we can do so from anywhere.

Sitting up in bed one night in Paris, with the horns of the taxicabs outside sounding like the horns of elfland faintly blowing, I read Sinclair Lewis's *Babbitt*. Had it been written with love and understanding instead of with hatred and fear, it might have been a very great book. The American idea that newspaper work is good training for the novelist is based on the notion that experience is sufficient to make a writer. He need have no ideas nor even the proper feelings provided he is a good observer; so runs the moral of empiricism misunderstood. But at any rate I did get an amusing, if distorted, picture of my own country. Later on, I was to be reminded of this episode when I was visiting friends in the Adirondack Mountains. We were driving through the village of Lake Placid when someone suggested climbing up to the top of Whiteface. Now, it happens that I do not like mountains, but I was a minority of one, so up we went. At the top I felt very nervous but was prevailed upon to relax and to enjoy the features of the spot. Chief among these, I was told, was a telescope, which worked for a little while after you slipped a dime in it.

'What can you see through it?' I asked politely, from the safe spot I had found across the road from the rim.

'Oh everything,' they said. 'You can see the village of Lake Placid just as plainly as if you were there.'

I was very much confused. 'But you were there, not half an hour ago,' I said. I thought that I had them, but they were only sorry for me.

It would not do to have written an argument in favour of returning home without doing a companion piece in favour of going away. This is what I mean to write now, and it is going to be somewhat difficult. The reason for this is that I love New Orleans. I have observed this before but I must repeat it. For New Orleans is the kind of pastel country in which it is possible to forget about colour altogether and devote oneself to abstract

[108]

thought. The extremes of wet and dry weather, of heat and—more heat, furnish the proper atmosphere for surrendering all devotion to the *here* and the *now* in favour of the *there* and the *then*. The world is so little with you except in an animal kind of way, it gives you the feeling that if you died and were to be buried above ground, after the custom of New Orleans, it would make an uncomfortable though perhaps not profound difference: you might be a dinner for crayfish instead of having one *of* crayfish, but the heat in summer would be equally steady and intense, and the file of visitors would be there and no less mournful; but above all, you would be able to go on wrestling with the abstract problems which have so long puzzled the world, and you would continue to have the same excellent outlook upon the nature of things.

If this picture of the advantages of remaining in New Orleans is found to be somewhat terrifying, let it be taken as an indication of my own warped personality and not any reflection upon the fair city near the mouth of the Mississippi. New Orleans for me has always divided the universe. South are the swamps, with their scenes and silences and smells that are not to be found anywhere else in the world. North is the world which is not to be found anywhere in the swamps. One is as important in a way as the other. The southern direction attracts me irresistibly, and I have gone there a number of times but always for brief visits and heady after-effects. The northern route is the one I have travelled the oftenest and the longest times, and will, I daresay, travel more in the future.

What is the northern attraction? Certainly, for one thing, it is the land of self-discovery. If a man remain forever one with his background, how can he find out his own capabilities? Were the arm never to be separated from the umbrella, who could tell them apart? The only way in which one can clearly get oneself defined is to keep oneself quite intact and move the background sharply. This is manifestly absurd and impossible; but one can achieve the same results by a slight change: one can keep the background quite intact and move oneself sharply. This is the recommended procedure. If one wishes to conduct some kind of private investigation into the nature of one's own existence: its course and meaning, the first thing to do is to buy a ticket and pack a bag and set off for wherever one is not at the moment. There will be characteristics of oneself emerging against the new background which were never suspected. Perhaps one did not have them; they may be functions of oneself in relation to the new background; but that, too, it will be important to know. The chief thing is to make sure that the new environment differs emphatically from the old. If one lives in the country, find the largest city. If one has never been away from home very much, then set off for the other side of the map. Live for a little by Mercator's Projection. If one is inland, make for the sea; if one is a maritime product, go to some landlocked farm. The principle remains the same: in order to become what one is, it is occasionally necessary to leave where one has been.

The New Orleans to which I return after an extended trip appears to be the same to others. But to me it bears the attractive flavour of contrast. I can perceive it no longer as an extension of myself. It exists now in distinct comparison with what it is not. True, it always did depend upon such definition, but that was never before so vivid a fact of awareness: I can now actually *see* its shortcomings, its limitations, and the sweet and penetrating values which it shares with only certain other places and times. I know somehow that before too long I shall have to leave New Orleans for ever. I will not, as I would not, change this decision; but already it makes me considerably sad.

If I could not remain as an American expatriate in Paris, the obvious second choice for a philosopher who wished to continue to be stimulated by others of his kind was New York. Probably in no other city in the world are there as many cross currents. The number of exciting persons one is likely to meet there exceeds what it would be anywhere else. New York seemed at first glance to be the proper stopping-place for the trader in ideas.

The thought was most attractive for I have always liked New York. I like the smell of the sidewalks, the tall and silent buildings, the high alleys of streets, and the expressionless faces of the masses of mutually distrustful people who always harden themselves for a trip through the mazes of their fellowmen. I like the brutal subways which always take me everywhere except where I want to go; and I like the night-life of the very smart night clubs, although it is a life not half so smart as that conducted in Paris by the same people; and I like the restaurants and the feeling that anything at all is likely to happen. I like the feeling of my own innocence which New York gives me, and the conviction which seems to be shared by no one else there that nobody in New York would possibly want to harm me for any reason.

If possible I always try to get to New York for a little while every year; I always have and I will always intend to try. But I could not finally live there because—well, I suppose the only simple way to describe it is to say that it is because I belong here. The philosopher's mind is cosmopolitan, but that is no reason why his body cannot be attached to one place. There is a sense in which I have never been able to pry myself loose altogether from the oaks, never been able to get away from the night odour of honeysuckle in summer, never been able to forget the little girl who lived around the corner but whose name I have forgotten, never wanted to give up the taste of cane syrup, never wanted to leave town.

Whether these reasons have made the decision for me or not I cannot say. There are others. I came back to New Orleans because being an only child I felt a certain responsibility to my family to learn my father's business in case it should become necessary to carry it on after he grew too old. But other reasons arose for remaining at home. The philosopher who is not accepted at first as a full member of the profession, the thinker who wishes to stand on his own ground, the inquirer who is not supported by an institution, is better off somewhat removed from the scene of the political struggle which goes on within the walls of the universities. In New Orleans, I can feel that if nobody ever hears about me it is my own fault. And if nobody hears about me during my own lifetime, that is of no importance.

The temptation to cheapen work, to labour at problems which are burning issues, to take part in the factional fights which obsess philosophical circles just as much as they do all others, is stronger in the big centres of population. No one is free from contemporary influences any more than from influences in the past. To a large extent we are all creatures of our own times, and it is fitting and proper that we should be. But to build upon our times, to carry them forward and upward a little, is the goal. And this seems more easily accomplished at some distance from the centre of things. We can swing the big awkward moving circle a little more if we live upon its periphery than we can if we live in its core. Like those who would turn aside a glacier ever so little, the edge is a more convenient place for the position of the fulcrum than to be frozen in its midst. In New Orleans, I feel myself to be in America but not wholly its creature. It is a place in which I can love my country and the world through my country, but where I am not quite as subject to its contemporary and pressing influences as I am to its larger meaning. America has a meaning as indeed everything has, and New Orleans may be a little more in on the secret than Kansas City, although it is possible that I say this only because I have never been to Kansas City.

For a painter who must see contemporary work, New York is the place, and I suppose that the same is true for musicians and sculptors and architects. But the philosopher who can afford to buy an occasional volume can afford to live anywhere within reach of the postal system. New Orleans knows its transient public, too, and many interesting and curious people are supplied to it by the railroads, the boats, and the airways, in as strong a solution as it is possible to digest. To live long enough in New Orleans is to meet eventually most of the people who would be met in New York in a week.

So I decided to come home and to engage myself upon the Emersonian task of building better mousetraps, on the assumption that it might not be only mousetraps after all for which

the world would be willing to beat a path to one's door. I seem
to have irrevocably combined in myself a passion for fame
together with a stronger passion for fields in which fame is not
possible. How many persons have heard of A. N. Whitehead
compared with the audience which is reached by Gary Cooper
every working day? What is the poet compared to the successful novelist? I won't give an inch in what I do, but I want
everyone afterwards to know all about it. That is a fatal
combination and one most surely doomed.

Perhaps, then, it is some homing instinct, some sad and
fearful feeling of disaster, which made me turn inevitably
toward the city of my birth. For where else can the man who
has failed seek for consolation and forgetfulness than at the
scene of his earliest and most overwhelming ambitions? I
managed to reverse the process, and came home before I started
out upon my intellectual adventures, but this may after all have
only been the result of some reliable premonition, the work of
some bogey in the dark who knew what he was doing.

CHAPTER THREE

Natural History of a Philosopher

WE pass to the fourth decade of the twentieth century. In this period the philosophy of the self-made man was replaced by that of the economic man. The humanitarian ideal was altered by the concentration of industrial forces through mass production by means of the power tool. We understood that everyone had to have the necessities of life, and we put the base line for this admirably high; by necessities we meant food, shelter, clothing, and medical attention. But we made the mistake of assuming that to have these would be to have all that anybody could possibly ask. We had forgotten that man cannot live by bread alone, although assuredly he cannot live without it, either. So Marx became the symbol of the nineteen-thirties. Our literary critics, who have long since exchanged profundity for the glass of intellectual fashion, abandoned Freud for Marx. They ceased to hint at the profuseness of their love affairs and began to tell us something of the modesty of their net income after the deduction of taxes. The full effect of the trade collapse of A.D. 1929 was now felt in all its force. Business men began to appear a little ashamed of themselves but they had not yet abandoned the fort. Government could help business if it wished to do so by lending money, but government interference in business remained an uneconomic nuisance, the meddling of politicians. Just how these two activities were to be distinguished was never made clear. But thinking persons did begin to look about them and to question fundamentals.

It was felt slightly even by those who were not capable of doing their own thinking that the old values would have to be overhauled in order to learn whether we were moving in the direction in which we ought to be going. War, of course, was a thing of the past, and the rise of the Nazi party in Germany an uncomfortable prospect only because it reminded us painfully of the barbarisms we thought that we had put irrevocably behind us. But there were other issues, closer at home, which would have to be settled. There was, for instance, that struggle between capital and labour. Despite the easy words of the political orator concerning the better understanding between owners and workers, it seemed to those who could appreciate the situation that the more understanding of the issue there was the more enmity there would be; for the issue between two economic groups both of whom want to control industry was a direct contradiction and not possible of a solution which could be satisfactory to both sides. We did not look about us sufficiently to see that other western countries which had become industrialized were faced with the same problem. We had definitely decided upon political isolation; what foreign countries did was their business, whether we happened to approve and be sympathetic or not.

Other things were in the air which are less easy to describe. Philosophical postulates are never all in text-books; many more of them colour the atmosphere of opinion. The subjectivity of the second decade had been abandoned; it was no longer supposed that conflicts and problems in the external world can be resolved by the solution of those which exist in the mind and in the subconscious internal world of the human individual. Freud was abandoned in favour of Marx. It is amazing to notice the extent to which those who are not Marxists accepted the economic problem in its Marxist formulation. Monopolists as well as proletarians leaned on the dialectic by assuming that the inevitable working of the economic forces of history would catapult destiny their way, and, further, that what happens is inseparable from what ought to happen provided only that history favours a particular class.

The new developments of physical science were beginning to make themselves known to the general public. Popular accounts of the new relativity physics and quantum mechanics were challenging the imagination of people who had never heard of Newton. The old notion that substance and the void are ultimate and fixed was being replaced by the idea of invariant relations between variables. While churches continued in their

[115]

steady decline, the return of religion to the real became once more a definite probability. Yet the humanitarian ideal suffered again, this time through long exposure to accounts of aggression; we were becoming accustomed to remote persecutions: Abyssinia; Manchuria; China; the liberal, the pious and the Jewish in Germany; all these hammered at us continually in the news to force us to accept the fact that cruelty had returned to the world with renewed vigour. The sentient and the febrile expressed the desire, which was felt by all, to return to some sort of philosophy of reality and to find a morality which could have firm roots.

It is not possible to gauge the extent to which we are subject to influences such as these by estimating the degree to which we may happen to be aware of them. No one knows exactly what is going to be done to the system of beliefs by which he feels, thinks and acts, when he reads a newspaper, hears the radio, or digests the contents of a book. A casual conversation, attendance at a lecture, the titles in a publisher's advertisement, perhaps these or other trivia may turn over to the care of another conclusion the whole set of ideas we hold to be true. We can proceed under our own power to some extent in virtue of conscious awareness, but these means are slight and superficial compared to the resources of the subconscious, where memory and the beliefs from which we act are sorted and stored.

Like most individuals at the beginning of the decade, I could feel the burden of responsibility upon us all to assimilate the new knowledge which physical science had put in our possession, to resolve the economic problems which industrial technology had occasioned, and to overhaul the basic philosophy upon which our moral life was based. For this it seemed to me that great freedom from traditions of all sorts and from ordinary responsibilities was essential. The task was large and would require the whole man. Thus was brought about of course a reckoning with personal problems.

It is hard for an only child to go against the wishes of his parents without a guilty conscience. I had planned my life to be that of a black sheep, but found it impossible in the absence of brothers who could do what I ought to have been doing. My father was getting old, and the two stores he was running were soon going to be more than he could cope with; somebody was going to be forced to take over the responsibility. Quite obviously, that was my assigned role, and if I did not like it that seemed to make no difference to the objective situation.

My father, I always thought, was an admirable man. He had drive and he had character; and if the only thing that he truly admired was financial success, it was not for the things that money could buy but for the power it represented. He was no lover of soft living but of the real; and he sought it in the only symbols that our present-day mythology allowed to him. He was an autocrat in business, but as much because he thought the attitude was required of him as for any other reason, and, despite it, was much admired by those who worked under him.

My mother was a nervous woman who spoiled me because I had a hard time growing up physically. She was in charge of the culture of the family, which included, so far as I could see, three activities. She told my father what plays and motion pictures were the right ones to see; she put every possible advantage in my hands: books, music, theatre, travel; and she herself attended the occasional lectures of second-rate English literary men who came to New Orleans while engaged in getting paid for derogating America.

It was always something of a minor miracle to watch my father shrink in size between his office and his home. In the office his love for business made him uncompromising; at home his love for my mother made the business of compromising into a career. Since they were both happy with the arrangement, it caused me to wonder very much about the nature of social relations, of which I felt sure that I knew nothing.

Father never understood what I wanted to do. He wanted me to go into business with him, and reluctantly I consented. I had no desire to be a business man, and, for that matter, no talent for it. I had made up my mind that whenever there arose a chance for me to get out of business and to write, I would do so. The name of my father's department store was 'Feibleman's', with underneath the motto, 'The House of Values'. He wanted very much to have me open other stores all over Louisiana and Mississippi, to make our name known. Since I have made philosophy my preoccupation, one of my chief concerns has been to establish on a firm footing the branch of philosophy known as axiology or value-theory. In a way, I feel that I am carrying out my father's wishes.

Father had made his business success at the turn of the century and shortly thereafter, when the country was still growing. He had made it by hard work, and on the faith other men had in him. He had become the junior partner in a department store run by his uncle; when the uncle grew old and wished to retire, father borrowed a considerable sum of money from the leading bank of the town, with no collateral except his good name, and purchased the store. He borrowed the money one day, spent it the same day, and signed a note for it the next afternoon. That was the way business was conducted then. I believe that to some extent it still goes on that way in Texas, but not in New Orleans any more. But now he, too, was growing old; he remained most of his time in the office, a rare thing for him, and did not walk through the aisles very often.

The prospect of spending my life in a department store was a dismal one for me. I came back from Europe and tried it. I tried it, in fact, for five years. It meant little to me. I wrote poetry early in the morning at my desk; I spent the nights with an eccentric accountant who was busy at the time installing a new system in the office. I tried my hand at many tasks in the store, at one time or another, for five years, and did everything from selling shirts to writing advertisements and organizing sales campaigns. I can say with neither pride nor shame that I was not very good at any of the efforts I made. Business is not a profound undertaking, and I am fond of money, for I know the power it has to secure the kind of life I wish to lead. But business does require something which I simply do not have: an acquisitive instinct which cares for money for its own sake as an end in itself and reaches out far beyond the things that money can buy.

My father had evidently hoped that when I began to try a commercial life and gave it a fair chance to work on me, I would enjoy it as much as he did. He found out his mistake and acknowledged it, though it must have been a terrific disappointment. He agreed that we would sell the business as soon as an opportunity to do so presented itself. The opportunity came sooner than I had hoped. It was, I believe, in 1928 that Sears Roebuck & Company made us an offer which we accepted. The actual sale of the business took some years, and I remained with the store in the meanwhile.

Those who do not believe that an organization is more than the sum of its parts, that the personality of a large corporation is entitled to better than legal standing, have only to work for one to become thoroughly convinced. There is something immense and crushing about sheer size, and if anything shows evidence of 'the curse of bigness' it is an industrial or commercial corporation. It is only necessary to rule out the possibility of resigning and applying for work elsewhere in order to secure the perfect analogy of the corporate state. The consumer who does his purchasing in one of the large retail units of a chain store organization has no conception of the price which is actually being paid for the effort to sell to him at a low competitive price: let the buyer beware.

In the meanwhile, however, I am ahead of my story. Five years were spent in business, alternating with summer trips to Europe; five years of the furtive writing of poetry. It was during this period that a volume of my poems, *Death of the God in Mexico*, was published. It is clear to me now, even if I did not see it then, that for lyric poetry mine was too heavily weighted with meaning. I had been trying to make sonnets carry high abstractions, with only some success. Had I been sufficiently self-analytical and at the same time familiar with the alternatives to poetry which were available, I might have turned to philosophy much sooner. But as it was I had to change over slowly, the painful and hard way.

Why was it, except for the atmosphere of prejudice against dead scholarship, that the reading of philosophy meant so little to me at the time? I had begun at the age of fifteen with Emerson's *Essays*, a bad beginning; but later I had tried to read Kant and Plato. Kant was unfathomable, and responsible only for a polemical sonnet launched against the German of the metaphysicians. Plato appealed to me only in my capacity of literary man; I thought the dialogues very beautiful in spots —in those spots where the conversation did not take too metaphysical a turn. But no spark was struck in me; I had to climb slowly into philosophy at the end of five years of business.

For a while I tried conscientiously to make my business effort as unlike an outright failure as I could. I represented my company in the Better Business Bureau of the Chamber of Commerce. It was in those occasional meetings that my respect for the intelligence and authority of business men melted like butter. The business man is activated solely by greed, or, to put a kinder and perhaps more accurate interpretation upon it, at least so far as the small business man is concerned, by the necessity for making a living. What I most objected to was the constant desire of the business man to ascribe a noble character to his motive. In my eyes, greed is a human failing, a weakness to be deplored but to be expected; whereas hypocrisy with regard to it is a monstrous crime. The ascription of a high idealism to crass manœuvres is an abomination before ethics. Yet it was necessary to forgive them because I could not constitute myself a judge and because they did not know what they were doing. Difficulties could be prevented quite easily, as they must have discovered early in their business careers, by the simple precaution of doing as little as possible in a constructive way, by making no important decisions. I could see from the faces of my fellow-members in the Bureau that I was not going to be happy in my new life. They, for instance, were confirmed business men; business had not brought even them happiness. If so, happiness gave off a very deceitful appearance.

Selling the store took me on several trips to Chicago, where I had to remain a week at a time. I did not know anyone there and was fairly miserable. One evening, returning from work, I passed a certain bookstore. I went in and browsed around. The owner of the store was perched on the top of a large cash register, making fun of some old lady customers. Now, whatever happens to me always seems to be perfectly natural, since I cannot imagine anything unnatural happening. The attitude was fortunate in this particular case. I bought several books, taking two with me and sending the remainder home to New Orleans. When I gave my name and New Orleans address, the proprietor—for it was he, dear reader, who waited upon me—looked up and shook me by the hand.

'Why, I know your sister, Martha,' said he.

I smiled. 'Probably not,' I said. 'You must have met someone else by the same name, because I have no sister.'

I thought that perhaps this would end the matter, but I was mistaken. The bookseller smiled indulgently. 'Oh yes you have,' he replied.

Was he joking? If so, it was difficult to see what was funny. I assumed a very serious tone. 'No, really, I have no sisters and no brothers. I am an only child.'

He did not seem in the least interested. 'You have one sister,' he continued calmly, 'her name is Martha. Give my regards to Martha when you go home.'

It was in the middle of summer and I was getting quite warm, and a little angry. When he found out that I was alone, he suggested that we have dinner together, since his wife was out of town. Although I was both angry and mystified, I consented. At dinner he told me the story.

When a young man he had decided that he wanted to see the country, and that the best way to see it was on foot. He wanted to knock around all over the United States and really to get the feel of it, but he knew it would not be much fun to do that alone. So he had invited a friend, a younger boy, to go with him. The boy was willing but his parents objected; and when he went away, he was followed all over by letters and telegrams urging him to return and to settle down in some steady job. By the time the two travellers had arrived in New

Orleans, the messages had begun to take a more desperate tone
The future bookseller began to rack his brain to devise ways
of keeping the younger boy with him. Finally, he hit upon
something. Opening a New Orleans newspaper, he looked for
the advertisements of department stores, and seeing 'Feibleman's: The House of Values', he had written immediately to
the boy's parents. 'Do not urge Joe to return home now,' he
had said, 'for he has fallen in love with a girl whose father owns
and operates a large department store. Her name is Martha.
I think if you leave him alone, he will stay here, and go into
business with his father-in-law.' The permission—and even
advice—to remain came by return mail. Thus it was that
Martha Feibleman sprang into existence.

The fiction has been consistently kept alive ever since.
Martha exists only in the concluding salutations of letters.
'Give my regards to your sister, Martha', or 'Martha joins me
in sending greetings'; but I suppose that this is one kind of
existence.

Of the executive offices of Sears Roebuck & Company I
have only the most superficial recollection. The executives gave
the appearance of men of strength who were wearing themselves out over a comparatively insignificant proximate aim.
The necessity for earning a livelihood was no longer the driving
incentive; instead it was power, power over other men which
they would be too old to wield once they had gained it in
sufficient quantity. Yet they had failed to hitch their wagon to
a star. How great is the ambition of the artist; he cannot be
dismissed from his job and thus separated from the urge toward
his infinite goal. He may have to earn his livelihood by some
other method; his time, therefore, the time which he is free to
devote to his art, may be limited; yet he can always keep what
he has gathered: a certain skill, a supreme interest, from which
he cannot be separated by anything except the complete
breakdown of all his faculties or death.

The men who operate large corporations are frequently
lonely men. I do not mean that they have no family, no friends;
in all probability they enjoy what everybody else enjoys. Yet

they have assumed large responsibilities without the comfort of knowing that they are serving anything but themselves. Is oneself ever worth so much struggle and strain? I seriously doubt it. To work like the devil in business is perfectly all right provided that one is doing it for some large and very human cause. It hardly seems to be the proper thing to which to surrender one's whole being in this way, except in some different social economy where the success of a business might be expected to contribute to the total welfare of the society at large.

But then enjoyment is a personal question. The executives of Sears, I had to keep reminding myself, were doing what they most wanted to be doing, and so must in their own way have been happy. Their salaried employees were not in most cases engaged in commercial activities by choice, and so were more understandable. The whole spectacle made poetry seem more important than ever.

The idea of the business world that most persons cherish bears little relation to the facts. From the outside, a business appears to be an efficient organization, operated with machine-like precision by men who know their jobs and who perform them with impeccable accuracy. This is supposed to distinguish modern business from other types of social organization.

Would that it did! For in that case the business world would hardly have gotten itself into the chaos and distressful disorganization of 1929 and the following years. But the fact is—and it should not be so surprising—that business men are like all other mortals: human, fallible, and limited. The trade depression of the nineteen-thirties proved as much of a surprise to them as it was to the rest of us; they were not expecting it and could not believe it when it happened. The slogans so popular before 1929: 'beat last year', and 'don't sell America short', were more than slogans, they were basic philosophical propositions. We were led to believe by the self-hypnotism of the American business man that his new methods more than the results they achieved could accomplish almost anything. The new speed-up factory systems, for instance, had a cold,

I

impersonal sound about them; none of us stopped to consider that in detail the new system meant nothing more lofty than clocking employees while they retired to the toilet, in an effort to eliminate the wasting of work-hours. We heard about the new machinery which was doing the work of men with greater efficiency and less human assistance than had ever before been conceived, without considering what this would do in the general society to those who had been dislocated by the machinery. From brokers' accounting systems to farming equipment, everywhere men were being replaced by automatic mechanisms; what was to happen to the men?

Sherwood Anderson, who knew nothing of economic problems, had taken the opportunity afforded by one of the summers just before 1929 to tour the industrial sections of the eastern seaboard. He went through many factories, and had an opportunity to observe what was going on. Everywhere, he found the same story: machines replacing men, so that where, for instance, seven men had been engaged with hand tools in performing a certain piece of work, two men and a power tool were accomplishing the same thing with greater ease and equal efficiency. In each case, Sherwood would ask the same question of the owner, manager, or shop foreman, 'Suppose that this thing is happening in all the other factories I have visited all over the country. What will become of the men? And worse still: what will become of the market for your product, since it is the other men in other factories who buy what you make?' And the same answer was always given, an answer based on rank individualism: 'I have nothing to do with the other fellow's factory. I tend to my business; he tends to his; and nothing ever goes wrong with the man who minds his own affairs.'

A number of false conclusions meanwhile were drawn by the thinkers of the time, as the mighty tidal wave of American business swept the country and was being felt all round the world. To the apologists of business, it was clear that nothing else could be of equal importance. Pure science was an idle myth; the only science that counted was the practical kind that furthered industrial technology: applied science. Men like Steinmetz and Thomas Edison were raised upon pinnacles and held up to the admiration of the population. Boys were taught to aspire to trade schools, to learn to love to tinker with machinery; and universities began to drop all courses that did not take part in the programme; even logic disappeared as the required course of candidates for an undergraduate degree. Scientific speculation was left to the dreamers of Europe, while the by-products of their imagination were incorporated under the laws of Delaware and manufactured with profit in New Jersey.

Art under the reign of modern business fared no better than science; its fate if anything was much worse. It was turned over to the gentle hands of female appreciation where it swiftly lost its vigour and its patronage. The sale of novels was quickly reduced to the sale of *the* novel of the day, and *the* novel was usually a sentimental romance of bygone days. Could *Gone With the Wind*, *Anthony Adverse*, and *So Red the Rose*, to choose a few later examples which inherited this tradition, have achieved anything like their success if their fate had been in the hands of men rather than women? It seems hardly possible. But men did have a hand in the interiors of many of our modern motion picture houses, the largest of which were erected during this period. The Polar Bear on Ice (with lights) which graces the cinema parlour of my home town is typical of the atrocities which were foisted upon an unsuspecting public by the bad taste of the business man. Tudor mansions, Spanish villas, and other larger and weaker stucco imitations of perfectly good imported architecture of an earlier period and another country, took the place of sound architectural thinking in the United States. Frank Lloyd Wright was exiled, so to speak, and for the most part ignored when he was home. The artist was not regarded as quite manly, and, just as youngest sons in Europe had been in the habit of taking the cloth and joining the armed forces under the discouraging law of primogeniture, so in America the most effeminate sons took up easels and hired studios. The situation became hopeless, and it was actually thought impossible to reconcile a beard and all that it stood for with the writing of poetry. Despite a persistent admiration of England, the tradition of Elizabethan times, in which drinking, fighting, brawling, and whoring had been reconciled with ruffs and the writing of sonnets, was forgotten or else neglected.

If science and art failed to find a vigorous method of survival in the atmosphere created by a dominant worship of business, philosophy did no better for itself. The truth which went with business was that based upon workability; what worked must be true, and the test for workability was immediate and final. This called for rapid shifts in the nature of reality, since if something worked today then it must be true today, while if it failed to work tomorrow it must be false tomorrow. Workability brought results in the way of bridges built, telephone systems put into operation, industrial laboratories started; and if one asked it no profound questions it would tell no confusing lies. Actions not words were said to speak plenty. Quite easily, the morality which went with such a criterion smoothed the path in front of whatever one wanted to do. If the moral code did not suit one's purposes, then the thing to do was to take a moral holiday, or so at least said the philosophical apologist for the era of progress in American business: William James, himself the most moral of men. Meanwhile, Charles S. Peirce, the greatest philosopher that America had produced, was allowed to live and labour and die ignored, and his wife to freeze to death in loneliness and neglect after him.

Has it been noticed that no system of reality is ever broken down from the outside? The death blow can only be administered from within that which is thought to be real. To believe something true is to hold to it deeply, so deeply that it can only be removed by means of the pain called doubt; and we cannot doubt without reason to doubt. Even though the reason to doubt our beliefs must come from some external occasion or cause, it is the internally held belief which is directly shaken by it. We never replace one positive belief about reality quite simply by dropping it abruptly and substituting for it another positive belief. The structure of ideas which had been erected upon the successful progress of modern American business constituted the kind of belief in what was important, what counted, that can only be fairly described as a theory of reality. It could be destroyed not by the appearance of some new antagonist in the field of theory but only by the failure of business to live up to its own estimation of itself.

Business, as it happened, did fail of its own accord and not by any pressure from the outside; that is a well-established fact. No war, no internal politics, and no foreign competition, heralded the trade depression of 1929. The industrial and economic system collapsed, but why? The theory of the expanding economy is too well known for me to enter upon a recital of its details here. Suffice it to say that an indefinitely increasing production was sure to meet its fate sooner or later; nothing lasts for ever. The fact that potential consumption was never satisfied by actual production was not the fault of production but of the economic system itself. Not prices but the unsatisfactory distribution of purchasing power was to blame.

Of course it is always necessary to explain everything on its own level: economic events must be explained by economic occasions and causes; religious events by religious causes, and so on, irrespectively of the level at which the success or failure may have originally started. That is why I have ventured a word upon the cause of the business difficulties. As a philosopher, I was naturally more concerned with the general meaning of the failure of American business than I was with the fact of that failure itself. The economic explanation may have to be the first one, but it is so far as I can see, hardly the last. And I fancied that I had found another explanation in the difference between hatred and love.

Too many social organizations, regardless of what it is that they are organizing, depend upon a structure of hatred. The organization may be a company engaged in retail trade, an industrial factory, a university, an army, or even a church: the same factors sooner or later make themselves evident. More energy is devoted to personal advancement, to internal competition, to climbing higher despite opposition and over somebody else's shoulders, than to actually furthering the purposes of the organization as a whole. The elapsed time between individual rivalry and revenge on the one hand and organizational service on the other must be something tremendous. To this extent, lesser social organizations within a democracy can hardly be said to be democratic. They are quite the contrary since they derive their power from a single control if not a single ownership, and remain autocratic and intolerant. They are *laissez-faire* in the wrong sense whereas democracy allows individualism on the assumption that each individual will have his own special method of contributing to the welfare of society.

It has been observed before, and by the greatest of men, the founder of the Christian religion, that nothing solid can be erected upon hatred. What is worthy and enduring and firm under pressure is only what is built upon love. The decay and collapse of the tremendous forward motion in economic affairs that we had learned to respect as the progress of business might have been prevented if it had not been allowed to usurp other fields. If we had not asked it to carry the values which belonged elsewhere, since man can surely not live by bread alone, it might have been with us still. But love also means proper evaluation; we cannot expect the things which are of importance but are not all-inclusive to bear up under the strain of an all-inclusive love. We can only hope to live in this world by rendering unto things the values of which they are intrinsically worthy. Men cannot live by anything more than bread until they have bread, but this does not controvert the fact that they cannot live by bread alone.

Let me take the space here to record some simple business preferences. Among successful business men, I like the older generation, the generation of pioneers in American business, better than their second-generation sons. Among unsuccessful business men, I like those who are resigned better than those who are bitter.

The pioneers of American business were ruthless men; this is no discovery of mine but of their biographers. They stopped at almost nothing to gain the goals of vast acquisition they had in view. They had notable weaknesses and notable strengths; they were on the whole powerful, evil, and lovable old men; and I could not help admiring them in a certain way and being drawn to them. There was something warm and human about them; at least in the old age in which I got to know them, the age of their security and prosperity and partial retirement. I might not have gotten along with them so well in the days of their struggle, but for some reason they made admirably human old people.

It was, however, altogether different with their sons. The boys, frequently of my own age, who had had the advantages of education, of travel, and of all the things that money could buy, seemed to me to have learned the worst that their opportunities offered. They were vain, pompous, full of self-importance, supported not by what they had done but by the power embodied in the money their fathers had left. They were, in addition, frightfully weak. It can only be hoped that *their* sons will represent a reversion to type, for they represent nothing but vanity. I was very much amused once listening to an anecdote of personal importance recited by the wealthy son of a successful merchant in New York. The story was based upon the anonymity of the son under certain special circumstances. He had been mistaken by some petty official for a nonentity and treated as such, an unfortunate impression which he had taken an early opportunity to correct by going over the latter's head to the officer in charge. 'So I went down,' he said, and I will never forget his exact words, 'so I went down and told them who I was.' The chance, so far as I was concerned, was irresistible. I had been respectfully silent up to this point, but now I could not refrain from asking softly, 'Well, who were you?' The truth is that his father would never have become involved in such an embarrassing situation—or else it would not have been embarrassing; either 'they' would have known 'who he was' from his personality or actions, or he would not have cared whether 'they' knew or not.

The old man, the pioneer, the so-called self-made man, was the victim of a system and not an ogre at all. Social revolutionists have for propaganda purposes painted the capitalist as something of a personal devil whose entire life lay in squeezing the last penny out of those around him; a cold, cruel, selfish beast, and hardly a man in the true sense of the word. Nothing could be farther from the truth. Although it is not a first occasion for pity, the fact remains that the capitalist is one who, working within the limits of a social and economic framework which he had found ready-made, has been able to do more for himself than anyone else. If the system is a vicious system, is he solely to blame? The most powerful of the capitalists, those whose success and fortunes are due in the main to their own efforts and not to some inheritance, give the impression that they would have risen to the top of the heap whatever the rules of the game. But despite the impression, it could only have been true for some of them and not for others—certainly not for all. Different kinds of competition call forth different kinds of talents in men; and, to some extent, therefore, also different men.

I have known some very big capitalists, leaders with all the possessions and prejudices of their class, and found them personally to be the softest and kindest of people. Their servants were always well treated, never over-worked as they would have been by the members of the lower middle class. Such servants were always given last year's clothing, which was better than the new clothes most of them could buy; they were sent to the family doctor when they fell ill; and they were always liberally pensioned in old age. No, the capitalist is not a hard task-master, if we mean by capitalist the banker of the world between world wars. Of the new type of industrialist I know little, but suspect him to be something closer to the standard type of slave-driver.

But consider the banker type for the moment, the chairman-of-the-board variety of man. He is, as I said, kind and even lenient to those around him. But his situation demands that the corporation he serves show a profit. Rarely does he own the whole thing himself; modern corporations are too large even for millionaires to own outright, with the single exception, perhaps, of the Ford empire. So the chairman of the board is answerable not only to the board as a whole but to the majority of the stockholders. How is he to show a profit? Obviously, by seeing to it that the corporation spends less on operating cost than it takes in from the sale of its product. And how is this to be done? Only in two ways: by decreasing operating cost or by increasing the market price of the product Market price is restricted by competition; the issue is almost out of his hands, since one corporation cannot afford to charge more for its product than another. Operating cost is limited in certain ways. For instance, the break-down of a balance sheet shows that certain operating charges, most of them, in fact, are fixed in one way or another. The cost of light, heat and power, are dictated by the public utilities; taxes by the federal, state and city governments, rent by the landlord, or, if the building is owned, by the corporation itself, then further, by the rate of amortization allowed by the government. When all is said and done there is little left to the control or option of the chairman of the board except labour. Where this is not fixed by some union agreement, it can be reduced; but, unfortunately, the chairman of the board does not see a ten per cent. reduction in wages in the concrete terms to which it actually reduces. He does not see children with rickets and no shoes, hungry women, sick men. He only sees the balance sheet in front of him and the abstract nature of his problem. He only knows that if he cannot produce profits, the majority stockholders will jolly well see to it that they get somebody who can to take his place. And so he does what he must do.

It is a little late to be sorry for the capitalist. He is a force that has spent itself, and he is besieged on all sides; so that capitalist-baiting has become a rather undignified and unnecessary occupation. But in all fairness to him, as well as in illustration of what lies in wait for other classes who will in one way or another be besieged in the future, it is important to point out that nobody is inherently evil. There is no such thing as a *class*-man; there are only men, ordinary people, who become engaged in certain occupations and who develop the occupational diseases which are the logical results of specialization. What we need to get rid of whenever a social activity gets out of hand is not the human beings who happen to be in power; such murder, legal or illegal, perhaps justifiable from an economic point of view, is never morally justified, nor for that matter demanded. Economic and political dislocations can be rectified by changing the system in which certain people find a way to take undue advantage, not by murdering the people. For it is the system that is basically at fault.

So much for successful business men. Now let us turn to the unsuccessful, and far more numerous, type. I said that I liked those who were resigned better than those who were bitter; that is true. The bitter kind are those who may have more talent than the resigned, but they are frustrated; they have faith in nothing and are full of resentments. They hate the system in which they have been a failure; they hate the other unsuccessful people by whom they are surrounded; worst of all, they hate themselves. They know neither how to get ahead in the business world nor how to become reconciled with their inability to do so. They had expected to be self-made successes without knowing that a certain amount of luck is required. Circumstances must work a little in favour of those who paddle their own boat; but luck had passed them by and they neither understood *how* this had happened nor for that matter *that* it had happened. They only know that they have failed and they will not admit to themselves the full consequences of failure. They do not give up hope and they do not give up hate. They pour their contempt upon whomsoever is economically below them, and they vent their envy upon those above. In their own position they remain uncomfortable and unhappy, unable to enjoy whatever they do have and equally unable to find solace in dreams.

The men of resignation are a far different breed. They are

the ones who had never expected to be successes in the first place. Perhaps resignation is the wrong descriptive term: they were only dimly conscious of resignation in themselves. They had never really known what it was to aspire very high. They are the silent people, the dumb ones of the earth, in whom so much fellow-feeling and sweetness is contained that merely to recognize it is to call forth our love and our tears.

In my father's store were many of both kinds of people. I got to know the difference between them very soon. The resigned were the best. In the men's department, for instance, were salesmen and floorwalkers of Spanish, Italian, and English origin, men whose lives never changed from one year to the next. They would watch younger and brighter men who had come to work next to them advance to better jobs and more pay as though it were the most natural thing in the world, without asking why it did not happen to them, without resenting, without questioning, without really thinking about it at all. They would go home on Saturday with their pay in their pockets, and they would manage to squeeze out the price of a movie for Saturday night, and in summer they would have feasts of boiled shrimps in buckets and beer in pitchers on screened porches, and they would think that all was as it should be.

They had curious tricks of speech that were always in use, as though these were verbal tickets attached to them like the stickers on the shirts and ties that they sold. There was the thin man who could not speak unless he was fingering something on the counter, and who always added to every sentence the phrase, ' . . . to one way of thinking'. This suffix was not reserved for speculation or opinion; it applied equally well to factual report. For instance, asked how much he had sold by late afternoon, he would look at his salesbook, and say, 'Forty-seven dollars and thirty-five cents, to one way of thinking.' Then again there was the large and oldish man, the soberest in the store, who always repeated every statement a second time with the introductory words, 'I say . . .' Thus he would meet me in the aisle, and remark, 'It's a nice day.' Then without pause, 'I say it's a nice day.' The effect was always one of distinct syncopation:

> 'When it rains on Monday
> It spoils the whole week,
> I say when it rains on Monday
> It spoils the whole week.'

The effect was heightened by the fact that he despised jazz and all modern devices. He was rather a religious man, given to saving and piety. But the effect of the modern world was there, betraying him in the rhythm of his speech. And Oh God, there were others, even more mute, hardly alive except in the purely biological sense and yet striving with every ounce of concentration that was in them to gain a living according to the rules which they found already made when they became adults.

As I write about them now I can feel the tears starting because of all the millions upon millions of people who go on each day in this way. How are we to help them? I know all the glib answers to this question and none of them quite satisfy me. The socialist talks about lack of equality of opportunity and cultural lag; the capitalist mentions something about survival of the fittest and refers to the fact that not *all* office boys can rise to be presidents so long as there are more office boys than presidents; the artists say that all things have a value just for whatever they are and that we should not meddlesomely seek to help anyone who has not asked for help. But then I can close my eyes and see the helpless ones of the earth whom someone has shoved into a corner to perform the same movements every day and to receive the same small pittance every week-end and to raise more children than can conveniently be supported because they have never learned how not to; and I think of Jesus, not of any church but of Jesus, who said that he had come into the world not that we should have life but that we should have it more abundantly, and I know that it is not right to interfere with the helpless people if by interference is meant the use of force, and I know that it is not right to abandon them to the darkness of the routine which is their fate, either. I look ahead into the vagueness of the future and

I can feel that it is right to help them if we can do so by persuasion, by leading and not by pushing, and that nothing else is right but this. I know that all the works of art and all the science in the world and all the insight in the world that have enabled us to look ahead and see the endless possibilities of the infinite future will mean nothing to us unless we can learn to take everybody along with us into that future. The helpless little people must come along, too.

In many respects, of course, little people are like big ones; and the specialization of modern civilization catches them all in its net. Everyone has his own reasons for considering himself significant in the world's affairs.

The intense specialization and the outlook consequent upon it which I have noticed in all institutional activities and indeed in all walks of life first came to my attention in my father's department store. Each employee thought that the division of business in which he was engaged not only was the most important one but actually carried all the others as deadwood. Since I was the boss's son, many of the workers confided their indispensability to me, but it was evident that they firmly believed in what they were saying. Several of the office men: a bookkeeper and a credit manager, told me confidentially that it was their work alone which maintained the business as a going concern. The salesmen, they pointed out, made out a lot of sales slips which had to be sorted and computed. Such men, having no sense, would sell to anyone, they pointed out. It was up to the office force to keep the day-by-day affairs of the business in order and to decide whose credit was good and whose was not. Without this detail, they thought, all would be chaos.

I heard much the same story, privately, from the salesmen. It was, they argued, the actual exchange of merchandise for money that kept the department store alive. If there were no business there would be no profits; and without profits, no purpose. What a shame, they concluded, that so much useless work was done in the office and had to be carried for nothing! Selling was productive; office-work was not. Plainly, it was some whim of the owner which allowed credit managers, who only interfered with selling, to be kept on and paid for their time every Saturday night. I was shocked to find that professional attitudes and interdepartmental antagonisms ran all through the building. Shipping clerks had the same opinion of their own function, for, they told me, if merchandise was not checked in properly, or was not delivered to those to whom it had been sold, the enterprise of operating a department store would prove quite impossible.

At the time it seemed to me that all the claims were wrong; but now that I have had time to think about it, I am sure that no doubt they were all correct. In a perfectly functioning whole organization, no one part may be indispensable. If no merchandise is sold, business is impossible; but it is equally impossible if records are not kept, packages not delivered, and so on. In a motor each of the separate parts, such as carburettor, gas tank, spark plugs, could very well argue that without it the motor could not run. Each would be quite correct in its contention. The only pity is that no one of the employees of the store could possibly see that, while his own claims were correct, this fact did not invalidate the claims of each of the other specialists, whose arguments, erroneously, seemed to him to be opposed to his own. It is not hard to imagine one wheel in a watch viewing with ill-concealed contempt the running of the other wheel which from its perspective would appear to be misguidedly turning in the wrong direction. Neither wheel would be able to understand that without two wheels turning in opposite directions there would be no watch.

What is true of the department store is equally true of all social organizations. Manual labourers see in the work of managers something quite superfluous; and managers deplore the fact that it is necessary to have manual labourers at all when these are so incidental to the main theme. The doctor entertains no very high opinion of most human activity, for he knows that sick people can do nothing and that he is the one who can prevent their illness or help to restore them to health. The lawyer is convinced that only those who stay out of jail are free to follow their private lives. The fireman realizes that a successful career in any field is impossible to pursue from a house that has burned down. Each believes strongly that his own enterprise, and his alone, is the core of the social universe. Of course each is partly correct in his assumptions. All that is lacking is the proper sympathy for the other fellow's contentions, and the understanding that society is a system of interdependencies where each of us needs the others and none stands altogether by himself.

Can it be that the intense concentration on specialized activities together with the lack of comprehension of the size of group organization are the factors responsible for so much of our social dislocation today? Certainly no one thing can be held responsible for all our difficulties, but each, again, is contributory. It would be a fair start toward the understanding of the brotherhood of man if we could realize how important, and at the same time how helpless, we are without the bonds which tie us to our fellows.

Social interdependencies, social relations, are general rather than particular affairs; but individuals vary extremely in their comprehension of what is involved in this fact. Some minds turn to generalities as easily as others do to particular cases. Observe to someone that medical diagnoses and prognoses are subject to error, and he immediately replies that he had a friend whose doctor mistook prickly heat for measles. Tell me that it is the intense heat which has held back business enterprise in the southern states, and I immediately set to work to discover whether this can be said to be true of all civilizations. Since we live in a world which is composed of particulars as well as universals, of universals as well as particulars, I suppose that both approaches represent some kind of extreme specialization and consequent short-sightedness.

The supposition that men of action in the knockabout world are dealing most of the time with concrete things is mistaken. Many business men, for instance, are occupied with high abstractions, and the more successful the business man the higher the abstractions. The heads of large corporations have little to do with actual materials; they deal for the most part with operating statements, which consist of signs on paper. The practicing lawyers or physicians do not see clients or patients; they see examples of the infractions of statutes and they see pathological relations which have general application if they have any. It is difficult to find an occupation whose practice does not involve to some extent the knowledge of principles. And, conversely, the study of principles always has in view, however remotely, some kind of practical application.

Most interests, I suppose, stem from the eager desire to call attention to some neglected factor of existence. Throughout most of my early life I was ill from time to time and never strong enough to engage in vigorous athletics. As soon as I reached maturity and gained my full health and power, I found suddenly more joy in the exercise of my muscles than was average for my age. The first thing of the sort that captured my imagination was horseback riding. The family doctor seemed to feel that this was more exercise for my horse than it was for me, but I persisted. I learned to ride the hard way: through trial and error. And the horse I owned at the time learned to jump in the same way that I did. We saw a stone wall, we cantered toward it, and by some miracle of sheer luck, we both managed to clear it.

Jack was a wonderful horse for a beginner. He appeared quite unmanageable, but only upon my own instigation, and actually could be controlled quite easily. With the proper kind of an audience, I could make people catch their breath at the splendid skill displayed in the control of an animal of such fire and spirit. This was a different kind of Feibleman from the one who had meditated upon poetry consistently for some years, and I found him quite enchanting. A great deal of the credit, of course, should have been given to the horse. I rode with friends for quite a while, until I became convinced that I could not only ride well but could tell horseflesh, too.

On the strength of this belief I purchased a large racehorse entirely on my own judgment. I kept him in a stable in Audubon Park in New Orleans, in a riding club which had just been organized. He was quite skittish, and so every day for some two hours I walked him around the Park very slowly. After two months I changed to an easy trot, and then to a slow canter for several months more. By this time I thought that my horse, whose name was Clapper, was ready to be taken to the more inviting rise along the river, on top of the levee. There were, and still are, railroad tracks along the inside of the banks, usually used by freight trains. One bright afternoon Clapper and I proudly crossed the tracks and began our walk along the levee. Just then a freight train came along, and when it drew opposite us, the engineer blew his whistle.

The rest of the story can be told quite briefly. Clapper reared back in order to get off to a jumping start, and then ran like mad; I tried everything, from sawing on the reins to shutting off his wind by holding my hand over his nose, before he could be stopped. When he finally came to a halt, about two miles up river, I found that he was completely wind-broken, and might drop dead at any moment.

The next horse I bought on my own judgment was half blind.

You probably won't understand what my adventures as a horseman have to do with my penchant for abstractions. But you will understand that the former is somehow a result of the latter. Let us say that I am slightly exaggerating my incapacities in the practical affairs of life in order to make the point clearer. So that I have an interest in particulars, after all, even though it be only in the service of illustration.

How, then, does one get from business to philosophy? This, I suppose, in a way is the most important part of the story I have to tell. For although one example of anything is meaningless in a positive way and proves nothing, it does at least firmly disprove the opposite assumption, namely that one cannot possibly get from business to philosophy, from anything so practical and concrete to something so speculative and abstract. Moreover, if it is possible to move freely from one to the other or even to move at all, it does suggest that there might be some intimate and perhaps important relationship between them.

[139]

K

Every day during the tenure of my active business career I had lunch with Julius Friend, who was some years older than I. Friend had been with Basil Thompson, the editor of *The Double Dealer*, and his interests lay in the same direction as my own. Our tastes were quite different and our lives had few if any points of resemblance; but on the score of inquiry there was sufficient similarity to make working together convenient and helpful. Friend was also in business at the time, and so our conversation quite casually turned toward the problems of affairs.

This was during the period of the nineteen-twenties when the daily triumphs of the business man made him scornful of everything that was not business and made us equally resentful of what to us seemed to be unjustifiable scorn. For we could not immediately doubt the efficacy of business and the claims of the business man; we could only defend the objects of his scorn: art, and that peculiar art of life which the French, for instance, had made into a national monument. We accused the business man of being so single-minded and obsessed with his profession that he had neither the time nor the inclination to give any attention to the enjoyment of its fruits. We were in the habit of saying that he knew how to work but that he did not know how to live.

From a criticism of the business man, we turned toward an examination of business itself. Of course, the business man was simply a man engaged in business; as a man he could not have had the faults we found in him if he had not obtained them from his occupation. We began to read books devoted to business, and to speculate upon the theory of business enterprise. Some of the more glaring contradictions of modern business began to manifest themselves to us: the infinite acceleration of production based on a finite market; the emphasis on production to the neglect of consumption; the multiplication of paper value without the backing of real value; the displacement of man power by machine power without the consideration that it was men who made up the consumer market; the approach of the struggle between kinds of commodities within the economic arena imposed by the political state; and many others. Obviously some of these problems were incidentally occasioned by the advent of the power-tool. There was the factory in New Jersey which was completely automatic, and required for its operation only the services of freight car loaders plus a couple of engineers seated at switches. There was also the general use of the photo-electric cell, and other automatic devices. The direction was plain enough for anyone to read.

If the dislocation of modern business on a large scale could be traced to the power-tool, to what could the power-tool itself be traced? This seemed a fair question, and so we spent some time upon it. Luncheon turned into two-hour occasions for speculation. We found the origin of the power-tool in recent applications of practical physics; the power-tool was a product of modern researches in physical science. Engineers had found out how to apply certain principles of practical physics to the going concerns of industrial machinery. The unsung but well-paid heroes of the day were the men who were called in to design dams, power-plants, and factories, on a large scale. The actual work was done by labour but the ideas came from physical science.

We felt that we were on the right track in our investigations but that we had not yet come to the end of the problem. For where did practical physics get its ideas? Our reading and luncheon table dicussions continued, and we advanced backward in our investigations. We studied the development of practical physics and found that it derived from pure physics. We might have guessed as much; the names would have given us the clue. Despite the prejudices against 'pure' theory today, we should have suspected, as I suppose we did, that pure theory is theory which does not depend upon application for its validity, whereas 'applied' theory is simply pure theory which has been put to some practical use. All practice is the application of pure theory; all pure theory is theory which can be applied irrespective of whether a method has yet been found for its application or not.

We began, then, to read about modern work in pure physics. We struggled with it as best we could but soon learned that modern physics is non-understandable except against a background of classical physics. Like all revolutions in thought, it turns out that what appears to be artificial and revolutionary finds its natural and even conservative place in an historical development. In order to clarify the understanding of modern physics, we read the history of physics in reverse until we emerged into a time and a country in which physics had been indistinguishable from philosophy: the period of ancient Greece. Then suddenly, as if a veil had been lifted from our ignorance, we felt clear about our vision. We studied philosophy swiftly, feverishly, eagerly. We studied modern philosophy first, as was our custom, beginning with Whitehead, and reading backward through the German dogmatists, the English empiricists, the medieval theologians, and the neo-Platonists, until we came to Plato and Aristotle. Then, once again, we felt as though we had gone back to a familiar viewpoint. In philosophy, at last, we felt at home! Thus from our start in the most practical kind of problem conceivable, that of how to remedy the shortcomings of the conduct of business in the United States in 1929, we finally emerged into the abstract and eternal air of Greek philosophy.

With this equipment we now returned to our problem, which was that of the business man in the modern world. Philosophy threw much light upon practical affairs, even though unable to explain them altogether. From the vantage point of philosophy, the analytical method seemed extremely valuable. The business world seen from the heights was quite small; but at least it was a whole. For instance, the philosophy of the business man is that of crude materialism; yet he seldom deals himself with materials; he is entirely preoccupied with the abstractions of cost accounting or double-entry bookkeeping. He does not believe in the primary reality of anything except actual physical particulars, and yet he is lost in the mazes of representative signs. This leads him to deride the abstractions which the other fellow takes seriously, and at the same time to take seriously his own abstractions. He regards his own possession of the paper deed to a property as final, yet makes fun of the decisions of the 'nine old men' who sit upon the Supreme Court bench, as though nothing they could write could possibly have more than paper authority.

The necessity for earning a living proved the hiatus that exists between the peaks of philosophy and the plains of business. Convinced that only those things could be related which were clearly distinguishable, Julius Friend and I returned to the market-place; but at least we knew that so long as we were compelled to remain in business we should be only half-men, equipped not to make more money out of some money plus our labours but only to understand thoroughly what it was we were expected to do.

Then we found—it was in 1929—that the business world had suddenly fallen apart. We rushed to our typewriters at nights and on Sundays, since we were still in business ourselves during the working weeks, and dashed off a book. The title was *Alicism*, and it dealt with the brittle, unreal, looking-glass world of the United States at that time. It was not successful as an effort, so we destroyed it and started again. The second book was finished and published. Its title, a publisher's title, was accurate: *Science and the Spirit of Man*. It was partly the cry of a humanist against what the terrific accomplishments of physical science had done to man's other aspects; it was a pathfinding attempt. In it we showed the subjectivity of physics and the physical elements, and the objectivity of the æsthetic, the moral and other normative elements. We went into the writing of that book humanists and emerged from it realists, in the medieval and Platonic sense of the latter term. We started out in an effort to show that physics had distorted mankind, and to do this we had planned to demonstrate how everything that physics regarded detachedly really belonged to the human being as an attribute. But we ended in a different corner; we actually finished the book having convinced ourselves that nothing that exists within the human being had originated there; everything subjective and mental had to be located and accounted for as a property of the objective world. For the external world contained more than we could sense in it; it contained more than physical objects and sense data, more than the patches of colour and tactile surfaces. It contained the originals of our ideas: the relations between objects, and also all the possibilities which had not made their appearance in the physical world of actuality.

It is easy now (though it would have been impossible for me then) to see that the viewpoint contained in this first philosophical work is better a thing of the past. It is in some ways more autobiography than philosophy, but it had its points. Looking back on it, I can say that the main thesis of the book is to show the subjective aspect of physical relations and the objective aspect of the human values, reverse epistemological views from the then currently accepted conception. This, I suppose, was a deviation necessary in order to indicate the way out of the epistemological *impasse*; for things subjective have their objective counterpart, and vice versa. Thus was the path exhibited leading to the theory of independent values, and ontology revealed to be required and subsumed by any consistent epistemology. *Science and the Spirit of Man* is a genetic-historical work and not altogether a logical one. But the position at which it arrives after traversing the genetic-historical wilderness is logical and ontological enough: the independent and underived rediscovery of the independence of values.

In all subsequent work we laboured hard to make our pattern plain. The reorientation almost amounted to a rebirth. It took a considerable effort to establish the new viewpoint, and many details had to be filled in and many old positions reassessed. In place of the popular division of the mental and the physical, which did not prove under scrutiny to be a fair division at all, we substituted an older one, namely, the division of the actual and the possible, which assumes that all that was actual must have been possible or it could not have become actual, but that all that was possible was never actual altogether or there could not be new things coming into the actual world. This alternate division seemed to accord with modern physical science and its method better than the current one. It also seemed to indicate a certain kind of philosophy, which we then proceeded to write down.

Suddenly, it was as though my eyes had been opened to the dimensions and power of the universe. Poetry was an important art, probably the most important; and yet it was an art among arts, and the arts were, like the sciences, parts of the whole of existence. What, then, did it mean to be a philosophy? Only this, that the whole is greater than its parts. There can be no larger undertaking than the enterprise of philosophy, by definition, since whatever comprises the whole is philosophy. It has its branches, it has its specialities, its little problems and its technicalities; and yet there is a sense in which the least of these is grander than the most of anything else.

Philosophy specializes in generalities. Consider an example, that of number, for instance. Algebra studies numbers; x, let us say, stands for any number. But *number* stands for any meaning of number, and *quantity* and *structure* are broader than any branch of mathematics, broader than the whole of mathematics. To consider not philosophy but some down-to-earth empirical science reveals the power and universality of philosophy. We learn that the presuppositions, the method and the conclusions of an empirical science lie not in science but well outside it and in the province of philosophy. The hard and stubborn fact from which all empirical science takes its start is not alone; it shares with others of its fellows the fact that it *is* a fact, and all facts have certain well-defined characteristics in common. There is no way on earth in which a fact can be absolutely alone. And its connections and relations with other facts eventually constitute philosophy; which is thus not a superstructure, useless, superfluous and top-heavy, imposed upon a well-imbedded foundation, but an essential part of anything which has being.

We are beginning to understand this and to abandon that conception of philosophy which would hold it down to the knowledge relation. The knowledge relation is only one among the many relations of being, and philosophy is concerned with them all. By means of this broad concern it no longer needs to stand upon an analysis of the processes by which knowing is made possible but can soar instead to a discovery of the modes of being. Kant's analogy of philosophy with architecture is illuminating. The philosophical systems are the most magnificent systems that it has ever entered the mind of man to grasp. Compared with them, the structures of vast cathedrals and office-buildings, yes and even of the greatest of symphonies, are dwarfed. I wish that everyone could see what I see: the topless towers of ontology, unbelievably complex analytically yet synthetically so simple, stretching outward and upward from a centre of true postulates and premises. I could predict for my own career that with all my love for poetry, the writing of poetry would have to wait some years. For there could be no more superb or ambitious career than to surrender entirely to the demands which philosophy was making.

Before describing the next books, perhaps I should tell how *Science and the Spirit of Man* came to be published. As soon as it was revised and finished, we sent it to publishers in New York. Several of them returned it unread, with a letter frankly saying that since we had neither graduate degrees nor teaching positions in the universities which would guarantee the sale of a certain number of copies, there was no point in reading the book, for it simply could not be published. One publisher, a small and rather new one, not only rejected the manuscript but gave reasons for doing so which sounded rather novel. He was returning the manuscript, he said, because if it had been any good why would we have submitted it to *his* company? This seemed rather a curious argument, and we never could determine what would make a manuscript both acceptable and available from his point of view. Merit, it appeared on all sides, had nothing at all to do with the case. We began to write another book but before it was more than half done I went with my family to Europe. I took along the manuscript of the first one, hoping to submit it in England, on the off-chance that there it might find a hearing. At a party in London I met an English philosopher who was to be rather unsuccessful on a lecture tour to the United States. He became indignant at the story of my failure to find a publisher in my own country and advised me to try an English one. This time I was more successful.

Shortly before leaving for Europe on what proved to be almost my last trip, I met at the apartment of Hendrik Willem van Loon a young American, an absurdly young American, named Eliot Janeway. We found we were both going to England, and agreed to meet there. I described to Janeway, very briefly, my philosophical position. He remarked that it sounded to him very much like that of Charles S. Peirce, the founder of pragmatism and friend of William James. I had never heard of Peirce and so I immediately went out and purchased the only available volume of Peirce's in print, a selection of his essays entitled *Chance, Love and Logic*. I read it with considerable perplexity, and could not make much out of it. I came to the conclusion that Janeway had been wrong.

This was the year of the bank holidays in America. My wife and I had taken an apartment in Paris where we planned to spend at least ten or twelve months. We had left a baby and a nurse in the apartment, and gone to London for a month to try to place the book with a publisher. Allen & Unwin agreed to read the manuscript and to consider it. The rest of the month we devoted to the Russian ballet which was then in full bloom again. Why is it that the finest things have such ghastly followers? The Russian ballet and the novels of James Joyce, for instance; reputations may be made so, but at the same time they suffer from the cultists who make such achievements their gods. I have always admired the ballet almost above all other art forms, with the exception of poetry, and I have wanted to write about it; but is there anything worse than to be classified with the contemporary 'balletomanes'?

Anyway, we treated ourselves for a full month. We bought blocks of seats, and spent six nights and two matinees each week in the same seats. To our amazement, we found ourselves surrounded always with familiar faces; everyone attended in the same way. I think that for that month one audience supported the ballet. Probably no other city has so much enthusiasm for the dance as has London. Nowhere else have I seen as many as four companies successful simultaneously. In Paris and even in New York, the attitude is different. In New York my most sensitive and intelligent friends tell me that they do not return to the ballet 'once they have seen it'. They do not seem to comprehend that the ballet, like great music, for instance, does not yield its fullest enjoyments to any single experience.

At the end of our month we found ourselves having a holiday in Europe while the banks were having a holiday in America. Suddenly we could not get money in any form for our current expenses. We were not worried about ourselves but about the baby in Paris. I borrowed some money from Milton Waldman, an American friend who had been making his living in pounds sterling in London as a writer of history, enough cash to get us back to Paris. In Paris, an American steamship company agreed to give us passage back to New York in exchange for a deduction from our letter of credit, without any actual exchange of funds.

Once more in New Orleans, Friend and I began work on the completion and revision of a second book which we had started before I had left for Europe. While we were working on this book I read Peirce for the second time and suddenly a light appeared; I saw that he was close to our own ideas as well as to those of Whitehead. It is a very good thing in a way that we made the acquaintance of Peirce at such a late date. Otherwise we might have become abject disciples. As it was we drove through an obstinate set of data to our own position at the cost of what I think was great intellectual effort. We had neither formal training nor the example of a superior philosophy to follow; even Whitehead came late to our thoughts. But we were the better off; we had more to contribute that was fresh and we made a place for ourselves, whether recognized or not, that we could not have had if we had read Peirce before undertaking our own writing. Nevertheless, the importance of Peirce grew in size in my mind, and I resolved at the time to do a book about his ideas. The six volumes of the *Collected Papers of*

Charles S. Peirce were beginning to be published by the Harvard University Press, but attracted little attention. The reviews they received in the professional journals of philosophy gave little inkling that here was a tremendous and for the most part unexplored figure in philosophy, and moreover one who could very well be the beginning of an American intellectual tradition. The Harvard Press ceased to publish Peirce with the sixth volume. A number of others were planned, but they have not appeared, and so far as I know there is no movement to resume their publication.

The second volume that Friend and I wrote was entitled *The Unlimited Community*. This gave a position in philosophy from which we have not since departed. It represented the views which were developed immediately after *Science and the Spirit of Man*, but differed rather sharply from those of the first volume. It began the metaphysics, based on the objectivity of value as well as of logic, which we have entitled axiologic realism, and which we have refined in other books and essays. In six chapters it sketches a system of philosophy which will require many more than six volumes to elaborate.

Since writing *The Unlimited Community*, Friend and I have written separately as well as together. A number of my books have appeared in the United States as well as in England, but have attracted little attention. This does not seem to matter so long as I am free to write. Some day the books may get the notice which it seems to me they deserve. Possibly; possibly not. Certainly I am prejudiced in their favour, but I can regard them, particularly after some years following their publication, with considerable objectivity. What makes this feasible is that I do not feel entirely responsible for them. I am only their author, not their creator; other elements, elements beyond my control or initiation, enter into the occasions of their birth.

Is it likely, were this not true, that I would have ventured to write a book about that aspect of æsthetic theory which deals with comedy? The tragic makes us feel; but the comic makes us think. After experiences with a number of comedies, from the movies of the Marx Brothers to *Alice in Wonderland*, ideas occurred to me which were instigated by humour to which they failed to remain confined. The nature of comedy begged to be developed, and *In Praise of Comedy* was the result. The books on politics, two of them, were occasioned by the love of democracy and the spectacle of its imminent peril. *Christianity, Communism and the Ideal Society* was a defence of democracy in terms of the shortcomings of the absolutisms which rejected it. Catholic Christianity took the realm of essences or universal values (heaven) to be alone real and worthy, thus neglecting what good there is in actuality. Communism, the new absolutism bidding for acceptance, in theory rejected everything but the actual world, thus neglecting the claims of the objective and independent ideal world of essences or values. *Positive Democracy* was an attempt to show that a valid democracy is possible, not based on the claims of its origin in modern times, which were altogether individualistic and atomic in spirit and antagonistic to all conceptions of social organization, but resting rather in the realistic notion of positive real values to be sought in an actual though imperfect real life and on the further assumption that social reality when properly understood does not necessarily exclude an individualism which remains within its proper sphere. There was also a little book on science written in collaboration with Friend and entitled *What Science Really Means*, a defence and explanation of the metaphysically realistic conception of science. What will come next and ask to be written? It is hard to tell.

Perhaps I should explain here how I come to write books as I do, in the hope that something general as to the artistic process will be discernible in my account. Before *The Unlimited Community* I could, and did, write poetry freely, but not prose. The occasional prose piece, an essay on poetry or some related topic, was written only by the utmost effort: a little more struggle and it would not have been written at all. But *The Unlimited Community* in its capacity as path-finder seemed to release some kind of wellspring, for afterwards, books poured forth in a torrent. My method of deciding which book is the next one to be written is a passive one. No book is ever written until it has been planned, so that the actual writing of a book, and this is particularly true of the revision, leaves me free to think about the next one.

Of course, the next one has to be chosen from among many which clamour subconsciously for recognition. 'This ought to be pointed out', but 'so ought that'. Which is to be done first? I used to take sides in the decision but not any more. It does not do any good, for I found that the books always had to decide for themselves in the end. If I started on one work against their decision, why then I could not get very far with it before its place was usurped by another which had evidently managed to exercise a prior claim. Of this much I am certain, and I do not mean it in any metaphorical sense: I am simply a passive instrument, employed by ideas which use the writing of books by me to get themselves made known. Once the ideas have decided which one is rightfully entitled to employ me next, I pursue it. That is all I know. I am convinced that the ideas make the decision among themselves and that it is not my own. The compulsion I feel is too strong for matters to be otherwise.

It so happened that I did not approve of any such enterprise as the present book has turned out to be. What I wanted to write very badly was a book on social psychology. As usual I had made many notes. There was an outline, and I had actually begun work on the rough draft of the first two chapters. Nothing was left to do but to sail merrily along right through the first draft of the whole book—I could see its completed pattern in my mind—but fate decreed otherwise. In bed, in the bathtub, in the barbershop, the project of the present work continued to knock at my door and ask to be written. That is exactly it, and there is no other accurate description: the books come when they are not called voluntarily to the conscious mind; they come and ask to be written. It is a request which cannot lightly be refused. Indeed, the press of other external compulsions, such as the necessity of earning a living or being drafted into war service, is required to make refusal possible at all. The result is that the social psychology book has been put aside for the moment, at least until this book has been written, when, I suspect, it will pop up again.

To suppose that we have complete control of our mental life, that we know everything connected with the interrelations of ideas that goes on within us, is to suppose that we are quite simple beings, analyzable into a limited number of component elements and obvious functions. But the truth is that people are not simple; how soon shall we realize that? They are the most complex beings that we know anything about. In addition to having physical and biological being, they also exist at the psychological and social levels. They have knowledge of a world which is remote from them in space and time, and they even catch glimpses of values and of truths which are ubiquitous and eternal. They are amazing when considered as self-contained and autonomous individuals; how much more so when they participate in social organization as themselves members of a larger whole! The complexities of the human being thus far have succeeded in surpassing the power of the human mind to conceive.

In the light of these facts, it is strange that we act ourselves in our own privately confused and contradictory fashion yet expect our friends to be models of self-consistency. On what experience is such an expectation based? The fact is that each person is a veritable maze of conflicts. Men mean well and generally act from the best of motives, but the best man will on occasion put himself and his own welfare before that of his friends. Which of us has not had reason to be ashamed of his actions? We boast in ways which would make us hide our heads could we but view the spectacle of ourselves objectively. We lose our tempers through anger or prejudice and do things which we would give a great deal afterwards to get undone. When pressed, we even betray friendship in the most flagrant fashion, or, what is less harmful, have our own friendships betrayed.

It is important to remember that what is done to us is generally something which we ourselves could have done. We mean no harm, but then we are human, and to be human is equivalent to being restricted to a fairly limited range of values. We always tend to regard the perfect angel as superhuman; we admire but can hardly seem to imitate the angelic virtues in all their completeness. We too should like nothing better than to have no vices, no shortcomings of any kind, to carry messages for God or be on fire with the pure love of Him. But we know ourselves fallible creatures, held down by our natures to something less than the angels. Similarly, we tend to regard the perfect devil as subhuman; we fear but can hardly hope to escape entirely from the devilish vices in all their negation. We recognize that it is not human to act as St. Francis acted or as the Gestapo acted in our day. One is higher than we hope to strive, the other lower than we plan to fall.

Our own range of actions, prescribed by the values available to most human beings, lies somewhere well within the limits of the fairly good and the fairly bad. We hope to improve our morals and to live somewhat better than we have in the past; that strikes us as lying within our powers. To do even this much, we may have to aim to be perfect even as our Father in Heaven is perfect; yet we know in our heart of hearts that we shall not attain to that perfection, but shall collapse by the wayside. We shall settle for a compromise, since that is what we must do. The difference between most good men and most so-called bad men, considered abstractly, is just the point at which they have been willing to compromise. But to be contained within the range of limited good and limited evil is no fault; it is what we mean by human nature.

If, then, people are both complex and limited in their scope of ethical values, what becomes of friendship? Friendship may well be defined in one of its senses as love without sex. There are many to whom friendship, like the morning newspaper, is one of the most casual things in life. But those of us who are inclined to take friendship seriously, become deeply involved in it; we receive a great deal but we also give a great deal of ourselves. He who goes out openly to friendship has certainly given hostages to fortune which he may or may not succeed in redeeming. All persons capable of friendship should be forewarned. They may be disappointed, and to be disappointed in friendship is only slightly less harmful than to be disappointed in love. Friendship and love must be kept inviolate as places of refuge where the idealist may take shelter. To be disappointed in friendship and yet not allow oneself to become bitter and disillusioned is a task worthy of the strongest. From time to time it is a trial which must be faced. We are unworthy of friendship ourselves if we transfer our bafflement from the unworthy one to the whole of his fellow-creatures.

Hatred is easily satisfied. It is foredoomed to end with the death of the object of hatred. Hatred can desire no more than that, for it has few ties and knows chiefly a terrific concentration. To hate someone is to wish to obliterate him, and, unfortunately for hatred, this can be done. We identify the qualities or properties which we detest, with the person in whom they are made concrete and actual for us.

Love, on the other hand, can share the concentration but is not so easily satisfied. Indeed true love cannot ever be finally satisfied, since it seeks not only union with the object of love but with the universe through the loved object. Love goes through its object and outward toward the world. To love anything or anyone is always eventually to love the cosmos. Thus love does not end with death, for its goal is far wider than the life of a single person. With some justice we tend to regard the loved object as only a single exemplification of the qualities or properties which we love.

In the middle of the Freudian 'twenties, I was on my way to Europe on a very large passenger liner. My mother and father were on board; I had promised to cross with them although we were going different ways on the other side. Half-way across the Atlantic my mother met a young girl of sixteen and wanted me to meet her. I was then twenty-three and of course regarded any woman under thirty as a child unworthy of my attention; but I consented, more to please my parents than out of enthusiasm.

The girl was beautiful and I was impressed, although I did not entirely admit it to myself. We had tea, together with her younger sister, and I invited her to spend the evening with me. She consented, and we met after dinner. I did the usual thing, chiefly out of habit; I led her up to the top deck and tried to kiss her. For this I had my face slapped. The episode suddenly struck me as very funny, and I relaxed to laughter. The girl, however, seemed quite angry, and wanted to know what was so funny about it.

'I just thought it was odd, your acting that way, when we are going to get married.' I said that; I had not thought about it before I said it, because my plans had definitely excluded ever getting married to anyone. Nevertheless I had meant what I had said, and I regarded the whole thing as being so settled that it did not seem to require any discussion. Without making any more attempts to get kisses, I led my partner down to the grand ball room and we spent the evening dancing. No more was said about love or marriage during the remainder of the trip, although we met for tea several times.

A few months later we both happened to be in Paris, and I invited her to go to the theatre. In the taxi on the way she said suddenly, 'You know what you asked me on the boat?'

I said, 'Yes,' because I knew she was referring to marriage, although I really had not asked her anything.

'Well, I just want you to know that it is all right with me,' she added, and then I kissed her for the first time.

We were engaged or considered ourselves so, but decided to keep it a secret since we knew we could not obtain her parents' permission to get married for some time. She went back to New York for the opening of school, her last year of high school, and I came back to New Orleans to business. I made occasional trips to New York, for Christmas and on business; we went often to the theatre. Then her parents got wind of the affair. They asked about it, were told, objected strenuously, and finally consented.

It was not until our engagement was to be formally announced that I began to feel uneasy. Dorothy, for, as they say in the story books, that was her name, had been very shy. She hardly talked to me, except a little on the boat about God and

L

poetry, and I had no idea what she was really like. So I walked in one afternoon and said I was leaving. Marriage is a serious affair, and I wanted to be perfectly sure I could not do without it.

Another six months convinced me. I did not know whether I was going to be happy with her, but I could see that I was definitely going to be unhappy without her. I made inquiries and discovered that she was again in Paris, this time attending the Sorbonne. I was not allowed by her parents to communicate with her, but I managed to get a letter to her through a third person. She was, she wrote, willing to see me. I took the next boat to Europe and her mother took the first boat after mine. We waited for her mother, and then had a long talk: from nine in the evening until four the next morning. Decision —inconclusive. The following night I was to take Dorothy to the theatre again, but this time we were sent for in the middle of the second act. Back at the hotel, her mother had been pacing the floor. When we came in, she said:

'Look, kids. I can see you are going to get married, whether or not I give my consent. So I give it, provided you can get Father's permission, also.'

We returned to the States on another couple of boats, I going on ahead as usual, and her father also gave his consent. As soon as Dorothy reached New York, we were married, before anything more could happen. Then we came down to New Orleans and lived happily ever after. That was in December of 1928. A son was born in August, 1930.

The desire for children, an entirely different thing from the desire for sexual relations, is natural enough; and I should think that only monstrous people would lack it altogether. Nevertheless, to be satisfied to find immortality through progeny is a questionable venture. It is the only recourse most persons have for obtaining a life after death; and they can only hope that their issue will honour their name. But I doubt whether this is as it ought to be. Children should be desired before they come and loved when they do, just for their own sakes and without any ulterior motive; while immortality should be sought in some other direction: through the arts or sciences, for instance. It is a pity, I suppose, that the fundamental desires of most persons are alike, whereas the equipment for satisfying fundamental desires varies so greatly from individual to individual. Basic democracy must consist in the willingness of those with superior abilities to assist the others to attain the ultimate objects of desire which all hold in common.

At the bottom of all human beings is the desire to find permanence, reality, significance; these are all one and the same. We learn before too long that our frail bodies will not stand the strain of living more than a few decades; it is in fact rather amazing that mere flesh is able to stand as much punishment as it does. The soft parts of the human organism decay soon after death, and the relative rarity of the skeletons of any considerable antiquity shows how little we can depend even upon them. Apart from the fact that the remains do not resemble ourselves in the least, those bones which have excited the interest of anthropologists: the Neanderthal Man, the Chinese Man, etc., are pretty good indications that all the contemporaries of these ancient gentlemen, the millions upon millions of them, are gone with the wind. One cannot depend upon bones to maintain one's significance for one any more than one can upon the soft parts of one's body.

What lies in store, then? To us who have barely emerged from the Iron Age into the age of light tensile metals, stainless steel contains possibilities. When I was young I wrote a poem more or less devoted to the fancy of a young lady who should be composed of aluminium, with few joints to get out of order, stainless and rustless, and very beautiful indeed. It was a dream. For ladies, living bodies are preferable. Stone works better. Iron has a fairly short life; and what made me think the light tensile metals would do the job of immortality any better than the others is more than I can recall. Clearly the answer is not here and we must look further.

One way to attain permanence seems to be to attach yourself to other times by means of a house. Soon after my marriage we—my wife and I—bought an old Spanish house in the old

French Quarter. It tied us to the past; the next act was to build a new one which was to tie us to the future. Both failed rather obviously.

The Spanish house was beautiful and old; the walls kept falling apart, so that the house itself was impossible to keep clean. Moreover, it was during prohibition and we found that instead of living in the past the world was too much with us in the present. To one side of us lay the residence of a bootlegger; to the other, a house of assignation. We promised ourselves not a glorious past but a safe, impecunious future; when our money should be gone we would build a toll-bridge from neighbour to neighbour and live on the proceeds. The bootlegger thought it an excellent idea; but the girls who should also have been consulted were always asleep in the daytime. Then prohibition itself came to an end and the plan fell through; it was only another dream after all, and so we sold our house and moved into the suburbs.

Some years ago—not long enough ago to rub out the hurt, as a matter of fact—my wife and I occasioned a house to be built in newer New Orleans. We live in a neighbourhood in which the European architecture of a previous century prevails. Norman farm houses, Tudor mansions, have their place, certainly, and very important places they are because many of them are truly successful; but what are they doing here in twentieth-century America? Conservative American business men (is there any other kind?) cannot understand why I object so bitterly to new copies of old houses. I tried once very hard to explain to one of them that if everybody had always copied as we are copying now, there would have been nothing now for us to copy. But he did not understand. The reason is that we hold a philosophy which forbids us to place much emphasis on anything which is not material and physical; the engineer gets our respect, the contractor and the builder. The architect remains a necessary evil: a man who has had too much educa-tion and as a result can do nothing except draw pretty picture- of houses on paper and then hang around while someone else builds them.

So we decided that we would have a modern house, or rather, to follow the usual variant, a 'modernistic' one (said with extreme suspicion and a modicum of disapproval). We could not afford Frank Lloyd Wright, who can? There was no good modern architect in our city, so we did the best we could: we obtained the services of an architect who promised to copy in little a picture we gave him of a good but rather conservative modern house that we had seen in a trade journal; to this extent did we conform to custom. The local taxi-drivers promptly mistook the new home for a small private hospital or a gas station.

He did the best he could with the picture, which actually was not bad. Following my insistence, he used the most durable materials: poured concrete reinforced with steel. I felt that I had what I wanted. The elaborate glass walls of the living room, the glass brick which in places is employed both within and without, is nowhere part of the essential structure of the building. When the glass went, I felt that at least enough would remain to support a plaque bearing my name and occupation and the dates of my life and residence there. But, alas, what I had mistaken for destiny was only chance. My predilection for comedy caught up with me in several ways.

In the first place, I happened to drop into a drug store in New York, not for drugs of course but for lunch. I sat at the counter next to two personable young men who were talking in voices that were sure to be overheard. Being alone, I could not help but listen. They were evidently apprentices in an architect's office, conservative young men who disapproved of the modernism of their boss.

'You know what I dislike about modern architecture,' one of them said, 'it is the impermanence of the materials. Now you take these modern houses that are being put up today. They can't be expected to last very long. As soon as water gets inside the broken windows, it will decay the concrete; and as soon as decayed concrete allows the dampness to penetrate to the steel reinforcing, the whole thing will crumble like a cocked hat. So a modern house is no stronger than its weakest window.'

There was something wrong with my lunch; I had indigestion all afternoon. I have been thinking that it must have been the ice-cream.

In the second place, there was the disaster of Pearl Harbour. The second world war had begun and with it the danger of desultory or 'token' bombing by the enemy in my neighbourhood. We had been busy with preparedness work, in my case the instruction of air raid wardens. What was to happen to my house in a raid, was it safe? Possibly. I only know that as soon as I built a glass house, people started throwing stones.

What is to remain of our civilization? Judged from a purely physical point of view, very little. The materials with which we work, while being very malleable and subtle, are also very short-lived. Despite the fact that we probably print more books in a single year than the Egyptians did through all the centuries of their reigning dynasties, more of theirs may have survived than will of ours. Theirs were made of parchment; ours are of paper, and an inferior grade of paper at that.

Is nothing to remain to indicate to future ages the tremendous technology we have developed? Nothing, if we are to judge by the durability of materials, except the stone and the bronze of the sculptors. Of these, the only gigantic achievements in point of sheer size, comparable to the Stonehenge and the Pyramids and the Greek temples of the past, are represented by a single one: the sculptured heads of Washington, Jefferson and Lincoln carved in South Dakota by Gutzon Borglum. They are not very good as sculpture, whatever may be their value to patriotism. Has Borglum perhaps played a joke on us all in securing for modern civilization a low rating in the studies of comparative civilization of the future, by his punitive immortality?

The interplay of chance and destiny conspire with the vividness of actuality to make life and ourselves dancers. I have spoken before of the conception of life as a ballet. The dancing you have seen on the stage is a mere concentration, but does not differ in kind from what we do in ordinary life. Life certainly contains prosaic as well as poetic aspects, and much depends upon our perspective as to which aspect we learn to appreciate the more keenly. Of course, there are gay occasions and sad ones, but we can learn to dance through them all. There are people who discourage dancing but we dance in spite of them; and there are others who instigate it and we dance because of their existence.

There are people, gay people, immoral people, in a way aimless people, who manage to give more of a sense of form to the occasions of actual life than all the serious students of pure form that there are in the world. It is difficult to explain what I mean, for such people serve no ostensible purpose; they are not 'useful' citizens or upright and sturdy members of the community; they do not necessarily earn enough to pay taxes, and they limit their altruism to the nature of occasions. Yet they illuminate life, and in a way reveal the core of its meaning. They do not do this through books or even through conversation but through action. Not entirely through action, either, but through being what they are. What they are is in a sense their accomplishment; it cannot be directly pursued but is indirectly attained. To have a personality which is attractive is a kind of ethical action all its own; and moreover one which we should be very unhappy without, for it cannot be replaced by strenuous and vigorous methods.

One example occurs to me now of a particular friend. We met about fourteen years ago. He was working on a local paper, while I was still in my father's store. I took an instant dislike to him as I did to all newspaper men who wished to learn how to write novels. I have always disliked reporters who regarded their newspaper days as the proper way to acquire experience for serious writing. They never seem to have heard of any literary form except the novel, any method other than that of photographic realism, or any reward except to have the novel accepted by the motion picture companies. Bruce Manning had all of these things. Yet for some reason or other we planned an evening, and the evening was successful; he brought his wife and I mine and we all seemed to hit it off. It was the beginning of a friendship.

Not long after our first meeting, Manning and Bristow, his

wife, took a summer house on the Gulf Coast, where he was supposed to be recuperating from something or other. We went over for a week-end with them, and spent all day Sunday on a little launch we had hired to take us fishing. On the way back, we noticed Bruce and Gwen whispering together at one end of the boat. I thought this behaviour a little rude, until they came marching up to us hand-in-hand with an announcement.

'We have decided that we like you,' they said solemnly, 'because we have spent the whole day with you, now, and you have never talked about your baby.'

I do not know how to describe Bruce Manning. The tales that could be told about him, and have been told by many people, are endless and fantastic. I can only say that he has the gift of words in conversation, the feeling for people, and, better still, a sense of situations. He is the same person when he is poor and when he is rich. He has all the prejudices that you would expect to find in an Irish Catholic American—and accepts none of them. He has a profound respect for learning, which is in a way the truest learning that anyone can boast.

Chief among his virtues is a positive and affirmative spirit. He likes everybody and enjoys everything that happens. But most of all he likes low places and humble people. It is the Dostoevski streak. I could never get him to read Dostoevski and at the time failed to understand why. Bruce handles lightly what Dostoevski treated divinely. I understand now; he does not need to read a novelist whose world outlook he shares in his own way. One night in Hollywood, he drove me a long way into the slums of Los Angeles. The place he wanted me to see was a bar room containing the oldest and most diseased of prostitutes, the toughest of bartenders, and the most degraded of customers. It took us an hour to get there in Manning's car, and then we had a drink at the bar and a word with the bartender. When we left, shortly afterward, he said, 'Wasn't it wonderful?' The scene was certainly a sordid one; what had he perceived that I had missed until I had seen it through his eyes? Obviously, that there's a divinity doth hedge a dive. The ability to make a symbolic meaning stand out in sharp relief does not necessarily also carry with it the ability to be able to interpret the symbols in terms of their meaning; many people build better than they know.

When Bruce first went to Hollywood to work for the films, I warned him that many writers had gone out there with the intention of making a few thousand dollars and then of retiring to write the Great Novel. Nothing had come of such ambition because, once successful, the writers always learned to live on a higher scale which required the continual earning of enormous sums, and also because life in Hollywood cheapened them; they grew to despise themselves, gave up their true ambition, and turned into cogs in a money-making wheel of fortune. 'That will happen to you,' I said to Bruce, but he calmed my fears.

'I have nothing to lose to Hollywood,' he pointed out. 'A man who has no great genius does not have to be afraid to have it cheapened.'

He was right and I was wrong. He will not lose what he has. The last time Bruce returned to New Orleans, he said that some day when he was fired from Hollywood he would come home to be my gardener. I have no gardener, but I will have one then. For the things that the artists are struggling so pitifully, painfully, and endlessly, to write down a little bit, are cast about freely in Manning's casual remarks. The things that are worth doing are worth doing well, so far as he is concerned, but only provided that they are ephemeral. He writes no classics and pens nothing permanent. That is perhaps the greatest liberality of all. To have a talent, a talent that is almost religious in its generality of perceptiveness, and yet to make nothing recognizable of it, except to those who happen to appreciate its existence, is wasteful from the point of view of the individual. When Bruce turns his attention to money-making and writes for the movies his work is almost as meretricious as anybody's. That is because he writes and works at the level of the movies, and in and for the movies. But he has nothing to lose to them not because he has nothing but because what he has cannot be lost.

I once drove to New York with Bruce. It was in the middle of the summer and we wore seersucker cotton suits. Bruce's in particular had a very wide stripe, and this variety had not been seen much in the north in those days. We stopped overnight at a tourist camp, and drove early the next morning toward Philadelphia without breakfast. Just before entering the city limits, we stopped at a lunch wagon for coffee. The room was full of truck drivers having breakfast, and when we came in and gave our order, we noticed that they were looking at Bruce's wide blue stripes with more than the normal curiosity. To travel with Bruce means to be prepared to play foil at any hour. He turned to me casually, and remarked that it had not been hard. I knew he was not talking to me but to the wider audience; I was supposed to respond in kind, but for the life of me I could not get the plot. —

'What was not hard?' I asked, sleepily.

'Getting out,' he said, in a loud voice. 'All I had to do was to watch my time, slug the warden over the head, grab the keys and beat it.'

The crowd began to look more ominous. The stripes on his suit stood out. I could almost read the sign that they had in mind: '$1,000 reward for information leading to the capture of . . . dead or alive . . .' We left without waiting for breakfast.

I have seen Bruce do easily what I could never do without getting hurt. We were standing at a fashionable bar in New York. At a table nearby were four attractive people. Bruce noticed them and said that he would like to meet them. Before I could answer that this was quite impossible, since we did not seem to have any acquaintances in common with them, he had gotten a chair and pulled it up to the table. There was a painful suspense lasting not more than a second, and the shock was over. The five were all friends, laughing and drinking together. I like people and I would like very much to be able to do what he did. But I know that if I did, they would promptly have called the bartender and either have thrown me out of the bar or have sent for the police. Custom and prescribed rules of conduct were established for the benefit of those who do not understand situations sufficiently to be able to lean more directly upon the fundamental values and laws of the nature of things.

Huxley, it was, I believe, who said somewhere that Dostoevski was trying to find God by looking in the dustbins. Bruce combines that search with a sense of comedy, and of immanent essences in the social events that are most trivial. His is a high personality, one that is able to gather up these values and present them in such a form that life obtains greater meaning for those who come into contact with him. 'I am ready now,' he wrote me once, 'to get excited about something.'

There was a tramp who came through New Orleans a year or so ago, a very well dressed tramp, who borrowed from everybody and did not leave town until he had exhausted all its credit possibilities. One of the names he left with was that of Bruce Manning, a producer at Universal Studios in Hollywood. He had obtained that from some of the men on the paper on which Bruce had formerly worked. I knew that the man would end up in Hollywood borrowing from Bruce, and I started to warn him by telegram or letter but finally thought better of it for humble reasons. Bruce had himself been a tramp; he knew the species better than I, and there was little that anyone could tell him, anyhow, about people.

The next time I saw Bruce I asked him about the tramp. Yes, Bruce remembered him; the man had come out there and called him up. It had cost him lunch and one hundred dollars.

'But Bruce,' I remonstrated, 'you must have known the man was not genuine. He has never done a day's work in his life. He lives on other people. If you had a hundred dollars you did not need, why did you not give it to an orphan asylum? This man will gamble it away or drink it up; he won't do any good with it.'

'Yes, I know,' Bruce replied. 'But you see, I knew he was a fraud, and, despite the fact that he knew that I knew, he told me some long tale which he at least expected me to pretend

[165]

that I believed. Somehow, it did not seem to be the thing to do to let him down. So I gave him the money. He won't come back for more.'

There are many artists of craft but few of life. All I can say for Bruce, whatever happens, is that he is an artist of life. He discovers patterns in it that would not be there for us to see except for him. He knows how to make the trivial vivid, the important importunate, and the things that happen somehow right and bearable.

It is not strange that Bruce should have gravitated to New Orleans, the literary and artistic centre of the old south. Looked at with some regard for facts, this means that the French Quarter being old, smelly and dirty, but having a little beauty, too, might not be a bad place in which to live while doing work which can later be sold in New York. Looked at with a kindlier eye, it means that for the struggling artists of the south with all its backwardness, impecunity and lack of opportunity, the old square of New Orleans is extremely attractive as a place to meet kindred spirits and to concentrate upon literary and artistic work.

Some years ago, the stenographer I employed on half-time secured a full-time position. I advertised in the newspaper for someone with whom to replace her, and found among the applicants a very nice girl who had just arrived in New Orleans from the University of Texas. The position suited her perfectly because she wanted to do some writing herself, and only wished to work for half of each day.

Shortly after she came to work for me, I found in a small New York literary journal the announcement of a prize short story contest. I had written a volume of short stories, some of which had already been published in England and America. I clipped the notice and put it on her desk one morning, with the suggestion that she send one of my stories in to the contest. It was not long before she came to me with a request for a favour.

'What is it?' I asked.

'Well,' she said, 'you know I write stories, too, and I sort

[166]

of wondered whether you would mind very much if I sent in one of my own.'

'Of course not,' I replied. 'There is no favour involved. This is a public contest and I should think that anyone in the country ought to be free to submit as many stories as he wishes.'

A few months later she came over to my desk, looking a little pale. 'I have some *awfully* bad news for you,' she warned. 'I hope you won't mind it too much, but you see—I've won the contest.'

I think that she had expected to be dismissed for such effrontery. A little later she won a fellowship for a novel. Meanwhile my enormous talent for fiction writing has languished, but she has helped me a great deal. At the end of my book on Peirce, throughout which I had been clinging to the facts scrupulously in rather pedestrian prose, I felt that as my reward and for the purposes of a peroration I could afford to let myself go a little. I wrote a few pages of postcript in what I thought at the time might be considered very purple prose. My stenographer typed it for me, and ventured one suggestion. She had no comment to offer in praise of my literary style (although I had expected one) but she did ask a question.

'Is it all right,' she said, 'for "hurly-burly" and "willy-nilly" to appear together in the same sentence?'

The criticism lays open a great weakness. What a spectacle a man makes of himself in his search for truth! How many things beguile him and distort his approach! The feeling for proximate values, for instance, or the love of fame. We live among changing things while we look for what is immutable.

Today and the truth, was there ever a very close relation between them? Of course, whatever happens does so because it has some value and is to some extent true. But the amount of value and truth that anything contains is always severely limited. We strive to increase the amount of truth in the world, for as philosophers and scientists that is our task, just as it is the task of artists to increase the amount of value. But what we can accomplish is always infinitesimal compared with what we know ought to be accomplished. How can we boast, then, or be vain in the fact of what remains to be done? I see the course of events running along with some logic, but with much chance. Now, the nature of things allows actuality to steer directly toward its goal for short periods. We do not know the exact character of that goal but we do know when we are approaching it, and that is when we are most busily engaged in increasing the values of the good, the beautiful, the worshipful, and the true. We know we are veering away from it when we resort to force to accomplish our purposes, when for example we employ war without aim as a means of national policy, chicanery as a means of individual strategy, and indeed any physical conflict as a means of settling social questions. There are those to whom the presence of war is disillusioning; they had hoped to solve the predicament of being less than we ought to be with a spoon-fed philosophy, a slogan, a panacea, of some sort; and when they are brought face to face with the cruel but undeniable fact that the world which we thought we had saved from war is again engaged in a titanic struggle, they abandon hope altogether. But is that necessary; is it not the reaction of weakness, incompetence and confusion? Is it not the result of expecting that somehow today and the truth will meet never to separate again? We look, in whatever generation we happen to be living, to find the meaning of history: the past is a series of errors and lessons leading up to us; the future, a prolonged continuation of the present. The present is what history existed for: the meaning of the whole course of things. That everybody thinks so, is sufficient refutation.

No; we should look upon our times, whatever they may happen to bring, as more or less exemplifying what can be expected. The change is swift? It is sure to slow down. There is no change? Things do not always remain the same. There is war, and all the things for which we care are being abated if not destroyed? They cannot be destroyed; they can only be stopped for a while; they will return. In the meantime, it is our task to keep something alive, so that, if possible, precious time will not be lost by having to start from the beginning again. Nothing has changed that is valuable, only our fear stands in the way of continuity, a fear of the discontinuous. It can be controlled not by reassurances, not by blinding ourselves to what is going on, but only by surrendering to the power that is behind the necessity for getting things done. And, among the things that have to be done, whatever happens, are the arts and the sciences and philosophy. If we are interrupted momentarily by the obligation to fight, then we will fight; and when the fight is over we will return to our tasks, as though we had only been stopped by the presence of someone at the door.

For to think that today is opposed to the truth in some peculiarly ominous fashion is to assume that there was another day when it was not. Must we assume that our trials are generally different for being stronger, different in quality for being different in quantity? Most assuredly no. The artist, for example, fancies himself baffled by the second world war. But let us look at his equal for a moment in a day when things were otherwise. In the eighteen-nineties and even in the nineteen-twenties the artist was very much preoccupied with the problem that being an artist presents to the artist: his own private complaints and sufferings. We must believe neither that the artist has no trouble nor that all that he complains about is equally viable. The same is true of other people, and tribulations must be measured in terms of what is happening to the whole population. The artist must be helped in all possible ways, and allowed to choose his own course so far as that is possible. But he must also be expected to be strong.

Great periods in the world's history when crises occur are also the time when courses are adopted that will be followed for a long while. We should consider ourselves privileged to live in one of these decisive ages and to have a hand in determining the pattern of human life, at least in the immediate future. 'It is a terrible thing,' the translators of the King James version of the Bible have said, 'a terrible thing to fall into the hands of the living god;' but therein lies greatness, and the bigger we are the more of force we will wish to encounter. What is this to which we have been praying, and where are we when events are stirred out of their monotony? All that we ask is peace and love, art and science, and the calm pursuits of our daily careers, but we wish a certain kind of condition for this and not merely allowance; a certain kind of life and not merely life. We must be prepared to do what in a sense nobody has ever done before us in the history of the world, namely to be equal to our own capabilities. And we can do so only provided that we regard nothing good as irrevocably over, and the future closed to nothing at all.

CHAPTER FOUR

The Swelling of the Theme

To grow older is to have one's spirit of inquiry transformed. We can understand by glancing backward as well as forward much that was not clear before. The eagerness of youth is not necessarily lost, yet we begin to see that our stock of it will have to be somewhat conserved if we are to continue looking about us with the same thoroughness through the forthcoming years. For it becomes increasingly obvious that, while our goal remains as remote and unobtainable as always, we have been missing many pointers by the way. There is one illuminating and enormous answer waiting tantalizingly for us at the end of the path but (a fact overlooked in the past) the road consists not only of useless obstructions which have to be surmounted but also of many little answers each possessing its own demands for meaning and enjoyment as we progress. The spirit as a consequence is able to keep its elasticity but acquires from the friction of its passage through experiences a certain toughness which can help us or hurt us according as we employ it well or ill.

Our theme concerning the nature of existence reveals itself in a roundness we did not suspect it to own. We had sought to learn, for instance, only from people who had knowledge, but we have discovered that those who do not themselves have knowledge may have many varieties and degrees of value the knowledge of which we may be able to acquire through acquaintance with them as human beings. We find that we emerge from contacts which we had estimated as trivial with lessons whose impact is terrific. We learn about the good life not only from the good life but also from life in general. The persons I had ignored because of their lack of ideals were capable more often than I had suspected of inspiring them; the places I had overlooked because of their provinciality were

M

sometimes the forges of cosmopolitanism. Home took on a new and delightful aspect not so much for its familiarity as for its unstudied novelty.

Had I made a mistake in returning to New Orleans to live? There were times surely when I thought about Paris with some sadness and much regret, and there were other times when I wondered whether it would still not be better to remain in New York. The amount of interest in philosophical matters to be found in New Orleans was negligible; there were few persons to whom my work could mean more than a private and harmless eccentricity. Why then did I remain?

Very often from time to time I continue to ask myself that question. Pascal once said that a man should try to live as though he might die tomorrow or else might live forever. The attitude Pascal recommended for time would apply equally well to space: a man should try to live as though he might move tomorrow or remain in the same neighbourhood forever. Thus I have continued to stay in New Orleans but never with the feeling of permanency or attachment that resignation gives. I have no confidence that either my own character or the type of work in which I am engaged will allow me to stop here for the remainder of my life. There is always the chance that I will be called to teach in some university; there is always the chance that I will grow restless and wish to leave without having been called anywhere. But in the meantime here I am.

And as a matter of fact it is not a bad place. I spend a great part of my life, an important part, anyway, trying to satisfy my nose. It is neither a small nor a delicate nose, so I probably have good reason to pay homage to it. Memory for me, as I imagine it is for most persons, is largely an olfactory affair. Harmony Street in New Orleans where I was born, and Prytania Street where I played as a child will never let me forget the smell of oak trees and of acorns rotting on the ground, of mud in the streets after summer rains and of honey-suckle on hot summer nights. New Orleans is a beautiful city; the trees make it so if nothing else. For one with enough money to buy books from New York and have them sent in the mail,

New Orleans is a wonderful place to live. This implies also of course that it is wonderful only for anyone who can go away for at least a small part of every year; I can think of no place in which it would be ideal to remain permanently. It is necessary to change the background sharply once in a while, if only in order to discover how one is constituted.

Sometimes I think that it is not New Orleans which keeps me rooted here but the swamps below the city, the area between the city and the Gulf of Mexico, that fantastic land of strange and ill-assorted people, and of swamp marsh, of the salt marsh and its animals, its monotony and its decayed and foetid air which is timeless and so beautiful that to get it in one's blood means to be drawn back more than once. Perhaps Baudelaire is right that life (in a sense) is only a hospital in which the patients are obsessed with the desire to change their beds. I have dreamed in the swamps of going to Paris, and in Paris of returning to the swamps; but it is the swamps, I know it now, which have the irrefrangible hold upon me. I know of no region which seems to me less particular and more universal; not in the simple way of looking like other regions, but rather because of its unique combination of highly sensual values, of smells and silences and overbearing dampness and heat in summer, because of a timeless quality which is hard to describe though vivid in experience. It makes living in its most intense form possible.

In the novels of E. P. O'Donnell, particularly in the descriptions in *Green Margins*, some picture of what I feel about the swamps and the land down river is extremely well conveyed. True, I do not often leave town; I do not have much time to take off from my work to spend in the marshes; but I live near them and I know that they are there. And I can go there whenever I wish.

For an artist or a philosopher, New Orleans is perhaps a better place than most from which to be heard. It is good to have a base of some sort and New Orleans is that base for me. Meanwhile, I live from postman to postman. He takes my manuscripts away, and in the fullness of time brings back proof sheets—or the manuscripts. My friends write me about their ideas, send me their articles, and I send them mine, all through the courtesy of the U.S. mail. It is a tenous if significant kind of existence. Living in New Orleans from this point of view is almost like living in some remote outpost of Empire; an outpost, however, which is in continuous land contact and from which one can emerge into the heat and controversies of the day quite suddenly, and without spending months on a pacquet-boat. One is, so to speak, *in* the times but not *of* them. The gigantic waves of contemporary interest which sweep over the face of the United States are felt this far south only as the mildest of impulses. The high degree of illiteracy which reigns here, somehow forces the literate to a certain degree of intellectual independence which they might not have in other places where the competition is keener. Ignorance certainly does serve as an effective insulation against too great a participation in the sudden but brief enthusiasms of the day. The literary and intellectual fashions which take the writers and thinkers of New York by storm hardly ever reach New Orleans until they have ceased to exist at all in New York and have by consequence somewhat spent their force. This compels those of us who are eager for inquiry to fall back upon the eternal verities which must perforce always be fashionable to some extent.

When I glance around me I realize that in the local scene very little searching is going on, but does that make what I say any the less true? I do not see why it should. If the kind of things which I experience in New Orleans are not experienced by anyone else, does that mean they do not exist except as a figment of my imagination? Emphatically not; not, that is, so long as my descriptions of my experience contain elements which can be recognized by others in distant places (and I shall hope also in remote times) as identical with elements of their own. Living in New Orleans, I feel like an agent whose company without him would be unrepresented in the region. Is the south, after all, not entitled to have some voice in philosophy?

In what follows in this chapter, I shall describe some of the people and the ideas I encountered in New Orleans, or in trips taken from here in the last decade of my residence. To put people and ideas upon the same plane is no doubt to be somewhat misleading. I, however, can sometimes actually fail to distinguish. There is a certain philosophical viewpoint according to which people are only specific collections of ideas. A man is, to a larger extent than anyone suspects, just what he believes. He thinks according to his ideas, feels according to them, and, what is very important, acts according to them. Of course, few if any of us are familiar with all the ideas which we hold to be true. Ideas are held at many levels in the human being; some of them are incorporated into our very physiological being, held, so to speak, in the bones; and, while we do not know what they are, this does not deter us from acting according to their dictation. Thus from any humanistic point of view, an interest in ideas is a very significant thing: ideas must be watched for they may become people or (what is the same thing) the leading motives in people.

People are, of course, primarily human beings and ends in themselves. But there is another sense in which they are also methods, certain means of arriving at answers to the problems which living presents. The shape and colour of personalities have been made what they are by the wearing away of perennial questions; and the constant flow of existence past a man determines to some extent what his peculiar markings shall be. The friends we make are those whose solutions are our own; they are those who have worked something out in much the same way that we have, or at least in some way that we should like to have done. We feel sympathetic and close to them because we have adopted the same methods. It is always exciting to meet new people, and to discover just how they have solved the problems of being for themselves. We may be sure that some of them will proffer solutions of which we have never even dreamed, and will enchant us with alternatives. Part of the abundance of life comes from the application of methods which are rich and varied in their ingenuity or perhaps in some cases spare in their simplicity. But always there is the little difference which lends charm, the novelty from which we can draw delight, and the actualization of values which we can share. The rewards of society, in addition to making human life possible, lie also in making it worth while.

A single personality is capable of transforming the perspective from which we view the world. For some personalities are illuminations which light up not only unfamiliar corners of existence but familiar corners as well. There is no room to describe all the people who have meant something in this way to me; and it may even prove to be impossible to communicate a particular instance of what I am trying in a general way to explain. But I should like to make the effort to do so, anyway. When, for instance, Sherwood Anderson first came to New Orleans he looked like an old mother, his face, I mean, very much like that of Gertrude Stein. His was a full head with a straight though large and almost bulbous nose. His mouth was thin and determined, a straight line cut across the clear expanse of his lower jaw. It was the expression of a wise old woman, not effeminate but strong, a peasant woman who had raised a brood, done the washing and cooking for the family and kept her children firm in the law of her religion. Is there anything to be learned from the study of faces alone? Because the rest of the picture changed all that. Sherwood always had his hair brushed in a straight line curving slightly down over one corner of his forehead. The hair, the blackthorne stick and the clothes completely altered the first impression. He wore a corduroy shirt, a loud green one, and a finger ring for the knot in his tie. His suit was brown with a loud green pin stripe, and his woollen socks were constantly falling down over the tops of his high shoes. I first caught a glimpse of him as he was climbing down from a shoeshine stand; the glimpse turned into a stare. He did not see me, was no doubt hardly disconcerted by what must have been a common occurrence: he was almost certainly a spectacle wherever he went.

I later met him and we became friends. We talked together a great deal. I had at the time recently begun my friendship with

Bruce Manning. Sherwood and Bruce are the only two men I have ever known who could tell a story properly. They employed the same method, as a matter of fact. It consisted in the technique of the bedtime ghost story for children, applied to the commonplace, an atmosphere of great mystery applied to the most trivial of events and thereby transforming them into something greatly meaningful. The effect was tremendous; for the present, everything in the present: the room in which we were sitting, the furniture, the glasses in our hands, the fire in the fireplace, even the sounds outside, became invested with enormous significance. You felt as you sat there that you were being let in on some event of tremendous importance, that you were the only one being made acquainted with happenings which were capable of changing the whole course of history.

'You know, Jim,' Sherwood would begin, 'I only made lots of money one time and that was on a book called *Dark Laughter*. I bought a big farm in Virginia with the royalties, a place with a large stone farm house. Well, I decided that I could not write in the house, so I had a little stone cottage set up away from the main building.' He leaned forward in his chair, his voice dropped, and his eyes looked away. 'In the cottage there were two stone tables, and I was to write on one of them.' He was on the edge of his chair now. 'You know, Jim, what happened? I went down to that cottage every morning and sat there pencil in hand and paper before me.' Here he looked around the room apprehensively, as though to catch the murderer himself in the act of eavesdropping. I could hardly understand the hoarse and furtive whisper, spoken very slowly: 'Well, I sat there and never wrote a god-damn word.'

Other story tellers could produce suspense by introducing supernatural elements, mystery, or magic. Sherwood needed only the ordinary circumstances of the everyday life of ordinary man. The magic was almost metaphysical: it was of significance to him not that a man walked strangely but that he walked at all. The metaphysician is concerned with the commonplace, but he has, so to speak, an uncommon interest in it. For motion itself is the mystery: how can there be the phenomena of motion? Now, this concern of the metaphysician is abstract and general; he is never absorbed in a particular motion; this man or that walking down the street means little or nothing to him in his capacity as a metaphysician. What does interest him is the general law or significance of motion. The interest of Sherwood was typical of the interest of the artist. He was concerned neither with the particular alone nor with the general alone but with the general *through* the particular. A man walking had no interest by itself for Sherwood; neither would the laws of motion have had if he had known about them. But a man walking somehow illuminated for him the whole value of motion, and consequently was heavy with large and powerful symbolism. Sherwood could catch that significance readily, he could catch it but he could not hold it. That is why he wrote greater short stories than novels. His art was the art of the flash, the single impression: the poem, the short story, the song. But he certainly could catch it; what is more rare, he could catch it not only in writing but almost as well in speech. There is no way here to describe the peculiar values elicited from something which Sherwood had apprehended in the commonplace.

Perhaps his gift came from the peculiar way in which he saw the world. He understood a certain viewpoint well, and once came very near expressing it abstractly. 'You know, Jim,' he said, 'when we are talking there is not only you and me. There is a third thing.' He could not explain further what the third thing was and I could not very well press him about it. Certainly, values meant more to him than facts. He was impressed by the value in any actual situation more than he was by its carrier. The significance of a passing event rose up to meet him, detached itself for him from the event and rose pure and clean and immortally true and applicable, shorn of the details which while immutable would perhaps never happen in exactly the same way again. He had gone to Europe once with a friend who was a radical lawyer. They had had their trip paid for them by some wealthy woman in New York who had sympathized with the socialist cause. The trip was taken on the

Titanic, a boat whose destination was unknown; it had sailed under sealed orders.

On the way over, the socialist passengers held a meeting in the grand salon to which the crew, in true socialist fashion, were cordially invited. But the captain was die-hard and forbade the crew to leave their posts. Both Sherwood and the radical lawyer grew thoroughly disgusted with the attitude of the socialists on the trip over, Sherwood explained, and once the boat reached its destination, which proved to be Rotterdam, they separated and did not attend the labour congress for which they had made the trip. Sherwood did not see in Europe either the socialists or his radical lawyer friend. He returned home alone.

At this point in the story, beguiled somewhat by its very staid and factual presentation, I became interested in the figure of the radical lawyer as I was in all persons who could not make up their minds once and for all on the question of radical politics. I could see what had happened to Sherwood; he had, in his own account, become an anarchist. Anarchism did not mean to him what it meant to other people; he thought the word stood for an extreme and aberrant form of individualism in which it would be possible to form a society founded on neighbour-love. Perhaps Sherwood was somehow right that this is, or at least ought to be, the essential meaning of the word. Anyhow, I wanted to know what was the later career of the lawyer, and I accordingly asked.

Sherwood seemed a little surprised at my question. 'Why, he's in New York, of course,' he exclaimed, 'a radical lawyer, spending most of his time working for the radicals.'

The point of this story is that the *Titanic* only began one trip across the Atlantic and on that trip hit an iceberg and sank. Sherwood had obviously not been on it, but he had read about it in the newspaper. It was the only name of an ocean liner that he knew which had some particularly significant story attached to it. All other ships were mere names, and it must have been on one of these others that Sherwood had actually gone to Europe; but he could not recall either the exact year or the exact ship. What more natural, then, than that he should connect what he knew? The truth is that he was not trying to deceive either himself or me; his logic was not the logic of fact, it was the logic of symbolism. In the story, he had finished with the radical lawyer and was slightly annoyed with me for being so illogical as to reintroduce a figure which was now a superfluity into the conversation.

The career of Sherwood is the typical tragedy of the American artist, the one-book man. It is all very well to be an uneducated writer, but the absence of craft means that when inspiration fails there is no sound knowledge of procedure to take its place. We have our Whitmans, our Melvilles, our Poes; but we do not have our Dostoevskis, our Goethes, or our Hardys. For our writers suppose that writing is writing, that newspaper reporting, for example, is good training for the novel. Sinclair Lewis ought to be a sufficient refutation of any such wild notion. The newspaper man learns his sentimentality from his work, and acquires a nose for spot news; but he does not learn either how to write slowly or how to discover profundity. He does not learn how to think as well as feel. He learns only how to deal with what in fact the newspapers do deal: surfaces. And surfaces are where the novelist of dimensions begins, not where he stops.

Education is no end in itself; from the point of view of the artist it serves only as immunization against the devastating shock of new ideas. Regard for a moment the tragedy of Sherwood's development. He began life in a small town; he first wrote fiction as a small business man in a big city. Fortunately, he managed to get something down on paper before the literary critics and editors got hold of him. Those were the days of *Winesburg, Ohio* and *The Triumph of the Egg*.

Then came New York and its miniscule intellectuals. Through them Sherwood discovered Freud, he discovered D. H. Lawrence. The New Yorkers began to tell him what it was he was trying to do. They made him conscious of himself, his style, his contemporaries. From that period, he began to write in the way they expected him to write, and it was bad. For of all the things that could happen, they certainly did not expect him to do what they expected him to do. Sherwood began to write parodies of his own good work; *Many Marriages* came along and financially speaking proved his most successful book. The critics who were responsible for him now took courage; maybe it had been all right after all to advise the author. But when Sherwood began to parody his own parodies of his own work, the show was over and everybody prepared to go home. The critics slipped quietly off in the darkness and his public, which had never been too large or too faithful, stopped buying his books.

His friends remained with him, but it was a broken Sherwood, striving desperately to keep up the old optimism and courage and enthusiasm, that they saw. It had nothing to do with liking him, of course. One likes people or one does not for just what they are in themselves.

Sherwood and I were having lunch one afternoon in the restaurant of the St. Charles Hotel in New Orleans. An Arrow-collar-looking stockbroker of the Wall Street type came over to the table and addressed Sherwood.

'I beg your pardon, but are you Roger P. Thompson of New York? I am supposed to meet him here.'

Sherwood's face fell. 'No, I'm not,' he said quietly; then, as the man retreated after begging our pardon for disturbing us, 'No, I'm not, but I wished I was.'

At another time he told me that he had been a week-end guest at the home of a fox-hunting friend. He had followed the hounds all afternoon in his white Ford truck, and then listened all through dinner while the other guests discussed *Gone With the Wind*. Early in the evening he had retired.

'I wasn't sleepy, I just lay in bed and pretended that they had only been waiting for me to go upstairs so that they could discuss my novels without causing me embarrassment. Oh, I knew that wasn't true,' he said, leaning over, 'only, I had to get through the night somehow.'

Is it better to receive nothing from the public than to be lifted up and then dropped? I do not know. I only know that this is what happened to Sherwood. He was famous for a brief while, an all too brief while, and then forgotten. The intellectuals stove him in. They led him to suppose that what his work did was to release the world sexually, free it from inhibitions. They made him think that the significance that he was searching for was sexual in origin. That was the day of Freud. I'm afraid that I, too, was partly to blame. The others were men like Julius Friend, Roger Sergel, and Paul Rosenfeld, and there were still more. Sherwood adored intellectuals, I never knew why. Perhaps it was because he had never been educated, and so believed that they had a precious and private knowledge that was inaccessible to him but that being around them he might catch it. He certainly did receive only through his bones whatever he had in the way of ideas. Certainly little except feeling came through his conscious understanding. I do not believe that he was capable of reading a volume of what is known these days as 'non-fiction', consecutively. He would try such books and put them down.

'I don't know what you fellows are after,' he said once, and, while he added that he did not think much of it, there was little conviction in his voice.

After the Freudian influence of the nineteen-twenties which had hurt him so badly, he almost recovered. The Marxists of the nineteen-thirties made an awful big play for him, but he was not going to get burned again. That was when he used to say that he was an anarchist. People who are very earnest about their mission in life can hardly spare the time to look for signs of the tongue in a man's cheek.

Perhaps the only one of Sherwood's early influences which remained all powerful was that of Theodore Dreiser. It was hard to tell whether it was the man or his work, but Dreiser was something that Sherwood had mistaken for leadership in American letters. We were talking about Dreiser once. I had been challenging Sherwood's estimation of his magnitude, when suddenly I remembered the wording of Sherwood's dedication in a volume of short stories entitled *Horses and Men*. It read, 'To Theodore Dreiser, In whose presence I have sometimes had the same refreshed feeling as when in the presence of a thoroughbred horse.'

'What did Dreiser think of your dedication?' I asked after reminding him of it.

But Sherwood was not bothered. In an exceedingly matter of fact way, he answered, 'Oh, he forgave me.' I had the feeling that the natural response to a dedication was forgiveness, and for a moment my evaluations were upset.

There were stories I had not heard, Mamma Geiger, and all the other famous ones he told so often but never wrote down. He came to New Orleans for a month almost every winter. He wrote in the morning and then I had lunch with him; often Friend would be along. In the afternoon he would go to the races or wander along the docks. At night we would frequently forgather to drink and talk. One day I brought him a copy of *Lady Chatterley's Lover* which had just appeared. He took a day off from his writing (a very unusual thing) to read it. He came to lunch after consuming the whole novel and a few drinks, in a morning. He was loud and robust about his enthusiasm, until the crowded restaurant rang with the timbre of his approval. Afterwards, he became quite sad. It was beyond a doubt the book he wanted to have written, the book he had always tried to write. It was his book in a sense in which it was not Lawrence's.

The absence of an education of any formal kind has its advantages. In the process of becoming familiar with the insides of books, much is gained but something is certainly lost. The advantages may outweigh the disadvantages, but Sherwood had the other side to defend. He had what so many of us have lost: a feeling for the values to be apprehended in the actual world, values which exceed the respect for their apprehension in books and other works of record.

He would often engage in expatiating upon his favourite theme: the sterilization of men by the machine. The operation of the machine had robbed men of their manhood, so that they had nothing to offer women. We had heard it before, but this was a brilliant example of exposition. Sherwood had been sitting before the fire, highball glass in hand. As the whiskey took effect, the monologue became more eloquent, and Sherwood reached heights he had rarely touched. As he relaxed, he observed that he had written most of what he had been saying, in a book called *Perhaps Women*.

Roger Sergel was there, a friend I owe to Sherwood. Roger was puzzled. He had read the book and could find in it few of the arguments and nothing of the conviction with which Sherwood had just presented his case, and he ventured to say so.

'You have said some things that were not in that book, Sherwood,' he observed quite mildly.

Sherwood was not so much hurt as he was irritated. He objected to the bookishness of men. 'Well, Hell,' he exploded, 'I'm saying them now.'

Sherwood had befriended a young writer in New Orleans. He had gone on a picnic with the man and his wife one Sunday afternoon. The man had been trying to write and to sell his writings but had sold nothing. Sherwood spent the day encouraging him. On Monday I saw Sherwood, and he told me about the writer. He had met many young hopefuls in the imitation Greenwich Village parties he had occasionally attended in the Vieux Carré, but this was the only one with any promise.

Sherwood left town shortly afterwards, and did not return for a year. Then suddenly one day without warning he turned up at the Monteleone Hotel. The young writer heard that he was in town, and went to the hotel to call him on the house 'phone. He wanted to tell Sherwood the good news: he had sold a couple of stories to magazines and was thinking of giving up his job to devote all his time to writing. Sherwood answered the telephone.

'Come on up,' he said, 'I'm glad to hear your voice.'

'No,' answered the young writer in a slightly different tone. 'You come on down; I can talk to you more like an equal now.'

The first book of philosophy that Friend and I published had just appeared and we had given Sherwood a copy. He had struggled with it a while and had given it up as a bad enterprise, but not before seeing that the name of Jesus had received favourable mention. That was in the days when the influence of James' *Varieties of Religious Experience* and the work of Freud and Frazer, explaining all religion away on the basis of psychological aberration, had begun to penetrate even to those who could not read such weighty works. Sherwood was puzzled at our approval of primitive Christianity and the Fourth Gospel.

'What is so good about the life of Jesus?' he asked.

We endeavoured to explain to him that, as opposed to the notion of a transcendental and remote god in heaven who opened a hopeless breach between this world and the other, Jesus was a god who had made his presence known in the actual world, thus dispelling the false notion that there is nothing divine about what we experience. Sherwood looked very puzzled for a little, and then a light appeared in his face.

'I think I get it,' he said brightly. 'You mean, "Come on down; I can talk to you more like an equal now!"'

For some reason I felt very much like crying. Sherwood could do that; without effort he could evoke the beauty of the world, and, behold, it was simple, like that of a little child.

Does anything ever exceed the enormous complexity that is required in order to support simplicity? Sherwood had never been exposed to higher education, and his small town associations early in life had persuaded him that he was very simple with the simplicity of the artist; and so he was. But the simplicity of the artist is something different from that of the ordinary person. My wife and I visited Sherwood in Marion, Virginia. We saw him in what he fancied was his natural environment, among country people. But the effect was really fantastic. Sherwood was the only one there under any illusion that he was fading against his background. To the local inhabitants, he was obviously something out of this world: an amiable eccentric with influential connections. They liked him and he liked them, but that is quite another thing from their believing that he was one of them. Sherwood was in fact a very complex individual: sensitive; warm but suspicious; and not a little given over to an optimistic love of the world, a love which he never altogether lost.

The word, American, appears many times in Sherwood's work. It is as though he had awakened suddenly to find himself a literary artist and a stranger in his own country. The self-consciousness of the American artist is something we shall have to get over. Sherwood wanted us to get over it, for he was not the type who liked being exceptional; he was no precious artist who rejoiced in the superiority of his own sensibilities. He was surprised and he did not understand it but he knew that it was wrong to regard native products as unnatural. He was a story-teller, and what lumber camp had ever been without one? James Stephens used to say that the time of Ireland's fall dates from the first day when a poet was asked to pay for his drinks in a pub. Could a poet even get into a bar in this country with any degree of personal safety if it was known that he was a poet? Assuredly, we shall have to change all that, if we are to grow up to our own capabilities. We shall have to make this country the kind of place that Sherwood thought it could become; for while he knew its shortcomings and felt the need for improvement, he loved it beyond anything. We shall have to take pride in our artists and acknowledge the extent of our dependence upon them, if we are to gain from them the advantages of a mature culture.

Sherwood from time to time had contemplated many vast projects. He was going to write a history of the Civil War; when he died he was working on a large volume of his memoirs which was left unfinished. He was all devoted to the future and not at all confined to the past, despite the large measure of oblivion which his later work had cost him. In the United States the artist must earn the love and gratitude of the people all over again every time he does something. Nothing remains over for the man who has made a contribution from the admiration which was bestowed upon him at the time; he must perform his miracle again and again. But the forgetfulness did not oppress Sherwood beyond recall. When he died he was on the way to South America both to reap some adulation, which was no more than his due, and to look toward a continent which everyone thought was to count for a great deal in the world.

Sherwood Anderson was more and less than a literary man. His good work is inconsiderable in bulk and distinctly minor, but filled with an inestimably precious magic; it will survive. But he was more than a writer in that he was also a seer. He called our attention to the things which never die, things which might disappear for a while but must reappear again in the future of which the prophet speaks. He was prophetic of the reappearance of the artist in the greater America that is to come.

There are other tales to be told about this period: there was my boat. It was only about five years ago that I learned to sail. Something in me seems to rebel against the idea of learning anything in the orthodox fashion. Roark Bradford and I had gone sailing on several occasions, and we decided that we liked the sport. So we followed similar procedures: I will narrate mine. I bought a book entitled *Learning to Sail* and read it. I studied it, in fact. Next I took the cardboard out of a shirt fresh from the laundry, and with it made the pattern outline of a sailboat hull as seen from above. To this I pinned the profile of a sail. I also made a cardboard arrow. Sitting up in bed with my eyes shut late at night or early in the morning, I would spin the arrow. Whichever way it fell would indicate the direction of the wind. Now I would open my eyes squarely in order to face the problem of deciding which way the sail had to be set if I wished to take my boat into the left bedpost. Thus I learned the different tacks it is possible to take on a boat.

The next time Brad and I went sailing with friends, our nautical knowledge proved endless. We had the austerity of authority and the asperity of beginners.

'There's a nice boat,' someone would say, indicating a sail in the distance.

We would scan it with a critical eye. 'Too much freeboard,' we would observe.

Then we began to subscribe to *Yachting*, and of course that brought us up to date. A copy of the *Yachtsman's Guide* gave us the proper perspective.

An anchor had to be cast out, for instance. We would watch for a while and say nothing but we finally could not bear it any longer. 'Not enough rope,' we would observe calmly. 'The rule states that the fall should be eleven times the depth at the water line.'

It was about then that our friends decided that we ought to have a boat of our own. Bradford ordered one to be built at Grande Isle. I went to Cape Cod and returned with a boat having much too deep a draft for local waters. But at least we had turned the trick of learning principles abstractly and applying them ourselves.

The boat was hardly settled in Lake Pontchartrain in the Southern Yacht Club harbour before Bradford and I decided to take a week-end cruise. Lake Pontchartrain is some twenty miles wide; many deep bayous feed into it. Our destination was Bayou Liberty, a romantic-sounding stream to the north-east. We set sail one September noon by dead reckoning. It seems that the danger of going aground was greatest just off the mouth of the bayou, and we had to pick up a couple of nun buoys two miles off shore. Then we were to proceed up the bayou for five miles to a house that my uncle owned. The chart showed only about two miles of bayou, but after that it was impossible to get lost since the stream had only to be followed.

For the first couple of hours we made little progress. There was no breeze at all, almost a dead calm. To an experienced seaman that would have meant something, but we only scanned the sky and hoped that enough breeze would spring up to push us along to our destination. It did. For several hours we sat and smoked cigarettes, enjoying a sense of freedom and of the sea. We scorned an appeal to the motor, for were we not yachtsmen, and did we not have all of the week-end to spend? Then a light wind sprang up. It was perfect but it did not remain that way. The light wind turned into a light gale in about thirty minutes. The weather bureau at the New Orleans Airport, which is on the lake front, clocked that wind at forty-two miles an hour. Or so they told us afterwards; we had no way to judge at the time, and anyway we were much too busy to care.

Bradford happened to be taking his turn at the tiller. I came up and asked, 'Don't you think we might reef her down a little? New sails, you know.'

Bradford squinted at the top of the main, then along the clew. Finally, he drawled out, 'It's a sailboat, ain't it? Well, let's sail the goddamn thing.'

I was agreeable, and we sailed. I went below for a couple of slickers and two life preservers, and brought them up on deck, but not without some adventure. I paused on the way to turn off the sea-cocks, but just under them somebody had put a box of soap flakes. I was a little wet, and before I knew it, the box, the slickers and I were wreathed in lather, scudding about the cabin from walls to ceiling as she took the waves head on.

After a while the sea and wind got worse, and it took the two of us, standing up across the cockpit, to hold the tiller in line. Fortunately, in a few hours, we hit our buoys dead on, and took in our sails. We followed the red cans into the bayou without mishap, feeling utterly exhausted and triumphant and probably a little hysterical. We had mastered the sea—well, anyhow the lake. But more was before us. It had grown dark and to augment our running lights we did not have anything more powerful than a two-cell pocket flashlight. The bayou was narrow and winding, so I posted Bradford on the bow with the flashlight, while I stood at the tiller and the engine. The storm was still raging out on the lake but that did not affect us in the bayou with its overhanging trees, except to intensify the darkness. Bradford at the bow strained for the direction of the water as best he could, calling out to me 'Left!' or 'Sharp right!' from time to time.

It was then that I began to appreciate the value of a chart brought up to date. For we ran into a bridge which had not been marked at all on the one we had. Even after we had scraped our bow considerably and clung to the side of the bridge, I almost preferred to believe the chart which said quite plainly that it was not there. The bridge swung out on a swivel in the middle of the bayou. We passed along it by the simple but uncustomary device of clinging to it and being pulled through with our boat as it turned.

The climax, or perhaps I should say the anti-climax, lay before us. Some distance up but still short by a mile of our destination the bayou made a distinct right turn. Ahead, someone had dug a small channel in line with the bayou, for the purpose of mooring a skiff or a runabout. In the darkness Bradford had been unable to see, or else had called out to me without my hearing. In any case, where the bayou made a sharp right turn, we and our boat did not. We were going full speed on the motor, which could not have meant more than seven knots, but the boat weighed some eight tons. We drove straight ahead into three feet of water with a hull that drew five feet three inches. She came to a sudden halt and heeled over in the mud.

We were tired, as we then began to realize, and very hungry. It was about seven in the evening. We got out the dinghy and the anchor and tried to kedge out of our troubles, but we could not budge her. We tried kedging with the motor in reverse for a little, forgetting that a feathering propeller does not reverse very well; and then we gave up. It was just at the turn of the autumn weather. We rowed over to shore, and borrowed a couple of blankets from an obliging neighbour, for we had forgotten to bring our own. We did have our own food but we were much too tired to cook. We had a slice of cold ham on a slice of cold bread and fell asleep almost immediately.

It was hard to tell how far we were from shore, since we had rowed backward across the bayou starting from the stern of our boat. In the morning I awoke to hear dogs barking and men talking. Bradford was awakened, too. We looked at each other: how did strangers get aboard? We had not heard skiffs or a motor. We rushed up on deck—to find that shore was only about five feet away. The men and the dogs were observing this strange curiosity which had suddenly loomed up in their backyard. It was almost like motoring to a week-end, and then spending it in the rear of the car.

Luck was with us. The neighbour who had loaned us the blankets got out his power cruiser and tried to pull us off ground, without the slightest success. Then later in the morning, when we were consoling ourselves with coffee and cigarettes and despairing of ever getting the boat back into the water, our host appeared. He was a powerful and resourceful outdoor man. He looked over the situation, and then observed quietly that he would have us in fine shape in less than an hour. I knew what to think about that promise, but, being a guest, did not feel that I could offer my opinion as a comment. But he knew more of what he was talking about than I did. It developed that he was moving his caretaker's cottage that week-end, and had obtained for the purpose the services of some eight labourers and a heavy winch. He proceeded to tie the winch to a big oak while we rowed a rope across the bayou and took it around another oak over there, then back to the boat. The net result of this manœuvre was that when the winch was turned, the rope, a heavy one, broke in the middle. But my host was calmly undiscouraged. He produced a length of wire rope, and this did the trick. The boat slid out of the mud without complaint, undamaged.

I should perhaps have mentioned her name. I am not very good at naming animals and boats and things. Some people are. Bradford suggested the *Ibid*. It was, he said, a name I was quoting all the time in footnotes in my books, and must, he judged, be that of my favourite author.

The boat, I suppose, was a concrete expression of my love for the sea. But perhaps it was not the sea I was in love with after all, but only the littoral. I have never been to sea in the proper sense, I have only crossed to Europe in large ships. But I love the smell of shellfish rotting on the sand, and the salt sea smell and the life of beaches and the behaviour of waves. I love to stand on the shore and think that out there just underneath the surface beyond which we cannot see there might be almost anything: sharks or whales or even sea serpents. In a sense, to be in the mountains is to be hemmed in; I have never liked them, I have only admired them. But the sea is unlimited; to stand on the shore is to look all the way around the world. A ship, I can imagine, might suddenly turn up from almost anywhere. And if all the seas by now have been charted, and if unexpectedly some word were to be heard from the interior of a dark continent or the remote reaches of a further coastline, I am sure, although I cannot prove it, that the news would come by sea and not by land.

Something of this constitutes the charm of the maritime provinces. New Orleans is not far from the ocean, being separated from it only by a sprawling group of brackish bayous and salt marshes. The river that passes New Orleans is wide and ends in the Gulf of Mexico. Somehow we approve of its progress as of its goal. The thought that any day it would be possible to board a freighter in the Mississippi and journey to one of the Seven Seas is consoling for those who must stay at home. In the small towns of America this need to wander, to find strangeness, is filled by visits to the railroad stations to watch the fast expresses pass by; more recently, the airports aid this function; but in New Orleans the river is old. For the French and Spanish inhabitants, it must have been a tie with the home countries. And even now it seems to have more distant relations than do the railroad tracks or even the airways. To anyone living in the smaller world in which physics has shown intense inter-relations, Matthew Arnold's 'salt unplumbed estranging sea' becomes once more what it was formerly: a friendly challenge, a high road of romance and mystery, an unbelievable life in motion.

One day I shall try to buy a flat-bottomed power boat. I want to spend days and nights in the monotonous-looking swamps. I want to smell their decay, and listen to the interstices which exist between their incredible silences. I want to feel them as though I, too, were dead, or they alive. I want to write about them; poetry probably. I want to fight their mosquitoes and eat their fish and examine the strange kinds of life that live in their depth. I want to outwait a crane, to see him put his other foot down undisturbed in my presence. All this, I shall discover, is part of philosophy. Thus I have no regrets for the passing of the *Ibid* into other hands. Boats have distinct personalities, but it is not the boat that I want to fall in love with so much as the corners into which the boats can take me. And, as much as I love the sea, it is not the open sea I crave. That is for more materially adventurous souls. It is the littoral I am after, that dim and, in the swamp, country unspecified, boundary, where life and death as well as sea and land so often meet.

The confines of the swamps are no more indefinite than the limits of some personalities. There are borderline people, just as there are borderline countries. If democracy is only an equality of opportunity and not of obligation, who is to take care of the weak ones of this earth? 'Everyone for himself and the devil take the hindmost' can hardly be the proper interpretation of the democratic form of government. For if it starts with an equality it certainly does not end with one. I have in mind particularly at the moment a man in New Orleans I have known since we were children. Economically, there is nothing pathetic about him; he earns a living, if not a large one at least a sufficient one; he is happily married and has children. Socially, he is likable, and if he does not excite his friends at least he does not antagonize them. The most prominent of his characteristics is his complete neutrality; he has no singular features. To say that he has no strong personality is an understatement. It is worse than that: he seems to have no central organization at all; he does not operate from anywhere in particular. He takes colour and mood from the person with whom he happens to be. Despite the fact that he earns his living on a newspaper, words have little effect upon him; he hears them and understands them but he does not take them seriously. He is influenced by other personalities, especially by what appears in facial expressions and gestures. Let me give an example. Suppose that I meet this man with a mournful expression.

[193]

'What is the matter?' he will ask.

Suppose then that I burst into tears and tell him some joke I have heard. He will listen and then most likely cry with me. But suppose that on the other hand I greet him with a fit of laughter, and when he asks me to tell him what I am laughing about, I say that I have just heard of the death of my sister. This will set him off, too, and he will be heartily amused.

Eventually, objective interests determine subjective actions: what goes on in the world determines what we shall turn our attention and energies to; but, all the same, much depends upon mood, upon affective approach and sympathy. Those of us who have some strength of personality with which to back up the power of thought can to a certain extent direct the attention of others and this involves us in a heavy extent of responsibility.

The friend of whom I have been speaking has set himself down in his own mind as a failure in the world. The weakness is written all over him. He wishes to write a novel and has made several attempts. But he has convinced himself that his feeling is right that he shall never do one worthy of publication. He is doomed by his own self-estimation to make the attempt and also to anticipate defeat. He is too energetic to give up trying and too self-abnegating to hope for success. The successful persons of this world have no idea to what extent the stage is set for them by those nameless others who have cast themselves in the role of background material. They only apply for the humble role of spear-carriers in the opera of practical life, not because they regard their talents as hidden or misunderstood but simply because they do not regard their talents as sufficient for the accomplishment of anything which would be worthy of capturing anybody else's attention.

The people of whom I am speaking are the kind of people who telephone newspapers for information because it is easier than going to a library or using a reference work. Another friend of mine who has charge of the reference room of a large newspaper has told me stories which indicate something of what I mean.

In New Orleans the docks along the river run parallel to one set of streets and at right angles to another, so that all that is required in order to indicate the location of a boat is to name the street nearest it at right-angles to the river. One day a man telephoned the paper to ask where a certain boat was going to dock. My friend investigated and replied, it would be found at the Dumaine Street wharf. There was a long silence over the 'phone. Then the voice asked again, 'Dumaine and what?'

Another time someone called up to ask how much thirty English shillings would amount to in American money. My friend looked it up and found that a shilling (at that time) was approximately twenty-five cents; he told this to the telephone inquirer. There was another pause on the 'phone and then another question: how much would thirty shillings be?

The stories of New Orleans life which indicate some kind of dumb acceptance of the customs of contemporary society, are endless. There was the taxicab driver who heard the abdication speech of the Prince of Wales on the radio.

'Them English are hard to understand,' he observed in a hoarse voice. 'I heard dat King speakin' yesterday. Dey talk about de King's English. Dat's a lot a bunk.'

On another occasion my friend was wandering in the French Quarter where he had gone to obtain an interview with a visitor. He was a little early so he dropped into a 'beer parlour' for a drink. There were in the room only four bare wooden tables and a mysterious door to the rear of the building. A waiter who appeared to be somewhat miffed came in and leaned on the table, holding a dirty napkin over a still dirtier arm. 'Well,' he asked, 'what do *you* want, Buddy?'

My friend wanted a bottle of beer. The beer was brought without a word. When it was time to pay, the waiter leaned on the table again and asked for twenty-five cents.

'But,' my friend remonstrated, 'that beer is only fifteen cents everywhere else in New Orleans.'

The waiter looked very bored as he replied, 'Yes, I know, buddy, but you see, this ain't no beer parlour. This is a whore house.'

The epitome of the general New Orleans attitude toward life was expressed by another taxicab driver who drove my friend home from work one evening. The driver was talkative and as my friend is always appreciative of the native tales of life in the Crescent City he hears a great deal. It seems that as the driver was taking his cab through the French Quarter, he had been hailed by a woman, who stopped him in the middle of traffic.

'Where to, lady?' he inquired.

'Oh, anywhere,' she replied.

This puzzled him somewhat. 'Well, that ain't the way it is, lady. You see, I can drive you anywhere in the city you want to go, but you got to tell me where you want to go so that I can drive you.'

'But I don't want to go anywhere in particular, just around. I'm a stranger in town and I got lonesome. So just drive me anywhere.'

He took her to all the places of interest to tourists. Then, seeing that she also wished to visit the night clubs, he went home, changed his clothes, and in his own private car went from cabaret to cabaret with her, ending up finally by going home with her to spend the night.

As he had told the story, the driver had shaken his head quizzically. 'You know, I been puzzled about that all day, and you know what I think?' He paused. 'I think it's just like anything else.'

Often what strikes us as funny makes us laugh only because this is a way to prevent tears. The ludicrousness of the actions of simple people is only a paper's width from the pathetic. We appeal from the comedy of situations to the world as it ought to be, and the comparison back reveals many shortcomings. The richness of life, the variety and spice of true situations, is contributed in part by error, but this does not mean, as many persons suppose, that a true life would be one lacking in feeling.

It is not necessary for all to become as little children; many are so already. To be unconcerned with problems at the exceedingly high level at which human life exists, to admit defeat as a foregone conclusion, to lean on others, all in an unself-conscious way and with the terrible dependence of the unaware —this is to be a grown child lost in an adult world. It is not enough that we, the sentient, go ahead of those who make up the bulk of the procession. We must also pull the whole of humanity up after us. This is a religious and not a philosophical function. The artists and the scientists and the philosophers carve out the future. The religious leaders see to it that the bulk of mankind catches up. The 'brotherhood of man' may be only a slogan for the individual worker who is in the true sense a pioneer, but it is a life task for the man of feeling who has the responsibility of being his brother's keeper.

Impelled by an interest in our fellows, we should all like to be known to everybody, but this is personal. Success: what is it? What does it mean to be known unless we learn first to distinguish the degrees of reputation? The movie star and the politician are today familiar to the greatest number, but what does such familiarity mean? The movie star is worshipped only by the ignorant and the helpless, whose opinions are ephemeral. Fame in this sense today may mean utter obscurity tomorrow. In fact, it usually does. The politician may be, like Hitler, entitled to a reputation only on the basis of hatred and fear. The only fame worth having is, needless to elaborate, one based on love and understanding. Love as well as understanding may be personal, but it will be greater if it issues from works; it is what we do and not what we are that counts. The greatest figures are the most unknown; for their achievements have survived them and actually come to stand for them, having at last become what they themselves wished to be. Such personal anonymity when coupled with objective accomplishment represents the greatest sort of fame.

There would be no use in pretending that I would not like to have copies of my books read and understood by everyone, translated in all languages, discussed and followed in practical life. But I am not willing to pay the price by saying anything that I do not believe or omitting anything that I do. Not that I really have the choice! It has been pointed out time and again that the popular novelists are not untrue to themselves. The cheapness that appears in their work is part of them; they actually believe that they are writing great books; they are honest and sincere. The only genuine betrayal is by those clever people who dislike their own obscurity so intensely that they attempt to 'write down' to the level of a large public. Yet they fool nobody but themselves. Books written in this way seldom sell. The hypocrisy usually shows through, like cracks under a bad paint job, and eventually everyone avoids the work. If it is remembered that we are engaged in getting down on paper not ourselves and our own personalities but some objective cause, the necessity for true speaking will become more obvious.

How I envy those whose books find a wide audience! I would not want to be the famous author of their books, however. I want my own to sell in the quantities that theirs do. It is their numerical advantages I wish to procure for my own work, not their reputation. The difference is important. Now, it seems to me that there is a low ceiling for books on philosophy in the United States. Look at the ones that have been successful. Durant's *The Story of Philosophy*; there is a better freshman textbook in use in any college.

Last summer my car was in a slight accident and the insurance company sent an adjuster round to see me. He was fat, jovial and bored. I answered all his questions as briefly as I could because I was bored, too. I had managed to talk him over close to the door, and I thought the interview was over, when he happened to ask me the nature of my business. I was quite shameless about it. 'I am a philosopher,' said I.

His face lit up, and with some despair I watched him cross the room and seat himself in a comfortable corner of the sofa. 'Now that's very interesting,' he observed. 'Tell me, what do you think of Will Durant's philosophy?'

My reply was nothing that can be printed here. It began with the simple statement, of course, that Will Durant had no philosophy, was in fact not expected to have one. I thought that this statement would do something to terminate the interview, but my insurance adjuster seemed to beam all the more. He remained silent while I went on to give a short lecture (as it turned out). I explained that universal literacy was a great step forward over the kind of illiteracy which had characterized the middle ages when only the clergy could take advantage of learning. It was a great step forward, but it was accompanied, I explained, by the debasing of the intellectual coinage. The result of universal literacy, the first result, anyhow, seemed to be what was called yellow journalism, the printing of anything regardless of its truth so long as it could be sold and would be read. Mr. Will Durant, I went on, represented the yellow journalism of philosophy. The culture of our day, I felt confident, would go on past that period; in addition to having a public that could read, education would see to it that we also had a public which could discriminate. The day of Hearst would pass, and the Hearst of American philosophy would pass, along with the less successful but no less insidious members of his class, into oblivion, to have their place taken by those who had had sincerely inquisitive minds, like Charles S. Peirce, who had wished to hand on his method and his findings to a younger generation of inquirers.

My insurance adjuster continued to beam all through this tirade. I began to be a little ashamed not of the truth of what I had said but of the occasion of its delivery. The fat man got up and started for the door. 'You know,' he said on the way out, 'I'm glad to hear you talk like that. I was born and lived for years in a house in the same neighbourhood as Durant. Everybody tells me that he has gotten to be something, but I could never believe it. I knew him well as a boy. Durant more important than me? Not likely.'

Just about the time when the general public began to hear about the mysteries of relativity and subatomic physics, of how space was curved back upon itself and how the atom was about to be exploded, the philosopher (and mathematician and physicist) Whitehead, wrote the first of his three greatest philosophical works, entitled *Science and the Modern World*. Due to the fact that he has developed his own special vocabulary for philosophy, Whitehead is for the layman and indeed for many philosophers extremely hard to understand. The title, however, *Science and the Modern World*, seemed to indicate a proper kind of answer to the question that the public had been asking, and so the book sold in some quantity. Judging by the number of editions through which it has gone, it may be said to have been a great publishing success. Judging by what I can see in the book myself and what people have told me, few of those who have read it have understood it. The title was probably entirely responsible for the enormous sale. Once again the public had been deceived; but this time by thinking it had something meretricious when actually it had a pearl of great price.

The business of giving popular lectures, like the sale of popular books, is a difficult one to fathom. Popular lectures are desired explicitly for the wrong reasons, but back of that there is a sincere if pathetic effort to grasp after values which are unknown. Women, middle-aged and elderly women, who make up the bulk of the forum audiences, are truly in search of values which they know have been neglected in their lives; but what they specifically ask of the lecturer is that he entertain them. They wish to see and to hear their heroes, the heroes created by the newspapers, the movies and the radio. Since these elderly women exert no effort, they acquire no return; and the words of wisdom dropped by the lecturer (it does happen occasionally) are wasted. There is an important thing called adult education, but it does not consist in random, arbitrary and occasional lecturing. To learn for two hours about one subject this week-end and about a quite different one the next is little more than confusing. Tour lecturers know that they are performing a rather unenviable function, and so they attempt to justify themselves with the thought that they are contributing to adult education, but they are doing nothing of the sort. Would that they were, for they are simply entertaining the public, and not the most vigorous segment of the public at that.

Of the two, popular lecturers and writers, the far more fantastic phenomenon is that of the popular writers. There are such unfortunates as the authors whose books are bought and read in the millions—and promptly forgotten. It is typical of a mass-production age that the influence of an author is commonly measured in terms of his sales. Nobody puts the question, how much effect does he have on those who read him? I often resort to the test of asking readers of some book by a popular author whether they remember the author's name. More often than can be imagined they have forgotten. Those who read great quantities of Harold Bell Wright, Zane Grey, and Margaret Mitchell, have failed to remember titles and can do no better with the authors' names. The popular writers of thirty or forty years ago have been relegated to an oblivion that is even more complete, for neither their names nor the titles of their books can be remembered. The reading of such books, however widespread its practice, makes little impression; it is an episode in the day's work, or better, a soporific to the day's affairs, and is forgotten as quickly as the night's sleep which it induces.

I gave a lecture on popular books, in which I tried to point out that the truly popular writers were not those who have had a sensational rise in the eyes of readers and publishers for a year or two before oblivion, but rather those who have managed to maintain a steady sale century after century. The curve of the sales of any one title by a popular writer, say *Riders of the Purple Sage* or *Gone With the Wind*, indicates a sharp decline approaching zero after some years. But not so the classics. Given a good run of decades, Plato or Aristotle will outsell *Gone With the Wind* many times over. In the last few years there have been several fresh translations of Plato and several new editions of Aristotle. But who still reads *Anthony Adverse* or *In His Steps*?

The point is that the readers of important books are much impressed by what they read. They have to give something of themselves to such books, and they are not the same people after a thorough reading that they were before, not the same people at all. Something has entered into their lives which was not there: a different way of looking at the world, and even perhaps different methods of approaching problems. Books which make this kind of impression on a few persons have an eventually greater effect than those which though widely read cannot really make a lasting impression on anyone.

Popular writers and popular lecturers are not accidents, however. Neither are they men of great intelligence who have deliberately chosen to pervert their talents. Great writers say what they think and feel, as clearly as possible; if the result is still obscure, then it is up to the public to reach for an understanding. Not so the popular writers; they say exactly what most people are thinking and feeling in their own day. They can say just what they do because they have no great experimental or penetrating powers. Specifically, the great writers are concerned with the most universal values and truths, popular writers, with the most singular. It is not possible deliberately to become a popular writer, any more than it is possible to be a great one by such a method. We must write what we think and what we feel, for only in this fashion can we do our best. Those who set about to cheapen their work pay an awful price. I can think of no other enterprise in which the guilty are visited with punishment half so quickly.

But the serious popular writers, those who do not know that they are doing harm, have a method which is instinctive but interesting, from an analytical point of view. The method of gaining popularity as a writer consists not in treating serious things with levity but in taking trivial things with gravity. I offer as prime examples the entire collected works of such men as Hendrik Willem van Loon or Will Durant. When Durant tried to reverse the process, his books failed to sell. In *The Arts* by van Loon, the point about Michaelangelo which is given the most attention is the fact that he painted the ceiling of the Sistine Chapel lying on his back on a scaffolding.

To be ponderous about platitudes; to seek out curious and out-of-the-way facts without attaching the slightest general significance to them; to repeat what everyone already believes but in sententious sentences which makes the thoughts official and remind the hearer that he holds them—these are the trademarks of the idols of the market-place. But whosoever wishes to hold public attention for the longest time cannot seek such attention directly. He must seek not attention but the truth. The discovery of the truth is its own reward; for men who need another, let them remember that the world seldom forgets those who have actually carried forward and added to the sum of human knowledge.

To occupy oneself with the arts is to aim high in the catalogue of human enterprises. And to aim high is literally a high adventure; it involves falling far if one is a failure. The man who sells shirts, sprays fertilizer, or drives a truck, is an honest man and his work is worthy in itself. But where does the artist belong who is no artist at all? Where is the man who has sold what he has, or who, by virtue of what he is, has a bad effect? There is such a thing as evil without effort. To hold public taste down to the level which it has already attained, simply because, in this way, the financial rewards or the acclaim is high, can never be forgiven either in this world or in the next; and the error is no less grave for being unintentional. We are what we are and we do what we do; censure may depend to some extent upon personal responsibility, but the objective good or ill accomplished does not. This makes participation in the arts and the sciences a risk and a gamble against great odds.

Those who deplore the small sales enjoyed by the books of the philosopher do so on the mistaken belief that the philosopher could if he so desired write his complex ideas in such a way that they would be as simple as any other ideas, or in a charming fashion that would make the majority of persons willing to strain after complex ideas. The first is quite impossible; the second unlikely, at least for a long while. The satisfaction in doing good work does not have to consist in counting royalties; it may consist in having had something to say. Happy are those who can live upon what they make in search of the truth. The endowed scientist, the artist with a grant, or the novelist whose good work manages to sell, are individuals with the finest personal arrangements. Not everyone can be so fortunate, and the selection of those who are does not seem to

[203]

o

be made upon the basis of any recognizable criterion. There is chance in the world as well as order. But the prospect of what-could-be combines with the imagination of what-ought-to-be to urge us to do our best whatever the cost.

We feel chance as tragedy but we know it as comedy. Back of both stands the presence of invisible order, but the conflict in actuality produces a corresponding paradox in human beings. It is a great surprise to most of us that the comedians are in their private lives very bitter and even tragic people. This phenomenon is considered to be illogical. I have noticed, by the way, that where events are illogical, it is not the insufficiency of the premises or the faultiness of the implications drawn, but logic itself, that is blamed. The form is held responsible for the formlessness. Contrariwise, when implications are sound and the premises sufficient, the content and not logic is given the credit. In this way, the inadequacy of logic becomes plain to everybody, but its achievements are largely neglected.

Comedians are simply people who laugh because, as we have noted, if they did not they would be compelled to cry; they are always on the verge of high emotional stress, and the aspects of the world which appear plainest to them are its incongruous ones. They laugh out of disappointment because things are not as they ought to be, because there is no Santa Claus. I remember the general expression of disappointment over the publication of Mark Twain's autobiography. I have in mind, too, the conservatism of Leacock. Yet the comic spirit is familiar in America; it would be familiar, I suppose, in any scene which was abounding in energy where formalism was still absent. We have no great æsthetic tragedies because nothing in American life is yet regarded as inevitable. What I am offering here is only an historical explanation, which is to say no cause at all. It is thus also an indication of our opportunity, and shows the greatness of the potentialities which confront us.

In the meanwhile, however, the comedians laugh and complain. I know only one well: he is Roark Bradford, the teller of folk tales, the recorder of negro life. He is a very grim and a very funny man. Satisfied with nothing, alive to the hollowness and pretensions of those he personally knows, he can ascribe goodness only to myths and legends, to the fictive people who presumably are as they ought to be. He does not like New Orleans; he does not like anything very much but he likes New Orleans less than most things and remains here, finding it necessary to stay close to the source of his irritation. This has subtly shifted him over from a programme of love in his writings to one of hate. He is a comedian no more, balancing on the thin edge of bitterness; now he has embraced bitterness itself. He is not tragic as a result; he is grotesque, for the hollow shell of the laughter is there, but to mask it now there is only the cracking expression of destiny. The child of God has found his misfortune.

To those of us who grew up in the first quarter of the twentieth century, materialism was the logical premise of all our natural and instinctive outlook. This meant that personality, character, and the virtues, somehow were overshadowed by more tangible things. We have heard of the reality of the intangibles but try as we might to believe in them it remains a gigantic effort of mind. What I have been trying to explain about Bradford is difficult to describe in proportion to the extent to which it runs counter to what we fundamentally believe to be real. Yet it has a real meaning. A man can die while his material being remains the same. He laughs, he loves, he moves about, he converses with friends; yet the direction has gone out of him, the intent toward the future has become a shrug of indifference. This disregard is treason to the existence of life at its fullest, by one who as an artist is a giver of life.

Perhaps somehow we need to be born again, for how else shall we come to embrace a proper philosophy? To believe that only things supra-mundane are real was the error of the mediaeval philosophers and theologians. To believe that only things of the earth earthy are real is the mistake we are making now. Each has its compensations and its blandishments; each also has its devastating shortcomings. For now we think that we are not hard-headed unless we are disillusioned about practically everything. Yet scepticism is not the philosophy by which we can guide us in our daily lives. This has been demonstrated before; it will have to be demonstrated again.

Scepticism, like false belief, is frightful. We shall have to be ready to believe in something, yet equally ready to cast it aside. This is a difficult state of mind to hold, yet a necessary one. Works come only from faith; yet from time to time the faith must be shifted, when larger objects of faith loom upon the horizon of our cultural knowledge and consciousness. It is not necessary to be solemn; indeed the opposite is true, for we need comedians who can dispel the air of solemnity which hovers about the ancient objects of worship. We need also the spirits of freedom and of inquiry for the discovery of larger and larger meanings in life. Emotionally, however, in a profound way we must be neutral toward whatever happens, not subject to profound reverberations from superficial surprises. There is no cause for bitterness because we neither receive from the world nor give to it all that we had expected. There is no cause for rejoicing, on the other hand, when the world takes us at something exceeding our actual worth. All of these clouds will pass; they are heavy, but eventually not telling. We are equal to them.

Every summer I try to go, for a few days at least, to the Hedgerow Theatre near Philadelphia. One thing that is characteristic of America is the presence here and there of hard little knots of intellectuality which are as native as corn bread and *cuite* or New England clam chowder and maple syrup, but which, unlike these products, remain largely unappreciated both locally and in the land at large. They remain unencouraged but irrepressible, part of the American heritage that I am writing this book partly to show cannot be denied.

I feel very much like that about Jasper Deeter, the sharp and bony little Pennsylvania Dutchman who gave up acting in New York because he objected to type-casting in the theatre and came to Rose Valley with several others to establish a repertory theatre of his own. The effort was typical of Jap, as his friends call him, just as it is typical of all those who have something to contribute to the common pot of human values. It was not the error in his own case which alone he wished to see corrected; that would probably have been a simple matter. No; he wished to change the system so that the American theatre as a whole could be improved. Of course, the type-casting problem was only the problem which set him off. The Hedgerow Theatre was the result, and the Hedgerow Theatre has gone much farther than the fight against type-casting.

Gathered at Rose Valley in Moylan, Pennsylvania, are some thirty people maintaining a theatre under Jap's direction. They are young and they are old, retired Shakespearian actors and kids fugitive from college. They live a communal life in several houses near the theatre, and do all the work involved in the maintenance of themselves and the plant; everything from cooking to designing and making scenery. All are required to act, and all have memorized many plays which they are prepared to give at a moment's notice. Everyone works hard from early morning until late at night.

Jap has instilled in his people a love of the arts and a respect for the literary qualities of plays. He is producing on the stage great works of art and not merely vehicles for actors. His direction is more than mere direction for acting; in a peculiar way, a way which is something singularly his own, it is also a direction for thinking. He is teaching his people how to be intellectuals about life, without losing force. Do not ask me how he accomplishes this, for I am not sure I can explain it; I have seen him directing plays time and again, and I only know he does it. It is a personality trick, I suppose, but a good one.

The influence of personality is not, in its good sense, used by a leader to secure unquestioning allegiance from followers. It is rather an axiological means of securing adherence to certain values and ideas which perhaps would not be communicated successfully in any other way. Not all personality influence has such a good effect and not all communication is by means of personality, but when used for such an end the means are good.

For Jap, the theatre, and more particularly the play in hand at the moment, is not the final end at which his direction is aimed. It is only the jumping-off point; the premises in terms of which his conclusions are reached. Jap is after universal values and truths, as are all artists. He uses the theatre to get at them, just as others use philosophy, physical science or theories of history. A point of direction or the necessity of understanding a character in a play from the inside, important as these are, are still for Jap only the occasions by means of which he leads his cast toward wider considerations. Thus he is primarily a teacher, secondarily a thinker, and finally a theatre director. I do not say this in disparagement of his theatre, only in praise of it, since I do not think that any other theatre in America, with many times the equipment and advertised (and paid-for) skill in its actors, can begin to approach the high level of achievement which the Hedgerow Theatre has already attained and manages to touch year after year, on the closest possible budget.

In the summer when I visit Hedgerow I always try to arrive late in the afternoon of some day when a short play is being given in the evening. I go to see the play, and afterwards, retire to one of the living rooms in a house occupied as living quarters by the group. A bottle of whiskey makes its appearance, followed shortly by Jap. Then some of the group stroll in, one at a time or in pairs. We drink, and talk about mutual friends: Sherwood Anderson, or the plays we have seen. Then gradually more drink, and the conversation begins to turn on æsthetic questions. This loses everybody but Jap and a few others. From æsthetics we turn to metaphysics, and this loses most of the æstheticians. But all listen intently. We talk and talk on. The young actors fall asleep sitting up in their chairs as they listen. We continue, and later they awaken to listen again. This goes on until the bottle is empty and the conversation fairly maudlin. At this point we get into the wrong automobile and go for food to the nearest all night 'eate shoppe'. It is a wonderful experience, and I always go home determined to write a book about the theatre.

It is hard to estimate the value for America of such an enterprise as the Hedgerow Theatre. In terms of what its effect
should have been, I suppose it is a failure. It should have
produced a number of great leaders in the theatre; this it has
not done. It should have been responsible for the rise of a host
of imitative theatres throughout the country; this it has not
done. Finally, it should have stimulated a whole school of
playwrights, writing untrammelled plays to be produced on the
spot, after the fashion of the Abbey Theatre in Dublin; this it
has not done. Why? It is hard to tell. The influence of the
films, perhaps; the decline of the commercial theatre; the fact
that the amateur theatre has been a disastrously dilettante
influence; it is hard to say.

But this much can be said about Jasper Deeter, and, indeed,
about all truly great men who have the qualities of leadership.
They are what they are and they stand for the values they stand
for. Let this be said to their credit. If the times are not with
them, and if they remain unappreciated, it is a reflection upon
the times and not upon them. Even so, they have not failed.
Nothing can be finally measured by its popular success, for
values are values regardless of popularity or success. Then
again, it is never possible to say when an action will be seized
upon and followed as an example. We can never conclude
finally that it will not. Jasper Deeter is taking the theatre, and
a very small percentage of young America, in the direction in
which they ought to go. Somehow, some day, and in some
wise, that will matter.

The Hedgerow Theatre produces many of Shaw's plays.
The one I want to see again is *Heartbreak House*. This English
imitation of Chekhov has a certain air of studied casualness
that I have always admired. I was reminded of it in the living
room of our house in the French Quarter. The house had
proved too small for our needs. It was tall and narrow, with
three storeys. The top floor contained a living room, bedroom
and bath, and when we bought the house it was planned for a
study. Somehow, we had forgotten to provide a nursery, so
that when one became necessary, my study had to be converted

for the purpose. This left me without a room in which to do my writing. I had always been somewhat sensitive, anyhow, about working at home. I could not forget a dialogue in *Heartbreak House*. The wife is talking (with a friend in the living-room. 'What does your husband do all day?' the friend asks. Just then, I think, the husband, whose name is Hector Hushabye, comes in through a french window, and answers the question before his wife is able to reply. 'I stay home all day like a damned soul in hell,' he says and is gone.

There was no available study in our house, anyhow, so I looked about for some place to do my writing. Finally, I hit upon the idea of taking space in an office building, one of the largest in the city. I hired only one room, and this I filled with a typewriter desk and a chair, nothing more. There was no telephone and no name on the door.

At first the plan worked very well. The isolation was terrific. I was alone, absolutely alone, and I had the impression that if I were to die and the janitor who came in to clean were to fall ill and miss a couple of nights, my body would not be found. The arrangement was just what I wanted, and my work went very well. I was writing poetry and short stories at the time, poetry mostly. But then after a while my tight little universe was disturbed. Despite the absence of any name on the door, and the presence of opaque glass in it, salesmen and pedlars began to knock. They could hear the typewriter, I suppose, or occasionally see a moving silhouette. They were selling anything and everything, insurance, automobiles, shoelaces, shoeshines, contraceptives, land, and what not. I tried to be polite but also to get rid of them as quickly as possible; yet by the time this last operation was over, the train of my thought had been definitely broken. I can interrupt myself for a while, or be interrupted, without loss; by the telephone, for instance. But when I have to leave my desk and cross the room to talk with someone face to face, it does put me back considerably.

It was clear that I would have to seek for a further solution. After some speculation on the matter, I sent for the sign-painter in the building and directed him to put the following words on the front of my door, in letters of modest size:

James Feibleman
Poet

I was never disturbed again, possibly because I was thought a freak, or possibly because poets are traditionally too poor to buy anything. I do not profess to know just what caused the falling away of the salesmen, but I do know that not one knock more was heard on that door until the end of the lease. Indeed, the neglect became painful. I had not intended to frighten everybody away forever. One single salesman could at least try, if only out of curiosity, I felt. Were there no adventure-some pedlars left in the world? Would not a single one of them brave the wrath of an eccentric? Where was courage in the profession?

It was no use. I was left strictly to my own devices. Occasionally I would hear footsteps approaching the door, then I would take heart. Here, I would say to myself, here is one brave soul who is willing to meet a poet without quailing. But no. The footsteps stopped; the sign was being read; the critical moment had arrived. There would be another moment's hesitation, and then the footsteps would start away again. Again a failure.

It was not long before I gave up my office. The solitude was far too confining. I felt deserted, neglected: where *was* everybody? In order to engage in work as solitary as writing, there must be alternate periods of publicity and privacy. The rhythm is stimulating; whereas monotony, particularly the monotony of utter privacy, is enervating. Often I feel that I want to be alone, utterly alone—but then, I wonder, where is everybody?

How wonderful and how pitiful are the solitaries, those lonely and awkward people who consider themselves too good to accept the associations they would normally have and not good enough for the ones they would like to acquire. They live in a limbo of solitude and torment, a world of their own making, which is the result partly of snobbery and partly of neuroticism but surely partly also of the fact that, in Browning's phrase, their reach does so exceed their grasp. How shocked they would be if they could only know how they conform to a pattern, how much each one of them behaves like the others. The pattern is so perfect that, instead of naming names or giving accurate personal descriptions which could be recognized and so cause personal injury, I shall try to describe it abstractly yet in some detail. Let us call our composite individual the Solitary.

I am at home with my wife, in my house in the French Quarter in New Orleans. The Solitary telephones: may he come over to visit us? Yes, I reply, certainly. Are we planning to have any other company? he asks. No, I answer, no one will be here except the family. He seems satisfied and promises to come right over. He would much rather find me entirely alone, but since that is permanently impossible, he manages to take my wife into the circle with us. It is a struggle, for he does not see the necessity for her—except to me. I should perhaps point out that the Solitary is entirely self-centred and judges everyone by his own standards while frankly recognizing them to be entirely his own.

A little later the front doorbell rings and I hasten to answer it. There is a look of delight on the Solitary's face. He enters and follows me to the living-room. My wife is sensitive, and after greeting the new arrival, relapses into the silence of cigarettes and apparent attentiveness. The Solitary next proceeds to give me a full account of everything that has happened to him, particularly in an artistic way, since I saw him last. He tells me about the book he has read (or the picture he has seen, the music heard or the dancing watched). He gives me his own opinions and impressions of it, his thoughts and resolutions about it. I comment but sparingly. My comments are not taken too well, except where they correspond exactly with his own. In the case of experiences which I have had and he has not, he listens eagerly, and regards me as an oracle provided I do not go on too long about it.

After a while the bell rings again. A couple of friends were passing by and wondered if we would be at home. They are invited to come in, thus causing great dismay to the Solitary. He adopts one of several courses. He leaves immediately, while the new guests are being shown in; or shortly after they have arrived and are being introduced. Or he remains for the evening, relapsed into a very grim and disapproving silence which it is impossible to shake.

The Solitary can be identified by certain unfailing characteristics. First, he is always a bachelor. If he has been married, the marriage was unsuccessful, and was followed shortly by divorce. A second marriage is never attempted. Secondly, he always works in some government office. He may have a civil service position. He is always known to his fellow workers as eccentric and morose, since he will not associate with them and takes as little notice of their existence as is possible under the circumstances of daily proximity. Thirdly, he always attaches himself to one family, never to more than one. He is doggedly faithful to that one, however; and, though invariably poor, he will go without meals in order to bring the children some expensive toy, the wife a handbag, or the husband a sports shirt. Fourthly, he is morbidly sensitive, and always suspects everyone, except his favourite family, of intending direct insult or, at the very least, derogatory innuendo. Fifthly, he invariably becomes a dreadful nuisance to the family to which he is attached. He will telephone on the flimsiest excuse, or have someone else telephone while he listens on an extension. He constantly warns the family against other friends whose motives, he suspects, are the worst possible. Sixthly, he regards his own approval of some book (or picture or music or dancer) as significantly of the nature of a discovery; what he finds merit in, though it be flagrantly played up in all the newspapers and on the radio as well as in the conversation of the day, has been noticed for the first time. Finally, he is militantly professional concerning all questions touching upon his favourite art (unfortunately, it *is* usually an art), and he is entirely lacking in anything remotely resembling a sense of humour.

Every family has its Solitary, the maladjusted individual who must be held up by the force of the solid relation which exists between a man and his wife. When the three of us are sitting in a room, I have almost the physical experience of a bond, like an invisible rope, stretched between my wife and myself, with the Solitary comfortably leaning one elbow upon it. I am sorry for him, as who could fail to be? Yet I resent him because of my active dislike for his attitude toward life. I know that he has a high regard for me, not because I am I but because my family is the one to which he has decided to attach himself, on account of my work. But I know, too, that he would consider himself too intelligent and spiritual to go out for a glass of beer with the clerk at the next desk in the post-office or customs house in which he works all day, whereas I know that I would not. He is a spiritual parasite and, like all parasites, neglects the brotherhood of man. I resent him, yes, and I am sorry for him, too, because I have been lonely, God *how* lonely, in London on Sunday, for instance, before I knew anyone there; and I understand what he is going through.

Yet he puts me in an awful predicament. If I am nice to him, he takes advantage of it and will give us no peace, for then every evening must be devoted to him, while gradually our other friends will stay away, feeling that the Solitary distrusts them. If I am not nice to him, then my conscience hurts me, knowing as I do what awful agonies he is enduring, agonies which are no lighter for being self imposed. What ever I do about him, in the end I will be sorry.

The art of living, like happiness, may prove to be something which cannot be pursued directly. It may be necessary to achieve it in the same way in which we preserve certain of the virtues, such as innocence or purity—by indirection, or perhaps simply by having it or not having it.

Certainly, the work of most men is specific and consists in a particular job which has to be well done, thereby requiring concentration and selfless devotion. To become a concert pianist, for instance, means to forget about oneself as a musician in favour of the single-minded concentration upon the mastery of the piano which hours upon hours of steady practice entail. The result may be a familiarity with music and a facility in its performance. The successful musician may prove to be happy in his career, but if so, it is not because he pursued happiness but rather because he pursued music.

What is true of happiness is true also of the art of living. It is a useful analogy to conceive the living of one's life under the genus of the pattern of a formal art. Many men who made up with gusto for their lack of logical rigour have lived so. Havelock Ellis, Elie Faure, and others, have assumed, with some penetrating insights, that life itself is the greatest of the arts. The prospects are inviting, it must be confessed. To perform every action however miniscule as though it had a tiny but important place in some larger scheme of things, to light a match with a sense of one's personal destiny, to shave not only a beard but the beard of a protagonist in the play upon the grand stage of life, to say hello to an acquaintance on the street as though the word were the utterance of a final judgment, these are the rewards of a formalism of art which penetrates through every fibre of accidental existence.

But of course these symbolisms have their drawbacks. They violate the admonition not to take oneself too seriously. To be self-conscious about trivial acts may be to lose the sense of proportion which a sense of humour somehow provides; it may mean to fail in those high moments of decisive action when the power of combined reason and insight meet to make one equal to the demand of a crisis. We will not always be equally tense; we should not always be equally solemn; and we cannot always be everything that we are capable of being. Every occasion is not something to which we have got to rise. To be an artist all the time is not to be an artist at all. For the true artist, in his time off, is what is left over from his work in art. Nobody would pretend that the artist as a person contains all of the perfection which is found in a supremely great art. It is not likely that Beethoven contained all the purity of character that would correspond to the purity of line to be found in the Fifth Symphony, and the Parthenon probably has an æsthetic status which was hardly paralleled by the moral level of the Greeks who built it. To be an artist in life is to fail to be an artist in life at least part of the time.

To this objection, the defenders of the art-of-life theory may consent, by insisting that to know when to relax is also part of the art of life. But this means that the art of life is not an art at all but life itself, which nobody has ever disputed. Unfortunately, we cannot consider everything an art, because if we did, the term, art, would become non-discriminating. A word which makes no distinctions whatsoever is of no use to us in thinking. If everything is an art, that fact is no more instructive than if nothing were an art. Works of art are what they are in virtue of other things which are not works of art. The contrast is an essential part of the meaning.

These considerations are brought to my mind most graphically by the spectacle of the poet who lived in New Orleans and who strove to make a pattern of his life in small ways. His life as a whole was an ugly shape, but in little things he had posed for so long that his poses were incorporated in his very bones. By studied attention he had mastered the art of making every move a figure. The removal of a cigarette from his pocket, for instance, was a careful and elongated gesture, having a beginning, a middle, and an end. He kept his cigarettes in the top outside pocket of his coat, and would reach for them with his right hand, while making a perfect horizontal right-angle of his elbow. The movement was perfect in its way, yet somehow lacking in scope. He had become a creature from the antique wood to the fullest extent to which he could manage to make himself one. To this end he devoted most of his time; he lived in Audubon Park, reading Proust or Ronald Firbank or James Joyce, his favourite authors. He was peculiar to New Orleans, as native as the magnolias; his cosmic interests were yet kept narrow, for he could convey the impression that the stars to be seen from Audubon Park at night were put there by the Park Commission.

His poems had a certain quality about them which justified his place as a minor poet in the American gallery, but he did not write enough to call attention to himself. He worked very hard at writing, if never very long at a time. I remember one poem he showed me; it consisted of stanzas of three lines each. One line ended with the phrase, 'extraordinarily green.' The poet thought about this for some days, then when I saw him again, he had retyped the poem, writing in the top right-hand corner of the new copy the words, 'ultimate version.' The only change from the old copy was that 'extraordinarily green' had become 'extraordinarily mauve.' He had an amazing relish for words, and the enunciation of the sound of 'extraordinarily mauve' gave him a positively delightful physical sensation.

He had no feeling for people; everyone was treated on the assumption of a common education, whether it actually existed or not. We were standing in front of the Little Theatre one night after the first act of a play which we did not have the heart to see to the finish. The poet as usual was reaching over his elbow for a cigarette and we were contemplating the serious problem of where to go for a drink. The Little Theatre is lighted in front by two bright street lamps, and is not more than a couple of squares from the river and the docks. Suddenly, a sailor, a very drunken sailor from South Africa, came lurching along the sidewalk, and, seeing the bright lights of the Theatre and probably supposing it to be some sort of cabaret, started to go in. We knew his entrance would cause some dislocation of the play then in progress, and someone called out to stop him. The poet was nearest the door, and he stood in the sailor's way.

'I wouldn't go in there, if I were you,' he said very casually. It brought the sailor up sharply. 'Well, why not?' he asked.

The poet spoke very slowly, relishing his words. 'Because it would not a-muse you.'

The accent of studied elegance which is hard to describe impressed the sailor and he lurched away from us as quickly as his unsteady legs would take him.

The aim at perfection is one of the worthiest things in the world, but I wonder whether it is possible to achieve it in little things except at the expense of larger. What happens to the most casual acts of the world, the spilled coffee, the lost penny, the used blotter? Somehow, they must fit into the scheme of things, but they seem to have no shape of their own. Can this be? It is hardly likely that anything goes without meaning, and at least they achieve, in Whitehead's admirable phrase, some sort of objective immortality. Yet it is unlikely that all purport stops there. Certainly in the pattern of our lives, to dwell upon everything is to make no whole of the parts. But to proceed, as most of us do, by aiming only at the whole irrespective of the parts, cannot be as it ought to be, either. I do not pretend to know the answer. We have a lesson for the poet; it is that we are known by our works, not by our attitudes. But perhaps the poet has a genuine lesson for us, too, in the care of tiny movements and careless gestures and little things. The art of life is life itself and we may not be artists of wholes but only of parts. It is something to think about.

The ordinary judgments we pronounce upon people are far too simple. The usual estimation of a man's worth is made upon the basis of a two-valued ethics: he is good or he is bad. But I doubt if there is a man in the world to whom either value can be unqualifiedly applied. For men are mixtures of many properties; they are good and bad in degrees of both that serve to nullify any single estimate.

The prime example which comes to my mind when I think of such things is that of Dr. Alexis Carrel. I had shown the manuscript of my first book to a friend, Dr. Emanuel Libman, in New York. Libman is a great doctor but being professedly ignorant of such matters as philosophy, he decided without saying anything to turn the book over to Carrel. Carrel read it and then sent for me. I went by appointment to his office in the Rockefeller Institute for Medical Research. Carrel wore very thick glasses over his little squinty eyes, and a white surgeon's cap; the effect was very scientific in a Sunday Supplement fashion. We talked for an hour, and I promised to telephone the next time I was in the city. When I did so, some six months later, he invited me to dine with him at his club. We spent from seven o'clock until twelve talking. Carrel had a pronounced French accent and was somewhat difficult to understand.

This was some two years before the outbreak of the second world war, about 1937. Carrel talked a great deal about science and listened to my ideas on the topic of scientific method, which was the interest that had drawn us together. That Carrel was a combination of genius and charlatan is undeniable. No one will ever be able to shake my faith in his genius, scientific interest and ability. Part of him at least was completely the man of science. I believe that his actual achievements in the field of biology testify to the truth of this statement.

But Carrel had unfortunately two other interests which were in a sense unscientific and in which his intuition, to say nothing of his common sense, failed him. One of these was politics; the other was mysticism. Politically, Carrel had little faith in democracy and indeed disliked it. Democracy meant to him simply an opportunity for stupid people to meddle in the affairs of intelligent ones and to interfere with the efforts the latter were making to raise the standard of culture. The system of Naziism appealed to him just because he assumed that it actually was what he thought it ought to be. He told me that he was anxious to go to Germany to see what the Nazis were doing. He was not anti-semitic at all, and he had no belief in many other Nazi ideas, such as the super-race or superior blood. He believed quite naïvely that the task of the Nazis so far as the men of science were concerned was to hold the masses in check so that science could proceed without concern over any practical problems. He assumed that in Nazi Germany the man of science was allowed to work in complete peace and without interruption of any sort. He also assumed that the few were more intelligent and capable than the many (a fair assumption) and that under the fascist or nazi system the intelligent few, the right few, got to rule the unintelligent many (a ridiculously false conclusion). I do not know how he feels now. Certainly his love for his native country exceeded anything else in the emotional make-up of the man, and I cannot imagine that his approval of the Nazis has included the spectacle of the ravaging of France on the planned large scale that was conducted after the invasion.

[219]

P

The mysticism is rather more interesting than the politics in the Carrel scheme of things. It occurs rather vividly and at its best in his chapter on physiology in his popular book, *Man the Unknown*. Carrel, due to his imperfect knowledge of English, used an odd word but one which was quite effective. He called it 'mysticity', an abstract substantive which more than mysticism meant precisely what Carrel intended. Now there is, of course, a perfectly valid field for such inquiries as that into the nature of 'mysticity', but the trouble with Carrel's version was that he looked for mystic elements in places where they would not necessarily have to be. He clouded the issue for unexplored but probably empirical material by assuming that it was supernatural, as for instance, in the ability of peasants to predict the exact time of their death 'from natural causes', in their ability to foretell the actual immediate future, and in the better-known phenomenon of mental telepathy. It ought to be assumed, and would in fact, I think, be assumed by any complete scientist, that if such phenomena existed at all in any regularity, they must have natural causes. This is the scientific assumption, and to some extent Carrel subscribed to it, but not altogether. For him there was always in such phenomena an overlay of 'mysticity', ineffable, elusive, hard to describe or define, but very definitely constituting an integral element.

Carrel divided his experiments into two groups. In New York with, I believe, the aid of some other scientists, he conducted experiments in mental telepathy, striving to render it as fool-proof as possible. He told me of some remarkable results, of which, however, I had no first-hand experience. Two men possessing telepathetic power who were supervised by two groups of scientists in two separate hotel rooms in locations unknown to each other, were able to communicate complex and deliberately false scientific formulæ; what was dictated to one man by his supervising group was written down by the other at exactly the same time. Carrel owned an island off the coast of France where he lived during the summer and where his experiments were continued in the winter by his wife. He told me of equally remarkable results there: the ability possessed by the peasants to foretell the future. One peasant, for instance, had written down upon a folded slip of paper the amount of money with which Carrel would return from a shopping tour on the mainland.

What are we to say to all this? Nothing as to its validity or invalidity until sufficient facts can be made known. Psychologically, an explanation can be offered, with the reserve that such explanations are liable to be cancelled at any moment by the establishment of objective facts. Carrel had had a career as a medical officer in the first world war. Many intelligent men, such as, for instance, Sir Oliver Lodge, stunned by the loss of dear ones or merely horrified by the mass sacrifice of human life, were driven to seek some kind of hope in a life after death. The various forms of communication with the dead ensued: spiritualism in all its monotonous dependence upon singular evidence, in contrast with science which always relies upon generality and continuity of evidence. Carrel may have fallen a psychological victim to this wave of despair and its result in the various kinds of 'mysticity'. There may also of course be a better explanation.

Carrel subscribed to the Freudian but to me, at least, fantastic theory that the creative energy of the scientist and the artist is at bottom sexual, so that an active sex life militates formidably against creative activity in other fields. Every orgasm, he believed, was a painting wasted, an idea abandoned, an experiment destroyed. I cannot see any truth in this belief except the undeniable fact that both sexual and other activities involve an expenditure of energy. This does not mean, however, that energy saved in one department of living can be spent in another. Many great artists and philosophers lead vigorous sexual lives in addition to carrying on their professional work; many others do not. The fallacy of oversimplification has certainly been committed in holding to the belief that there is such a thing as a one-direction flow of energy which can be turned by us into any channel. A certain amount of physical exercise is healthful; could we do more intellectual work without it, or would our output not tend to be less?

What are we to do, then, in the ideal society of the future with the men who hold great advantages for mankind, but who also have certain drawbacks without which we would be better off? This problem has not yet been solved and undoubtedly accounts for much of the disintegration that goes on in social organization. If people were either good or bad we could simply exclude the bad and form our ideal society on the good; but nothing is completely good in the actual existence of graded values. In Carrel's case, since his only unscientific activity was unpolitical, I think we can count him very decidedly a net gain when the personal books are balanced. The modern age offers terrible temptations of fame in the form of newspaper publicity, to which only the strongest characters among us can offer sufficient resistance. But whatever actions a man commits that we cannot approve does not nullify the value of the good that he has done, and this is a truth it were well to remember.

Carrel wished eagerly to be the centre of a cult, but his wishes were never fulfilled. Since the advent of the second world war he has resided in France most of the time, while the culture cultists have been cut off from Europe and must take their fun where they can find it. Living in New Orleans, it has been my privilege not only to have moderately well-known artists as friends but also to watch the flow of admirers who issue from the railroad station or arrive in automobiles and buses throughout the winter and more mysteriously depart after having gained or failed an objective. The purpose of the visiting cultists is directly connected with some famous artist they have hoped to meet. They telephone immediately upon arrival. Sometimes they come armed with a letter of introduction; more often they mention a friend in common; but frequently they merely mumble the name of another famous person the artist is certain to have known at some time or other. The hero-worshipping visitors may be divided roughly into four classes. These are: the homage-payers, the curio-seekers, the kindred-spirits, and the golden-planners.

The homage-payers are a long familiar spectacle. They usually populate women's clubs but occasionally have the temerity to travel, in pairs, or even, in rare instances, singly. They are burning with a desire to meet the man who—. He may have written a book or a play, painted a picture, or just had his name in large letters somewhere; it really does not matter: they only want to meet him in order to see what he looks like and to be able, in subsequent conversation at dinner parties, to refer to him as an intimate. The homage-payers are easy to manage.

The curio-seekers are not unlike the last group. They may be men or women or both. They travel in assorted collections. They have a little more daring; and they ask for more. They want autographs or original manuscripts or first editions. In other words, they are after tangible assets and are not satisfied with mere acquaintance. They are the traditional head-hunters, and are slightly harder to manage. Sometimes they can be quite a problem.

The kindred-spirits are a thing apart. They travel alone, or at the most in pairs. In pairs, however, there is never more than one kindred-spirit and a companion. The kindred-spirits are humble in their demands and at the same time quite arrogant. They do not wish merely personal acquaintance or curios, nothing so cheap and tawdry. What they ask for is recognition. They come to the established artist, who in most cases has worked hard to achieve his public eminence. They may have done a little but on the average it is very little: a few bad pictures, one bad book or some brief chamber music. What they ask of the artist is acceptance as equals in the esoteric community of the great which they are convinced must exist. They want the artist to feel more sympathy for them than for anyone, on the grounds of a common gift and practice. They are not so easily hurt, and they can be managed without too much difficulty.

The golden-planners are somewhat different in kind as well

as in degree from the other groups, although of course they are remotely related. The first group consisted of women; the next two were mixed; the third is usually entirely masculine. Representatives of this last type usually travel quite alone. The golden-planners are rarely interested in the artist's past and only vaguely concerned with his present. They do not particularly wish autographs or inscribed volumes, although they have never been known to refuse these. What they really want is to make plans for him. They are going to write magnificent articles about him or about his work. They have a connection with a publisher and wish the artist to do a book which is slightly off his subject, or they wish to start a new educational institution or literary colony which will be just the thing for him, and they want to ask his participation. The point is that the artist has reached the size where they are ready to take him over and they have come to flatter him by acquainting him with the new and improved status which their recognition represents.

I am hardly famous enough to be bothered with visitors of the first two categories; the abstract portraits I have drawn of them are taken from life but not from my own experience; they are taken from the experience of my friends, novelists who are well known. The fourth category seems to represent my own visitors. I do not get the homage-payers and the curio-seekers; I only get the golden-planners. Now, I submit that my group is in a sense the worst of the three. Once a homage-payer or a curio-seeker is satisfied, that is an end of the matter. An odd letter or so may come, but that is all; and the affair can be entirely terminated simply by allowing the letter to go unanswered. But the golden-planners are somewhat more difficult. They start projects, exact promises, and volunteer services; they are hard to refuse without adding insult to injury; and they never fulfill the expectations they arouse. What they promise to do somehow always falls just short of coming to pass: the summer colony does not occur come summer, or it is so far from what had been described that the artist cannot bear to take part and so is compelled to refuse at the last minute. The educational institution never gets under way, though it almost does. The article of appreciation, for which the artist has been asked to prepare a sketchy outline, or add a foreword, is never actually written. The sunny optimism of the golden-planners has a souring effect in the end!

It is painfully obvious that the more famous the artist the greater the number of pests which hover about him, and as a direct consequence the greater his contempt for the individual members of the public which supports him by buying his works. In a sense the development of this attitude is hardly his fault. It is the fault of a basic error in the philosophy of the public. In the search for significance, the values should be properly attributed to the art. But the philosophy of the day makes no distinction between the artist and his work. Obviously the artist is responsible for bringing the work into existence, but once he has done so it exists on its own account and leads an independent life. So, in quite another way, does the artist. It is he and not his books or paintings or music who requires a certain amount of privacy, who needs solitude, who has a family and friend, who takes trips into the country or goes fishing or hunting. Moreover, without intending any personal offence, I believe that it can be asserted that artists have certain individual faults as well as certain virtues which the works of art do not have. To meet an artist in the flesh is not always to enhance the estimation of his work. From the viewpoint of character, he may or he may not live up to it. Sometimes it is far better to keep intimacy for works of art and to leave the artist himself to his own devices, being content to remember that by patronizing his work one has contributed to his reward.

There is something pathetic about the desire of the public to attain to a greater involvement in culture by making the personal acquaintance of the artist. Although boring and awkward and wrongly-directed, the impulse itself is a good one and well-founded. It does not justify contempt but it cannot be allowed to remain as it is. It simply needs to be redirected. It ought to be pointed out to the hero-worshippers that it is by their works that ye shall know them and not by personal contact. What remains is always what is important, if indeed anything is. The artist is not an exotic creature possessing strange and lurid habits but in most cases an ordinary citizen in everything, let us say, except his art. It is also my contention that art without having to be reduced to the level of craft can also be considered a natural if rare phenomenon. But perhaps when the popular philosophy of art changes, and we begin to regard the presence of the artist and his work as one of those familiar miracles which, like the fact of motion, are no less miracles for occurring every day, the relation of the public and the artist will become a saner one. In the meanwhile, it should be added in deference to the public that the personality of the artist and even his works are often distorted by the present-day dislocation.

It is possible, then, to like a man's work and not the man; and it is equally possible to like the man and not his work. In the case of at least one artist, a novelist, this happened to me.

For some while my friends had been trying to tell me about Henry Miller. He is the great American novelist, it seems. It was regarded as inevitable that I would like him and that we would be friends. I stood for as much of this talk as I could possibly take. I read Miller's books, or rather one of them; I should say half of one of them; but I did not want to meet him. My friends were very patient with me.

'You will see,' they said. 'You will see.'

Later, I dined with Huntington Cairns. He, too, kept talking about Henry Miller. We ought, it appeared, to meet. I was firm with Huntington about my lack of interest in that direction, but I did not shake him. I pointed out that Miller's writings are pornographic and that ordinarily this would prejudice me in their favour rather than the reverse. But, I went on, his point of view reminds me of that of the French writer, Céline. Both are irrational and worship everything that I hate, and vice versa. What could we possibly have in common?

Huntington invited me to attend a broadcast in New York, on my way home from Cape Cod. Afterwards, a group of us as

Huntington's guests repaired to a bar. I was seated between an executive of the Columbia Broadcasting Company and Henry Miller. This was Huntington's doing, I thought. I had been barely introduced to Miller, but that was enough. I turned to talk with the executive. We were getting along very well when I felt a tap on my shoulder. It was Miller. I turned around to face him.

'I hear you do not like my books,' he said.

My first thought was that it had been foolish of Huntington to tell him so; my second, that it was true.

'Yes,' I said, and hesitated, about to add: what do you propose to do about it? I suppose that this last must have been in my face, for Miller looked me straight in the eye with his own beady little pupils for almost a minute. Then he said:

'Well, I just want you to know that that is all right with me. I don't mind and I am sure that we are going to be friends.'

There was nothing more I could say and little more I could do. The following week he borrowed the money to take my wife and me to lunch, and we invited him to visit us in New Orleans. I like him despite my intense hatred for his ideas and writings. On the way home, via Chicago, I stopped in a book-shop and happened to see a collection of his short pieces, *The Cosmological Eye*, with a kind of autobiographical intro-duction, in the course of which he had written, 'I love violence.' Yet he had returned from France as the Germans marched in and he did not evince any keen desire to enter the war! Yet where else would those who love violence find it so concen-trated? I became angry with him all over again, and indeed it is only possible for me to remain friendly with him so long as I do not read his books. Several months ago he sent me a copy of his new book on Greece, *The Colossus of Maroussi*. I read some of it, including a passage in which he refers to the three 'sterling human qualities' of 'chaos, contradictoriness and confusion'. That was enough for me.

Miller evidently regards me in much the same way. He listened at one time to a long monologue of mine devoted to the levels of existence. I was trying to demonstrate how the empirical levels are built in a series of dependencies, so that for instance, biology is dependent upon physics yet wider in its own determination, and so on. Miller listened intently, understanding, I am sure, not a word. Finally, he said, when I stopped to catch my breath, 'But that is wonderful, the most wonderful thing I ever heard. Such rationalism is the next thing to insanity.'

What Miller and I have chiefly in common, we discovered, is our mysticism. He worships the east; I, the west. He wishes to become one with the universe by taking it all into himself. I wish to accomplish the same feat by giving myself utterly to it. We reach the same end through absolutely opposite means; that gives us much in common. We agree in regarding the Buddhist idea of the Bodhisattva as magnificent, the saint who refuses to take the last step into heaven until he has helped everyone else to get as far. But I profess to find the same idea in the life of Jesus and in the ethics of the unlimited community of the American philosopher, Charles S. Peirce. Miller wishes to disappear into the east; I wish to contribute to the world through my country and my people. Despite our differences, I like Miller and I think that we have a place for each other.

Liking the man is one thing. Considering his ideas symptomatic of the evil of the times is quite another. It is characteristic of the artist that Miller, a man who is capable of almost any enormity, should take refuge in expressing such capability in writing. Miller is late; Céline appeared just before the second world war.

Both are products of the same forces which have brought the war about. Their work represents the enemy within the gates. We do not wish to stop the kind of ideas to which they are giving voice; nor do we wish to stop the voices. What we do wish is to avoid the desire to voice such ideas. The artist never speaks for himself alone, if he is truly an artist. When the value of his work is exhausted by its contemporaneity, he is representative of the feelings of his times. But if he is great enough to be what is described as 'ahead of his times,' a truly great artist to whom the people must catch up, then he is representative of the feelings which ought to be, the feelings of the future. Hence the artist is an educator. Just as science improves our knowledge of principles, and thus stands for logic, so art improves our feeling for natural elections and thus stands for value.

It is the tragedy of Miller, the artist, that he is not ahead of his times. He expresses merely the contradictoriness, the chaos and the confusion that are his contemporaries. Despite his *avant-garde* claims and reputation, his work is exhausted by the feelings of those who live in his lifetime. He belongs to the nineteen-twenties.

We have passed through a period during which a limited order was liquidated. To be progressive was to be formless and orderless. But now we have managed to get beyond that period, too. To be fresh, the artist no longer finds it necessary to oppose order. The appeal for a revolt against order only comes in a period when an old order persists long after it has outlived its usefulness. To think of order then means to think of an insufficient order, just as today to think of organized religion usually means to think of the old, established religions. But there is always the possibility of a new order, in the same way in which there is always the possibility of a new religion. In our time there has been enough of chaos, contradictoriness and confusion, enough to sweep away the embarrassing claims of the old and insufficient order. Novelty lies in the direction of the discovery of a wider order; but a wider order does not mean an irrational, a fascist, order; instead it must be a rational order, one which makes freedom possible rather than limiting it. Such an order remains to be seen by the artist as it has already been seen by the scientist and philosopher. Planck and Einstein, Peirce and Whitehead, have given us the blueprints of a new understanding of the cosmos, a new cosmology. The artist has not yet helped us to feel it yet. When he does, it will be through a new emphasis on form; he will make us feel again not chaos but order.

Meanwhile, until the artists arise, it will be the day of the philosopher.

CHAPTER FIVE

Philosophy Today and Tomorrow

MOST Americans, like most other people, are not philosophers. Conversely, most philosophers are notAmericans, due to the fact that thus far Americans have had no interest in what seems at first glance to be so unfruitful an enterprise. The story of an American philosopher, then, should be exciting.

But, alas, there is no story. The philosopher has no private life of any significance. His adventures are for the most part confined to the desk and the library, in the course of which he acquires nothing more thrilling than a musty air, a bent figure, and a unique and entirely topsy-turvy way of looking at things. He is born, he writes and he dies. This is what happens to him. How anyone, therefore, could suppose that the autobiography of a philosopher could possibly be based upon egocentric details is beyond conjecture. The details of his life are made up in the account of what he spends his time thinking about, and this is rarely himself, rarely, that is, if he is a philosopher and not also a man.

I insist upon the distinction between a man and his work. Once again, the overlapping of classes is applicable; for some men are not philosophers, many, I should say; and some philosophers are not men. It is safe to assert that the claims of philosophy are not paralleled by the conduct of philosophers in most cases. The air of impartiality, of fairness, of detached interest in justice, do not always mark the behaviour of the philosophers toward each other. The only way in which a living can be earned from philosophy is through the teaching profession. Since the number of teaching positions in the universities declines steadily with the wholesale decline of general interest in philosophy, the teaching positions become more precious than ever. Consequently, they are fought over, defended and attacked with the viciousness of wolves, and there is no distinction between such behaviour, and, say, that of the executive staff of a large industrial corporation, except that in the latter case the financial rewards are larger. Strange as it may seem, instance after instance could be cited where philosophers have failed to stand together as philosophers but instead blocked each other, with nothing to gain in any case except the defeat of an opponent. The opposition among philosophical controversialists is aimed not at the level of controversy but at the level of jobs. Bad blood characterizes philosophy just as much as it does local politics.

The aim of philosophers must differ from the aim of philosophy. Too often the aim of philosophers is to show that all dead thinkers agree with them, and that all living thinkers who do not agree with them are wrong; but this is not the aim of philosophy. Philosophy is in search of the truth. Philosophy today is a neglected field, an area scorned for its lack of productivity, one which for the most part has been replaced by science. Science looks down upon philosophy for the latter's position as the handmaiden of theology. The claim may be true, but rightly or wrongly science does not hold theology in high regard. Thus the best minds of the day do not flock to philosophy, but seek other opportunities, and look for activity where the real is supposed to reside: in engineering, in chemistry, in medicine, and in the applied physical sciences generally. But what an opportunity this leaves for the philosophers! The truly big man would much prefer the advantage of working a neglected field so that he may have the opportunity to write his name upon it. He wishes to discover an interest which he may lift up rather than one which may lift him.

One disadvantage of philosophy today is its lack of popular intelligibility. This has frightened the public away, and has made the uninstructed think that philosophy is falling behind. Those who have had no special training in philosophy feel that the philosophy which is not intelligible to the great majority of reading persons is a failure. But since when is progress denoted by clarity? We cannot afford to identify philosophy with the literature which aims at everybody. What about science? The failure of the reading public to understand science does not mark it as a failure. Automotive engineers write only for other automotive engineers; biochemists, only for other biochemists. The public, which can understand neither, is eventually the beneficiary of the efforts of both; only the effect is felt somewhat indirectly.

Philosophy is neither a science nor an art but lies between them and contains elements which are held in common with each. Philosophy ought to be available to the general reading public as much as possible, but is not a failure when not so available. It ought to be readily accessible to anyone willing to take the proper preparation and to make the effort involved in its understanding and appreciation, but will have an effect ultimately even upon those who do not understand it. The philosophy of a previous day finally reaches the lives of this day's illiterates.

Meanwhile it is a fact that most persons are equally scornful and curious about philosophy. They want to know more about it but in the meantime they entertain no very high opinion of it. The hall-mark of stupidity is found in the fact that derogation always accompanies ignorance. The assumption of the scorner is that if the thing of which he had been ignorant were any good, he would have known about it earlier. This attitude of prejudice defeats curiosity, which must be quite humble and self-effacing to be successful. The truly curious does not associate himself with his ignorance. Indeed he does not think about himself at all; he thinks only about that which he wishes to know.

The more intelligent of those who hold a contemporary scorn for philosophy base it upon the failure of philosophers to agree among themselves. It is not understood that the disagreement among philosophers, once again, does not exactly represent philosophy. Philosophers disagree in what they choose to overemphasize. They cannot afford to agree completely until everything is known. This will cause some delay; but in the meantime the disagreement does not indicate anything as fatal as is generally assumed.

Philosophy exists in an intermediate realm, a kind of half-light, which joins humanity to the nature of things. Between philosophy and the understanding of the great majority of human beings lies a vast gap, so that when the philosopher looks back he becomes discouraged at the distance he has gone ahead of those who follow after. Then again, between philosophy and the nature of things lies an even vaster, an almost infinite, gap, so that when the philosopher looks forward and measures the known in terms of the unknown, he becomes even more discouraged. That is why philosophers have often resorted to talking in parables and appealing to religion as a basis for their own slim fund of ideas. It is a lonesome realm which the philosopher inhabits, speaking a strange dialect that is comprehended by few, and attacking a problem the dimensions of which cannot even be guessed. No wonder that only the strong can stand up under such a challenge, and that the weak look so ridiculously tiny in comparison with their undertaking.

Philosophy is not owned by philosophers and logic is not the property of logicians. The contradictory of this would seem to be the prevailing opinion, but if it were true I for one should not be much interested in philosophy or logic. We labour mostly under the mistaken assumption that to go up in interest is to go inward in concentration. All the higher functions and values are foolishly thought to be psychological. Philosophy, because we cannot find it outside us in the external world, is held to be a mental affair. It is said not to exist in the external world because we mean by existence tangible physical existence, and this philosophy by itself assuredly does not have. But the fact is that everyone has a philosophy and no one gets it purely out of the air.

Philosophy in the broadest sense consists in the belief in what is real. And this belief does not need to be consciously held in order to be a belief. We act from premises consciously or unconsciously held, and we do so as logically as possible. When our conclusions in action prove false, as they must whenever we run into serious self-contradictions, it is rarely the fault of our logical deductions; most persons, despite prejudices to the contrary, reason fairly accurately. What is wrong is the premises from which action take its start. And these would not be wrong, provided only that people could be made to consider them seriously. It is no easy task to haul up premises out of the subconscious where they dwell together in peace, and to see that they are wrong after all these years during which we have literally lived by them. Yet that is what has got to be done, if we are to improve our philosophy.

The less training in philosophy one has, the less is the task possible. To study philosophy means not only to learn what the best minds of the past have considered to be the truth. It means also to learn to move easily at the level of philosophical abstractions, and to look at one's own ideas with the critical eye which is accustomed to comparisons. The history of philosophy offers us a way to classify the best thought of the past, and that is by the succession of the discovery of philosophical ideas; another way is by types of philosophy. Certain points of view are perennial; they keep cropping up, so that a philosopher in any age is in a sense closer to certain philosophers of other ages than he is to his contemporaries who may be carrying forward quite different traditions. The man who is learned in philosophy is therefore equipped to haul up one of his own beliefs, and to say of it, 'Well, I hold this belief; where does it fit into the history of philosophy and where among the types of philosophical schemes?' These questions may, or may not, help him to consider whether his belief is true, but it will at least give him some sort of perspective on the topic. From there, it will be an easier matter to inspect it along with his other beliefs for consistency with facts and with other theories.

Philosophy as belief about reality is the broadest consideration which it is possible to have. There are inconsistencies in our thought and actions which we had not suspected, but there are also hidden consistencies. These, too, are important and revealing; for they tell us something about the atmosphere of opinion, the prevailing philosophy of the day which may be dictating the direction of an entire culture. Just as every man has his own philosophy, so does the society in which he lives and the culture of which that society may be a part. There is a philosophy of the man, of his family, of his club, his business, his town, his state, his nation, his hemisphere, and his western (or eastern) society. There is also a philosophy of the brotherhood of man. Beyond that there is a philosophy of existence and beyond that one of being. The last is by definition the largest. We want to know what each is about, so we have set ourselves an objective which we are in no danger of reaching.

Meanwhile, we are struggling; we are in philosophy and we can give ourselves to it. What more could anyone ask? It is this sense in which it is possible to say that we have not taken hold of philosophy but philosophy has taken hold of us. We are helplessly at the mercy of our interest. Fortunately for us, we have chosen a good one, one which lies at the heart of every man's desire whether he happens to know that it does or not.

The religion of an age is that study which thinks that it has the only proper method for attaining to a knowledge of reality, and which has managed to have its supposition made general. There never was a time when such a belief was held about philosophy. There was never a day, not even during the golden age of Greece, when popular acceptance had drowned the philosophical method. In most ages of the past, it has been theology or mysticism or both which has carried the palm. Today unmistakably it is science. The scientists, in their single-mindedness of purpose, are monks of a sort. The man whose lunch and supper consists of food on trays placed just outside the door does not differ substantially from the man who denies himself for the kingdom of heaven's sake, as is recognized by the tacit adherence of most people to the sole reality of the researches of science. We believe today that if any activity can possibly attain to a knowledge of what our existence and the existence of everything else is all about, it must be that activity which is being conducted in universities and laboratories all over the world under the name of science. Philosophy occupies the same back seat it has always held.

The philosopher, however, can console himself for his lack

of popularity as a philosopher by his knowledge of the generality of his subject. Religion and science may not always take philosophy into account, nevertheless philosophy does recognize them. Philosophy must take all knowledge to be its province; and the man who dares to call himself a philosopher must know something concerning the presuppositions, postulates, methods and conclusions, which are involved in every activity. The philosopher is the man who has set himself an impossible task and then gone about fulfilling it as much as possible. He does not need any recognition, although most certainly he would welcome it and be grateful for it; for he has found his fortune.

We are always better prepared to understand the operation of a thing if we know what it is designed to do. The difficulty which most people have with philosophy springs from their failure to grasp just what it is the philosopher is getting at, anyway. How can they acclaim him for having done a good job when they do not even know what the job is? Let me try to explain a little.

The word philosophy comes from two words meaning love of wisdom. But one who loves is already to some extent wise, since there is wisdom in loving. For the answer to the riddle of the universe is not a proposition but a logical feeling. We experience the feeling of wonder, which in turn prompts inquiry. The inquiry can go only so far, since always more has being than we can ever know about. For the world beyond the limits of our knowledge, we can have only a feeling of wonder, of love and perhaps of worship. Thus philosophy tries to explain what the world is *almost* all about, not what it is *all* about. The part can know other parts within a whole, yet it can never know the whole; the whole can only be felt by the part as a whole. Thus above philosophy lies religion. Religion is concerned with the aspects of the world as a whole which most pervasively excite our feelings. Philosophy is the most general of those studies dealing with reasons directly. If it can be thought about, then it is philosophy. But if things are felt which lie beyond analysis, the chances are that they exist in the province of religion.

Now religion does not advance, since it does not seek knowledge. But philosophy, contrary to popular opinion, does. Like science it seeks principles, and its problems are constantly becoming clarified and giving way to the study of more complex interrelations. The insights of religion cannot be communicated; those of philosophy can. From the point of view of the sum total of human knowledge which is possessed by society and carried forward, religious insight is of no use except to and for the individual. Philosophy is the highest *communicable* knowledge and thus the highest instrument of social improvement.

What is this knowledge which the philosophers are seeking to communicate? Philosophical knowledge is carried best in the form of problems and solutions, of questions and answers. Such knowledge is hard to propound, since to state the questions they are trying to answer is also to suggest certain answers. Philosophy may not be the same as religion or theology, as I have been trying to explain, but it does deal with the whole of being from a rational point of view. That is to say, it endeavours to discover (among other things) the widest categories, and the fewest number of them, into which everything in the whole of experience can be divided. Of course, we can say, all is one, and have done with it; but while this may be true it is non-discriminating: we do not know any more than we did before. We have not gained any suggestiveness for the further examination of the world. Again, we can say that all being is divided into mind and matter; essence and existence; possibility and actuality; thought and extension; thesis, antithesis and synthesis; possibility, actuality and destiny; or any other set of terms, with great effect. The fundamental division of the world of experience into two, three or more basic classes of things is the business of the most important branch of philosophy known as ontology, or the study of being.

Another question which agitates philosophers, and has done so particularly in recent times, is that which attempts to go back of the one I have just stated in order to ask how the existence of human knowledge is possible in the first place. How can we know anything? What is the nature of the process of knowing? Some men have said that we cannot know anything except our own thoughts, but others have suggested that we cannot know anything unless there is first something in the external world to be known. Still others have claimed that for knowledge to be valid, it requires the simultaneous existence of a world to be known and a knower, and therefore that knowledge actually exists in the interstices of a process. At all events, this knowledge problem and its proffered solutions, or demonstrated lack of solutions, goes under the fancy name of epistemology, or the study of knowledge.

Other branches of philosophy exist and have their own importance but all depend largely upon the answers which are given in these two departments. For instance, logic is inseparable from ontology and rests upon fact. We cannot set up an ontology which is supposed to be valid unless we start from logic, since if the ontology does not claim to be reasonable, our reasons for holding it are not valid. No philosophy can deny reason without denying its own value as a philosophy.

Then again, ethics, which concerns the theory and practice of conduct, and seeks for answers to such questions as, what is the good and how shall we best pursue it, always presupposes some general metaphysics, some ontology and epistemology, in terms of which its own problems are worked out. Æsthetics, which studies the beautiful, also depends upon a certain theory of beauty; and even theology, as a rational study, depends upon a certain theory of the real, and of God and the world.

These are some of the studies which are as yet hopelessly dependent upon philosophy. There is a sense in which all the sciences are branches of philosophy. That is, they are dependent upon philoso*phy*, not upon philoso*phers*. The very existence of empirical science and its empirico-logical method stems from a certain philosophical outlook. There was a day when the sciences were indistinguishable from philosophy, and the fact that they have grown up and gone into business for themselves and can tell everybody off has led certain scientists to deny even the lineage. But despite this filial ingratitude, it is yet the ambition of philosophy (if not of all philosophers) to bring studies to the point where they can fend for themselves as full-fledged sciences.

There will always remain some branches of philosophy which we need never fear will leave. One is ontology. Another is cosmology, or the study of the structure of the cosmos. The more of the special sciences there are, the more we shall require the services of a science of the sciences, one which seeks to organize the fact of the existence of the sciences, their method, the empirical fields which they study, and their conclusions, into a world-picture. That is to say, in addition to learning what each of the little segments of existence is about, we shall always want to know what it is *all* about. We have seen that in the very nature of the problem that is impossible. We can only feel what it is all about, but we can know what it is almost all about. The general world-picture is left for cosmology to draw, and cosmology for this purpose will always have to depend upon some kind of theory of being, or ontology, and some theory of the validity of knowledge, or epistemology.

Behind these studies we can never go, and thus philosophy presents the widest knowledge that reason, based on experienced fact, can ever have. Philosophy can grow unfashionable, as it has of late, but its day will always come again, because *it* cannot dispense with *us*. The problems remain, and the curiosity, too, despite the fact that for the moment we may choose to engage more in actual practice in the hurly-burly world than in the realm of speculation. Let us go as far as we wish in this direction; time is long and we shall always be returned by our bafflement to the ultimate questions of philosophy. Since it is practice which calls our attention to the necessity for philosophy, philosophy cannot be merely a field in which we hide from practice. The two things are interrelated in an inextricable way. For philosophy in its turn will direct us toward action; only, it is to be hoped, toward better action than that in which we might have engaged without philosophy.

The philosopher who does not teach, who plays no part in an educational institution, whose books do not sell in sufficient quantities to earn him a livelihood, who has no learned degrees to his credit, who has no regular associations and contacts with the men of his profession, who, in fact, carries no public authority of any kind or in any fashion except his writings to substantiate the claim that he is a philosopher, seems to have no place whatsoever in the modern world. Indeed he never has had in any world. He seems to be a complete anomaly. But if, in addition, he is an affable fellow, fond of companionship, interested in sports and amused by a joke, the claim appears as a complete pretension. He purports to be a seeker after wisdom yet he has not even the professional equipment of queerness or solemnity. He is neither eccentric nor withdrawn. Can he then be what he pretends to be?

Many philosophers, it is true, have been professional in the orthodox sense. Most are today. They have the requisite degrees, they work in universities, they teach as well as write. And a large percentage of philosophers have been content to let the challenge of just what is a philosopher be answered by the written record they have left us of their achievements in philosophy. This should in fact suffice. Technical philosophy, which seems so forbidding to those who do not understand it, remains arcana only to those who have not troubled to learn the technical vocabulary. Many non-professional philosophers of the past have been confronted with this problem in various ways. Spinoza, for instance, earned his living by grinding lenses, meanwhile writing his books, of which the most important was to be published posthumously, and doing little or nothing of a discursive nature to let the public in upon the privacy of his interest. Socrates, on the other hand, if we are to believe the accounts of him, sat in the market-place not only willing but eager to converse with any and all comers about the matters which concerned him most. The failure of Hume's repeated efforts to obtain a chair in a university did not prevent him from securing a lasting place as the storm centre of European philosophy.

In the majority of my books I have written exactly what I wanted to say in the simplest manner possible, which in most cases proved to be complex enough! I have had no particular audience in mind except those who, like me, are concerned with finding out the truth, no audience, that is to say, except possibly the Unborn Perfect Audience, which is no *particular* audience at all. Those who are to come must suffice and I will rest my case upon them. This is a book to be forgotten; but in these confused times when security of all kinds, physiological, psychological, economic, political, ethical, æsthetic, intellectual and spiritual, is at a premium, and everyone is thoroughly lost, it appears to be our obligation to hold a hand out to our contemporaries, to those we love and are preoccupied with first, and this of course quite irrespectively of whether they are willing to listen or not. And so this is my appeal to my reader: give the philosophers a hearing; wait a moment, only a moment, we only want a chance, listen to what we have to say. For I am only this: a philosopher and yet an authentic product of these times in America, and I will not and cannot be denied. When I say that I *will* be heard, I only mean that I am a public man.

Philosophers pay a high personal price for the abstractness of their work. It has a subjective effect which makes them to some extent strangers to the rough-and-tumble world of actuality. They learn to expect of events a consistency which it is sometimes difficult to obtain even in philosophy. And they become as a consequence the quixotic creatures who correspond to the legendary and stage character of the absent-minded professor.

Are these occupational peculiarities necessary? To some extent they probably are. The type of the philosopher is what a particular interest inevitably does to a man. Philosophy has its occupational diseases, just like mining coal, painting radium dials, or any other trade which makes unusual demands on the individual. Simply because the tools with which the philosopher works happen to be abstract ideas expressed in technical words, and not coal damp or luminous radium paint, does not mean that such tools do not have the kind of physical effect upon him which results from his enormous specialization. Consider for a moment, then, the philosopher's equipment. He works with terms which are peculiar to philosophy and other terms which in philosophy are given meanings they do not ordinarily have. At the same time, he is expected to have a working knowledge of at least the theoretical aspects of other fields— of as many others as possible. This requires not only a prodigious memory but also an active imagination. The individual philosopher may have only one song to sing (and despite vain hopes this proves very much to be true), depending upon what aspect of being seems to him to be the most important; but he is required to see what interrelations of things his particular slant on the world calls forth. Thus he must be at once down-to-earth, after the fashion of the man of common sense, and imaginative, after the fashion of the artist. No wonder that, judged by all ordinary standards, he appears to be a little queer. So does the artist. And it might be added that, judged by the same standards, the man who does not appear at all queer, the conformist and the 'regular guy', is a pretty dull fellow even to others of his kind. Some relief provided by means of contrast from among the queer professions is absolutely necessary to make a break in the average humdrum of existence.

Sherwood Anderson was fond of talking about his debate with Bertrand Russell, an event which took place several years ago. The subject was, 'Shall the State have charge of the children?' Russell took the affirmative, Sherwood the negative. I did not hear the debate, unfortunately, but I did read the newspapers afterwards and I also talked with Sherwood. The *New York Times* carried a little news story about Russell sailing for England in order to spend Christmas with his children. Sherwood went back to his home in Marion, Virginia. According to his own account, when his married daughter asked him what he had been doing, he told her about the debate. 'Well,' she asked, 'which side of the question did you take?' Sherwood told her that he had been opposed to the State raising the children because he thought that they should remain with their parents. 'Who, you?' she exclaimed.

Of course, there is no reason in the world why the philosopher should have to be consistent. I can think of nothing less human than consistency with respect to professed beliefs and actions. An overall consistency would be a fine thing provided that it did not prove too narrow. Usually it is a sign that something has been omitted; something warm and human and valuable which has been sacrificed to the primary demands of logic. Also, we are able to remain consistent only at the expense of some enormity which makes up for the great number of values which have to be suppressed in order to achieve the kind of logic we know is required.

Once upon a time I flew to Harvard (an odd enough thing to do) to see a philosopher. He was a man I had never met. I had read his only published book and found in it so many similarities to my own point of view that I wrote him a letter. He responded very politely, and so the first day that I was free to do so I went to Boston. We had made an appointment for the following morning at ten o'clock. I arrived late in the evening, very tired, and left word to be awakened at the same hour, thinking that since most philosophers have no conception of time he would be late enough to give me a while for my breakfast. But this was not to be. Promptly at the appointed hour the telephone operator rang my telephone with the time of day and the news that my guest was waiting. I dressed hastily and joined him, asking him, as soon as we had introduced ourselves, whether he would not have some breakfast.

We repaired to the dining room, and as soon as we had given our order he turned to me with this question. 'Do you accept the law of contradiction?'

I answered with some astonishment but undoubted pleasure that I did.

'Then,' said he, 'we shall be able to talk. I have tried so often lately to discuss philosophical problems with the positivists, who only admit the validity of the law of contradiction when it applies to my arguments and will not accept it for their own, and I have decided the issue must be settled in each case before we begin.'

At the time, his action seemed rather eccentric, but since then I have had enough experiences of the sort he described to convince me that he is right.

The philosopher should not be expected to be any more consistent than other men, since, in addition to being a philosopher, he is also a man. But his philosophy can be challenged as often as necessary. The two things are by no means the same.

Despite the difference in outlook between philosophy and other fields of endeavour, the public expects to understand philosophy without training, much as it attempts to listen to music and judge painting, simply by getting in the way of these things. The so-called obscurity of philosophical writing is resented by those who buy novels. It is believed that philosophy is a side-track, unimportant and old-fashioned, and that its working vocabulary is an outmoded holdover from a time when technological science, which really gets things done, had not yet appeared upon the scene.

Nothing could be farther from the truth. The same public which worships science and technology expects philosophy to come down to its commonsense level but does not ask the same treatment of pure and applied science. For instance, there has been little or no condemnation of the theory of relativity, or the formulae of chemical engineering, for being non-understandable to the ordinary, untrained mind. The problem is much the same, however. The results of philosophy make themselves felt eventually, just as do other disciplines, but it takes time for such effects to spread to the man in the street. The driver of a Buick accepts the machine blindly, without having the remotest conception of how it came about. He would be no more capable of understanding the principles underlying its construction than he would be of seeing the other side of the moon, though he is moved by them. Similarly with philosophy, he is affected by the work of men whose names are unknown to him.

It is instructive to follow the career of one philosophical work which has had an enormous effect already, but which was a pronounced publishing failure. In 1910, two of the greatest living philosophers, Alfred North Whitehead and Bertrand Russell, began the publication of a very large three-volume work on mathematical logic, entitled *Principia Mathematica*. This work was printed by means of funds granted by the Council of the Royal Society and by the Cambridge University Press, together with an additional amount out of Russell's own pocket. The edition was small, and a second was not required until 1925—a full fifteen years later. Now, judged by ordinary publishing standards the work was a commercial failure; it did not make money but instead lost some. As I write, the second edition is still available; it has not been sold out. Yet today, there are many textbooks in beginner's logic on the market, the first half of each of which is devoted to the traditional logic of Aristotle and the second half to the mathematical logic of Whitehead and Russell. It is now almost impossible to send a son or daughter to college without having him or her come under the influence of mathematical logic, provided he or she take elementary logic (which is no longer a required course). Russell is one of the greatest logicians since Aristotle, and his effect upon the world through the teaching of logic is sure to be tremendous; yet the work which is responsible for this effect is obscure to all but those who have studied it and has certainly failed to sell in quantities sufficient to afford financial justification for its publication.

Sherwood Anderson said that he had asked Russell whether it was necessary for philosophers to write in a way that most people could not understand, and that Russell had answered, 'Hell, yes.' Russell was quite right: it is. Those who would understand philosophy must work for their understanding, just as those who would thoroughly appreciate fugues written according to the form of the inverted concrizan must have some knowledge of the underlying pattern. That which it is possible to understand quite easily may not always in the end prove worthy, while that which is difficult may repay study with compound interest.

The point is that one does not escape the influence of philosophy simply by avoiding the work of living philosophers.

These men may be queer creatures indeed and their books even queerer, but such men and such books are powerful. To escape them is only to have them delay their effect to one's children and one's children's children. The effect of philosophy is silent but strong, and it is only the wrong philosophy that can have the wrong effect. The philosopher of the day is always a help-less individual but his ideas may be respected for their influence in decades to come.

Philosophy has its own special fields, in the theory of on-tology, epistemology, logic, ethics, æsthetics, and so forth. But philosophical activity is by no means confined to the special fields of philosophy. It enters as an important element into every activity.

Philosophical power is simply the ability to rise to an extended view of a subject.

What enterprise, then, can wholly do without it? The law-yer, the doctor, the scientist, the politician, the teacher, may be successful in a financial way by holding their attention to the immediate problems at hand. But the world was never moved forward in this manner. Would there have been any law or medicine to practice; any principles of investigation to guide the insight of the scientist; any state constitutions to administer; any knowledge to communicate to the young; had there not first been men who had acquired a general interest in their particular field? It is difficult to see how.

Back of those who have for their task the application of philosophy to the broadening and deepening of some special field or its activity, stands the figure of the philosopher with his own problems involving the widest possible generality. He has the two-fold task of construction and of criticism; he is the critic drawing upon the branch of logic known as methodology; he is the systematizer drawing upon ontology but also upon the postulates and conclusions from all fields of knowledge.

In scorning philosophy, therefore, as we have grown accus-tomed to doing, we are not only making the task of the philo-sopher much harder, since he must labour under a burden of derogation and neglect, we are also denying to ourselves the benefits which accrue to society through the fertilization of practice with a refreshed view of the theory from which it springs.

A philosophical position is not a wilful, arbitrary affair. Not only does philosophy choose a man; he is also chosen by some particular philosophy. My own belief has been selected for me by many things. I have been influenced, I hope, by all the currents which flow through my age. Only in this way can I expect that my philosophy will approximate anything remotely like the truth. It will have to be centred around a prominent idea, of course, but reality is probably not composed of a single idea, although many philosophers have thought so. In this way by overemphasis they have succeeded in bringing some forgotten truth to the attention it deserves; but they have not set forth reality in the broad outlines which it reveals to a few.

I am in the grip of an idea. It is not mine but an ancient one in philosophy. Plato was the first to call attention to it, but since his day it has been both misunderstood and neglected. I did not get it from Plato but from hard thinking about the problems of philosophy. When I came to read Plato a second time, for his system rather than for his arbitrary values, I felt that I could understand him because I was already looking at the world from something like his own coign of vantage. The idea is his own theory of the Ideas: that in addition to actual things there are such other things as ideas or values which do not depend upon being actual for their reality. I see this same notion in terms of two realms of being: the world of possibility and the world of actuality. One might call them, as they have so often been called in the past, the realms of essences and of existences; or the fixed eternal order and the temporal or historical order. Everything has a place both in the eternal realm and in the temporal realm; to explain anything is to show where it fits in these two orders of being.

The metaphysical distinction between the orders has helped to explain many things for me. For instance, I can understand now that words do not refer to things directly but rather to ideas which things exemplify. I can also see that the notion of development does not mean that the whole tree was actually in the acorn but that nevertheless it could come from it. The evolution of anything requires its advance from simple to more complex ideas, not merely its actual development from an earlier form. Furthermore, I can comprehend how the knowledge which comes to us from the objective world has come through that objective world, which means that the knowledge did not originate there but beyond there.

I learned from many contemporary studies to accept other metaphysical conclusions. From the history of science I learned that time is never a cause. Science is not seeking a knowledge of matter but of casual laws which act on matter while remaining independent of it. By the knowledge of laws, practical science is enabled to influence and control matter to some extent. The history of science is the history of a search for a causalistic system of natural law which shall be ubiquitous and eternal in its application.

From modern psychologies I learned that less than half of all psychological events can be explained on the basis of conscious awareness. Behaviourism, *gestalt* psychology, Freudian psychology and even the tropistic investigations of classical psychology, reveal the subconscious sources of reaction so clearly that it has to be concluded that the whole *psyche* or organization of the human organism, and not merely the mind, is involved in all responses. The old subjectivisms and mentalisms in metaphysics had counted upon the priority of consciousness. But now the discovery of the unconscious led to the further assurance that classical idealism, or mentalism, in metaphysics could no longer be successfully maintained.

From modern subatomic physics, specifically from quantum mechanics, I learned that the old notion of 'substance', a fundamental conception in classical philosophy and the major premise of mechanistic materialism, is nowhere to be found. The persistent reduction of matter brought the investigation finally below material particles and to the emission of energy. Thus physics has demonstrated that energy quanta and not any irreducible substance must be recognized as the final stuff of existence.

From Whitehead and others I learned that this energy may be organized at various levels, so that physical power, chemical reaction, biological life, psychological thought, and religious aspiration, are all particular examples of its complication. From logic I learned that logic itself and its elder son, mathematics, take their start from the analysis of energy-levels. All forms of energy, or all varieties of existence, prove to be complications or organizations of energy. Thus existence at every level is value in one form or another.

From relativity physics I learned that forceful relations and not the things related constitute the analysis of the physical world. All specifications of spatio-temporal position are relative to some frame of reference, and are absolute only when given the frame. No physical object 'owns' its properties but these are assigned to it by the frame of reference. Thus the properties of objects are determinable as fixed relations. From symbolic or mathematical logic, I learned that much the same development has taken place in the knowledge of logic. The new logic holds that classes having members are more general than subjects having predicates. Once again, properties of substances have been abandoned in favour of classes of relations. Thus both relativity physics and symbolic logic—two widely separated fields of investigation—have joined hands in affirming the reality of relations.

From the history of philosophy, later confirmed by a study of Peirce, I learned that nominalism, the philosophy which denies the reality of relations and affirms instead the sole reality of physical things or of thoughts in the mind, has held sway ever since science, by seeming to endorse this philosophy, has overthrown the limited realism of the medieval Church. Indeed, the anarchic state of affairs in the modern world would seem to be due in large part to the implicit acceptance of nominalism. Science arose together with nominalism as a protest against the limitation put upon the discovery of relations by the restrictive realism of the Church philosophy. The Church wanted to limit the number of real relations to those already known, but science protested that generals were unlimited since their number could be increased through empirical demonstration. Hence the opposition of science to the Church and the association of science led to the supposition that science itself must be nominalistic. But Peirce has shown that science in its search for invariant laws depends upon the real existence of relations to be known and therefore requires realism rather than nominalism.

Relations are timeless and spaceless, and therefore govern space and time. But the field of actuality, the spatio-temporal realm in which things exist and react, is by nature a flux. Peirce, and later Dewey, have indicated the perplexing nature of this actual realm, in which chance as well as law, conflict as well as concordance, play their part. The dialectical nature of the flux has been indicated by Marx, following Hegel. Evolution implies vaguely the understanding that there is a direction to this flow of actuality.

These are some of the chief obligations which I should acknowledge though doubtless there are many others. No philosophy was altogether new or absolutely original. Philosophies are always heavily influenced by what is available from historical and contemporary theory and practice. The claim of any philosophy is to be the widest possible system allowed by the known principles and facts at any given date and place. Thus we have noted that the philosophy which seems indicated at this time by the exigencies of inherited and experienced theory and practice has been forced into a channel which must lie somewhere between crude mechanical materialism on the one hand and absolute mentalistic idealism on the other. Hence my philosophy is not to be assumed as an inspired truth but is to be considered like all other philosophies as a postulated system whose final justification rests upon its self-consistency and range of applicability. Any successful challenge of either qualification must mark to that extent an alteration in the system.

When will the world learn to distinguish between the pioneering (I almost said 'creative') thinker and the routine scholar? It has been easily assumed that all those men who work with ideas, and more particularly with the ideas of others, must be bookworms, dreamy fellows who live in the past and have no connection with the present. In keeping with the notion we have of them, we suppose that they know absolutely nothing about what is going on in the modern world, and that they care less. All their attention is strained to verify certain details which they find in books by what they find in other books. They are in fact the men who write books from other books and not from 'nature'. They generally do not care anything about their personal appearance; they are poor but do not seem to realize it; and they regard everyone not a bookworm with the utmost amazement.

This picture, which I have not had to exaggerate very much in order to make my point, is to some extent a true one. It is true, that is to say, of scholars. One scholar told me that there literally is nothing new in the world. I am very fond of this particular man, but I find it quite impossible to talk philosophy with him. For he is not a philosopher but a philosophical scholar. Or rather, although a philosophical scholar is what he professes to be, he is not that, either. He is a philosophical philologist.

Here is what happens. I make a statement; let us suppose I say that all thingumbobs are universal. I am prepared to go on with the development of this notion when he stops me.

'Just a minute. You have used the word, thingumbob. What do you mean by that?'

I am a little annoyed at being thrown off the track of the argument as well as surprised that I should be challenged for a word that I was so sure we could fully agree on.

'I mean a grumpewitz, of course,' say I.

'Ah,' says he, 'but you cannot do that.' He fancies himself very much the detective. Although scornful of contemporary intellectual developments, he has been much influenced both by Freud and by the sleuth novels. 'You see, a thingumbob has only been a grumpewitz since the beginning of the nineteenth century.'

R

'But,' I protest, 'that is the meaning that Schmaltz assigns to it.'

This is evidently the wrong thing to say, for he retorts, 'A typical nineteenth-century figure.'

His reply is perfectly accurate and for some reason finds me speechless. Then his patience begins; he explains the situation to me as though I were a child of ten.

'Schmaltz, it so happens, uses thingumbob to mean universal, as you say, but he got the term from medieval Latin, from *thingumbobus*, which in the eleventh century did not mean universal at all but particular, the opposite of universal. The scholastics derived the word from *thingumbobolus* which in Latin was *thought* to mean "particular". But scholastic usage in this regard was really a corruption of a Roman usage which made it equivalent to a particular kind of fish found only in the Adriatic. From *thingumbobolus*, of course, it is easy to refer back to Ταριχος ιδιος, or "particular salt fish", which, as you can readily observe, is once more closer to the medieval Latin. We can therefore assume that the transmission was literary, and the change due entirely to textual corruption.'

From that point the derivation, always slightly dubious and open to question, is carried still further back, to the Egyptians, the Persians, or the early Hebrews. My little philosophical point, which was not at all *about* the words I employed but rather about the external references, the *meanings* of those words, now seems somewhat trivial, and I hesitate to return the conversation to it. It would disturb my scholar-friend, who undoubtedly has memorized a great deal in the way of languages and who is able to derive almost any word until it is lost in a mist of history in which its original meaning is suspected of being just the opposite of what it is nowadays. Semantics, you see, is neither new nor thorough.

But, unfortunately for me, I was thinking about the relation between what thingumbob now means to all of us and what universal now means to all of us. I was thinking about a problem in philosophy, not about a problem in history. This, perhaps, is the chief distinction between the scholar and the pioneering thinker. The scholar is concerned with means; the thinker with ends. One looks to the past; the other to the future which his thoughts might affect, and in which more of the truth may possibly be made known.

My scholar-friend does not believe in the objective existence of truth. He thinks that each generation gets its ideas from the previous one, and so in a regressive series back into the infinitely remote past.

The so-called creative thinkers, he contends, are simply men who are given credit for being original because they have left out the footnotes which would show where in their predecessors' work their ideas were first derived.

'If you want to be quoted,' he says, 'don't quote your sources. New work is simply irresponsible work. A commentary is as original as anything else.'

He does not imagine that thinkers get anywhere with their thoughts. The same old problems keep coming up, as indeed they should. 'We never solve problems, we only drop them.'

Of course, the scholars have a valid point to make. Those who criticize scholars as a group are overlooking something themselves. Not every piece of work which is done with the pretension to novelty and without the proper historical underpinning is worthy or valuable. The routine scholar is a man who cannot see the wood for the trees. Into this group fall, let us say, many of the nineteenth-century German scholars. But there is another group at which the scholars may fairly direct *their* scorn, and this is the group which has been called the easy sublators, the men who cannot see the trees for the wood. For them the problems which have existed for centuries to plague the best minds, melt like butter; complexities appear simple, and, in general, solutions are readily attained. Into this group fall men who approach philosophical problems with intuition but without the proper equipment for dealing with the minute and technical details; Havelock Ellis in some of his writings, Unamuno, for instance, and many of the dashing contemporary minds.

It is certainly a mistake to suppose that pedantry amounts to invention. The scholars confuse the ideas, of which words treat, with the words themselves. The reconstruction of the past should, however, never be confused with the discovery (or recovery) of ideas. To suppose that the intellectuals are all scholars is to assume that bookkeepers are the brains of trade. The characteristics of men who pioneer in ideas are not those of scholars but of artists. The intellectual, if he has anything original about him, works with his imagination just as the creative artist does. His medium may be abstract ideas, and his tools words, instead of clay, paint, or notes; but his manner of working with them is much the same.

The mistake of the scholars is to identify the utterer of a true saying with the saying itself. But what is true is true whoever says it. If, for instance, the translators of the King James Bible had fabricated the book out of whole cloth, what is viable in it would still be so. The Jesus of the scholars could be an ignorant man who quoted many learned authorities but became a god through neglecting to mention his sources. The Jesus of the imaginative thinkers is a great religious teacher whose statements depend primarily upon their truth.

We need to have the scholars, of course. They do the spadework on which the imaginative thinkers depend. We need the information they gather, the previously discovered theories and the facts which they record. We need their summaries, their histories. But we need them because in a sense they exist for us. The creative thinker works with the material of scholarship but emerges with something new and valuable for the world. What other purpose can scholarship have if not to furnish material for the work of the imaginative pioneer? Philosophy is foreign to the viewpoint of scholarship yet turns upon it. To the outside world, scholarship and philosophy are indistinguishable since both exist in books. But so do novels. The fact is that there is an important distinction to be made between the kind of exercise which is summatory and the kind which is exploratory, just as we have to distinguish between the historian of science in his library and the scientist in his laboratory. In both cases, the former exists for the latter and is indispensable, yet equally in both cases it is the latter which counts the most.

The contemporary estimation of course has no such understanding of the difference between scholars and philosophers. A scholar is considered an old and fairly worthless if harmless fuss-budget, and so is a philosopher. The absent-minded philosopher, like the hirsute lyceum lecturer, is a fictional character in which the public, which has little chance to meet the breed in the flesh, has come actually to believe.

When I was a young man, not insultingly young, perhaps about twenty-eight, and had succeeded in becoming the author of one published volume of philosophy, I happened to be a dinner guest at the summer home of one of my mother-in-law's friends in the Adirondacks. I was seated between an elderly lady and a very attractive young girl. Out of deference to old age which was at the moment elsewhere engaged, I addressed the majority of my remarks to the girl; but to my astonishment I met with nothing but silence and an occasional half-curious, half-indignant stare. After several more attempts to begin a conversation I gave up and continued the meal in silence. I was having other difficulties at the time, due to my faulty knowledge of anatomy. Trying to detach enough nourishment from a broiled chicken without dissecting it calls for all my powers of attention. Later on, while I was waiting for the heat of the room to melt the ice cream sufficiently to enable me to cut it with a spoon, my silent young companion turned on me suddenly, and said with defiance:

'I knew a philosopher once, but he had a beard.'

I was a little surprised, but I turned and answered, 'Under the circumstances, as you see, I can only apologize.'

Her attitude of defiance altered sharply to one of contempt; it was not going to be any fun to take an undefended fort.

'It was a red beard,' she went on, anyhow. 'He used to write his philosophy on banners and hang them around the wall.'

To this I found no reply, and I was immensely relieved when the elderly lady on my other side remarked that I must be enjoying my summer vacation because young people always rush around so in the country, don't they? When dinner was over and we had left the table, I did not know which way to turn.

The episode stayed in my memory, hanging there, perhaps, on a peg of personal injury. It started me thinking about the whole relationship between philosophy and the popular notion of the philosophers. In the educated popular notion, philosophy is a kind of accumulated private wisdom which results from the habit of philosophers living for quite a long while, and of going their own way all through this seemingly interminable period. It is no wonder, then, that philosophers are eccentric, unable to meet the requirements of social life, and systematically resigned to their sad lot. A philosopher, in other words, is, according to the more literate popular view, a queer but amiable fellow who has found what are, for him at least, good reasons for being contented with his inactive and ignominious role. As though to lend support to my impression of this absurd but very widespread picture of the philosopher, a successful business man who had been a friend of my father's and who felt kindly inclined towards me, said, upon learning the nature of my chosen profession,

'But you are young to be so resigned!'

While knowing better than to put faith in such implied arguments, I was bound to reopen with myself the question of my choice of occupation. Were my ambitions for philosophy so ill-advised? Did philosophizing really mean giving up the struggle? Had I adopted a profession in which, like the clergy or the military, conformity determines rank? Was I cutting myself off from the society of my time, deliberately, because I could make no place for myself in it? Certainly the standing of philosophy in the public opinion would indicate that the answers to all of these questions must be in the affirmative. I recalled that the great contemporary philosophers, so revered by a few persons, were yet unknown to the vast majority of mankind. How many people had ever heard even the names of A. N. Whitehead, Samuel Alexander, and Henri Bergson, for instance? Bertrand Russell and John Dewey were perhaps better known figures, but not for their philosophy so much as for the influence which they had exercised upon the world of education. And how obscure even these men seemed by comparison with, say, Charlie Chaplin, Winston Churchill, or Albert Einstein!

In the light of this reasoning, I looked back upon what I knew about philosophy itself, apart from the men who practise it. At once my old love, my absorbing interest, came to the fore, and the curtain of obscurity and neglect behind which the philosophers labour did not seem to be very significant. Something was clearly wrong with the popular conception. There was nothing to do, then, but to return to an examination of it. Three separate propositions are distinguishable in this conception. First, that philosophy is the result of long experience; secondly, that it is a kind of accumulated private wisdom; and thirdly, that it leads to social failure and private resignation.

The French philosopher, Henri Bergson, published his most important work, *L'évolution créatrice*, when he was twenty-seven; he must have been younger when it was composed. His long career since then has consisted in a development of, rather than in a deviation from, the position he established early in life. Such a career indicates the untruth of the proposition that a long run of experience is the primary requirement of philosophy. Other examples of a similar nature can be found. Frank Plumpton Ramsey, the Englishman, did brilliant work in mathematical logic at an early age; and in our own country Charles S. Peirce wrote papers before he was thirty which have remained among his best. While there is no doubt that most enduring philosophy has been accompanied by maturity, the evidence is that long experience can not be considered the principle ingredient.

Another way to approach this same problem is to raise the question whether it is not intensity and breadth, rather than length of experience, which is necessary. Some persons, unfortunately, succeed in living quite a long time without learning anything. It is, then, not a question of how long philosophers live so much as of what they learn that matters. Where do they acquire the intensity and breadth of experience which leads them to proficiency in their chosen field? Of course, one of the most obvious sources of philosophical learning is—philosophy itself. The philosopher must comb over the history of philosophy, and judge the best work of the past in the light of the opinions of his established contemporaries. This by itself is enough to start him thinking, since he, too, must re-evaluate the past as well as come to a critical attitude of his contemporaries. If he be possessed of sufficient energy and interest, he will then move forward to a consideration, quite apart from the sources which first brought them to his attention, of the philosophical problems which have by now been raised in his mind. He is then well on the road toward making some contribution of his own to philosophy.

This, however, is by no means enough. I have said that he is on the road, not that he has arrived at his destination. For besides an acquaintance with philosophy, he must be at least somewhat familiar with many other fields. He will of course learn much from ordinary dealings with the world about him. He will profit, perhaps, from having his hair cut, from being in a traffic accident, from playing tennis, or from reading the daily newspaper. In this way, he will learn most often when he is least aware of the process. Experiences which he has not expected will force upon his mind exceptions to conclusions which he had previously formed, and suggestions of others which he was far from forming.

There is still another source of information for the philosopher, one which is perhaps the most potent of all. This is science. Science is, so far as human achievement has gone, one of the most dependable sources of knowledge. Science has devised a method which does not depend upon any one individual or upon any one instance of investigation, which employs reason as well as action, and which is therefore the most reliable method discovered for advancing the sum of knowledge. In addition to its method, its conclusions as well as the assumptions from which it takes its start are of interest to the philosopher. And since there are many sciences in various stages of advance, this means many avenues of information which have got to be evaluated separately.

Thus we see that the philosopher draws on at least three sources (there are others) of philosophical information, only one of which involves experience in the ordinary sense of the word. All of course involve experience, but the word experience alone is not sufficient, for instance, to account for the differences—and sometimes the conflicts—which exist between science and ordinary experience, or between ordinary experience and the history of philosophy.

Philosophy has the additional task of fitting together the knowledge that it has acquired. Knowledge derived from different sources comes in assorted packages, which do not at first glance resemble the parts of a whole. It is the task of philosophy to put them together and to show that they somehow belong together, which is to say, form a system. This is no easy undertaking, and it is one performed by no other study. The widest task of organization thus remains the exclusive province of philosophy. That is why some philosophers claim that philosophy is the highest science, the science of sciences; a claim, by the way, which used to be made for theology or the science of religion. The claim is too modest. Philosophy is not the science of sciences alone, although it is that, too. It is, as we have seen, also the science of many other things. Although it has still other functions, it might better be called the study of studies, understanding 'study' to include common experience and all the branches of philosophy as well as the sciences. We have gone far enough to see that whatever philosophy is, it cannot be said to be merely the result of long experience.

Philosophy, everyone will admit, must include a set of ideas held in the minds of men who style themselves philosophers. The philosopher endeavours to communicate his ideas to the world through the media of lectures and writings, but to the extent to which they exist only in individual minds they must be admitted to be private. I have just explained, however, that these ideas come to the philosopher from various outside sources, so that they cannot be said to have originated in his mind. They have clearly taken their start outside him, and, it must be added, in a way over which he can exercise little or no control. His part consists in the selection of what he deems important from the information which is available. He can decide what to use and what not to use, but he cannot decide what is available for use. On this latter point he must depend upon the specialists in his and other fields. Thus the part which he plays in the selection and arrangement of philosophy is considerable, but in the creation of knowledge it is negligible. And as soon as he thinks that he has found and arranged something significant, he immediately endeavours to present it to the world. He means it to be known as a contribution to philosophy.

Thus we see that philosophy has both a public origin and a public destination. It may be routed through a private mind, but was neither created there nor is it there alone intended to fulfill its purpose. There is a distinction between the philosopher and his philosophy, so much so that in some connections it is misleading to refer to it as *his* philosophy rather than just as *a* philosophy, or, better still, as a philosophical point of view which he happens to advocate. This is why the attempt, which has sometimes been made, for instance by Bertrand Russell (who knows better), to explain philosophy exclusively on the basis of the personality and private history of the philosopher, must fail. If we could arrange to sell a facsimile of the philosopher with every copy of his book that is sold, perhaps it would be easy to maintain the identification of the man with his work. But since we cannot, we are forced to draw a distinction. For the man who wrote the book and delivered the lectures will surely die in the course of time. And if his work has any merit of its own, his ideas will continue to live on and to have an influence over other men. The ideas will take their place, either in part or in whole, among other ideas. And since such ideas, if they are valid, are destined to enjoy a longer life than he, they must learn soon to do without him.

One reason that philosophy is popularly held to be a kind of private wisdom is that more than one school of philosophers concurs in this judgment. Today the only kind of study which is regarded as being fruitful of dependable knowledge is science. Studies are venerated in proportion to their successful use of the scientific method. Thus physics stands higher than biology, and biology higher than psychology, and psychology higher than, say, economics. It is quite consistent with these ideas that philosophy should be in disrepute. Men who are in search of dependable knowledge and who know that dependable knowledge must mean objective and permanent knowledge, insist that philosophy is only a kind of private wisdom —and they will have nothing to do with it.

These men of course are not dismissing philosophy, as they so confidently think they are doing. They are only dismissing it in their own *thoughts*, by adopting a certain view of it which is not very complimentary. But this does not get rid of it, any more than the deliberate effort to forget a pain eliminates the pain. What they have done is to adopt a philosophy which they do not develop, but which they accept simply because it appears to them to be true. We have seen enough to understand that philosophy is not purely a matter of long experience, nor even of private wisdom.

In every age certain occupations are regarded highly while others suffer neglect. In the MiddleAges, for example, the most eminent profession was undoubtedly that of the clergy. Today, when religion is a mere matter of lip service, this eminence can no longer be claimed by the self-styled men of God. To follow the history of any high calling is to trace an irregular graph. Philosophy in the days of classic Greece enjoyed a high reputation, as it did again in the Middle Ages. Today, when science has preëmpted this status from all other fields, neither religion nor philosophy seems to have much of tangible value to offer. Both have fallen into the discard.

In such a predicament it is necessary for the philosopher to overhaul the whole question of philosophy. *Should* his study be returned to public esteem? If not, of course there would be little point in making the effort. Astrology, for example, is now in a low condition, but from all considerations it deserves to stay there. Its services should be limited, as they are today, to hopeful actors in Hollywood and nervous investors in New York. But philosophy seems to be a different case altogether. Philosophy does indeed have something to offer—as much as ever, in fact. But what it has to offer is not so evidently tangible, and therefore has no way in which to make an appeal to the modern mind. By this modern standard of tangibility, however, certain advanced developments of science seem rather thin and abstract, despite the fact that they are just as defensible as other developments which are more obviously connected with what is tangible.

Regardless of the justice of the case, philosophy, like religion and astrology, seems to have given way to the accepted claims of the sciences. This means that the philosophers are tolerated but not respected. And it seems to mean, too, that they are condemned to social failure. Yet social failure is a relative thing. A man who dies a failure in his own times may become greatly respected and even revered in later periods. David Hume, the British philosopher, was never highly regarded in his own day, yet in later times he has been given his proper place among the great European philosophers. Our own Charles S. Peirce died in obscurity; even his name is unknown except to a small circle of professionals. Yet he seems now destined to take his place as the greatest mind that America has thus far produced.

It is a symptom of the low estate to which philosophy has come that the philosophers themselves have concurred in the opinion which is generally accepted concerning their study. They are unwilling to attempt any defence of what seems, to them as well as to most other persons, to be an antiquated approach to the fundamental problems of the world. They look enviously at scientists, at business men, at artists, at anyone who is engaged in doing something concrete and practical. In other words, along with the decline of philosophy has gone a corresponding decline in the philosophers. The greatest weakness is displayed in the preoccupation which the philosophers have with themselves as philosophers and with their own profession, to the neglect of the subject matter with which they are supposed to be preoccupied. Envying those who have managed to escape into more respected occupations, the remainder entrench themselves behind personal attitudes and sordid professionalism.

The point is that to the right men this question of fame or obscurity, of public regard or disregard, is relatively unimportant. The true philosopher is not so much concerned with his own destiny as he is with that of his work; and if he is a very great philosopher, he will not even care so much for his *own* work as he will for the field in which he works. This was certainly the case with Socrates, whose interest seems to have been entirely confined to the truth as truth and to the efforts of all those who pursued it. Men are indifferent to their own success in a field in direct proportion to their genuine interest in the field itself. The philosopher should seek to further philosophy and not his own reputation.

The furtherance of philosophy in a day when it is in disregard means the development of a valid philosophy, and the demonstration of its practical nature. We must understand first what philosophy is, and then come to an understanding of what it has to do with practical issues. We must turn once more to a brief examination of philosophy, this time with an eye to its inevitably practical character.

Philosophy is not the property of a set of professional learned men who style themselves philosophers. The latter are simply men who have chosen to make the study of philosophy their life-long career, but they do not own philosophy any more than does anyone else. What philosophy *really* is, or better still, which philosophy is really true, is the secret they are endeavouring to discover for themselves. This, as any philosopher can affirm after years of investigation, is no simple matter. One will be on one's way to the understanding of philosophy only when one understands that the really exhaustive and complete answer to such a problem cannot be obtained in full from any philosopher.

I am going to define philosophy first, and then I am going to try to show what the difficulties are with regard to it. Philosophy is the nature of things. There, I have said it. It is as simple as that—except that *that* is not so simple. Some of the fundamental questions of philosophy are: What are the ways in which a thing can be, how do we know it, how do we feel about it, and how should we act toward it? An important point must be insisted upon which may sound paradoxical. This is, that since we, too, are things, the questions are equally true in reverse. What are the ways in which a thing (such as I) can be, how do other things know it (this I), how do they feel about it, and how should they act toward it? The understanding of this reversal depends upon the extent to which one can project oneself into other persons and things, upon the extent to which one is prepared to take up their position, at least in imagination. The effort to do so is crucial in the comprehension of all that philosophy means.

It becomes evident at once that the true nature of things is their philosophy, which is only stating our definition backwards. If this definition holds, then it follows that everything is a philosophy, or may be said to *have* a philosophy. Everything in existence takes, or is able to take, a certain attitude toward other things. Not only man but all things are involved, or could perforce be involved, in this reaction to other things. Men are always given over to feelings and—a further intensification—to thinking about their feelings. Dogs and other lower animals seem to do very little thinking indeed, although it has been shown that they do some. Oysters feel and do not think, and the chances are that they do not feel very much, either. A stone, which is about as insensitive a thing as can be imagined, must feel a little. It is hard to break but has a breaking point, and it is a thing and recognizable as such, all off by itself in the morning. So I suppose that we can admit that it feels, extremely little perhaps, but enough to make my statement that it does feel hold true.

Now, everyone has—I should have said, is—a set of propositions about the nature of things which he believes implicitly.

[264]

A man to a large extent *is* his beliefs and he could not exist without them. Some of the propositions he believes are held so deeply that to destroy them would almost mean to destroy him; it would shake his sanity as well as his faith. Of course, some propositions are true, while others are false. We do not know the whole truth about the nature of things, for if we did, we would be not men but gods. But among the propositions that we do believe, on the other hand, there must be some true ones. We do not fail to know something true about the nature of things, for if we did not, we would be not men but devils.

The central question for every thinking person is this: to what extent can the propositions I hold about the nature of things be considered true or false? This is a very difficult question to try to answer. Few if any of us know what our most fundamental beliefs are, since they exist below the level of consciousness; fundamental beliefs are very difficult things to discover, and it is these fundamental beliefs, considered as independent propositions, that we wish to examine. Once the beliefs are discovered, and, as propositions, brought out into the light of day, they must be checked against the existing knowledge which society has painfully collected. It is by no means easy to do this, since, with all our knowledge, so little yet is known and the frontiers of knowledge shift every day.

But the problem is made more difficult in virtue of the fact that few, if any, of us know exactly what the propositions are that we wish to check against the existing knowledge. This may sound ridiculous but actually it is not. Belief is not an arbitrary thing. One believes what one has to believe on the evidence which has been presented and which appears to one's reasoning powers to be convincing. One is not free, therefore, either to believe or not to believe a statement at will. The propositions which one holds are not easy to change. The reasons for some of them have been forgotten. Often even the propositions themselves are half-forgotten in the sense that they have escaped from consciousness into a region where consciousness does not operate. Then too, they are hard to deal with: laborious to discover, impossible to dislodge, and difficult to verify.

Thus the first task, in the business of validating one's philosophy, is to discover just what that philosophy is. This may be an easier task for the philosopher, who makes it his profession, than for the amateur, who does not; yet it is by no means easy for anyone. Long practice and a good deal of discipline in catching oneself unawares are requisite for the task. The key to the situation lies in the fact that we act upon our beliefs; and some action, a great deal of it, is so-called unconscious action; that is, it is action based on beliefs not known to be held.

Let me give you an example. A man is sitting on the front porch of a house that faces the railroad tracks. He is arguing, endeavouring to convince some of his friends that he is a misanthrope, a hater of humanity. Suddenly, a child gets its foot caught in a track in front of an advancing train. The man leaves off speaking and runs to save the child's life at the risk of his own. Here his actions directly contradict his claims. He claims to be a hater of humanity, yet himself risks death to save another human being. His actions have betrayed a love for humanity, while his words have denied it. Now, the point is that the man is not a hypocrite. He is not maintaining one proposition while consciously holding another. He really supposes that he believes what he says. But his belief in the matter lies at a deep level in his being, so deep that he does not know of its existence, and it is only when he is called upon to make a decision with regard to action that he uncovers it.

Obviously, such beliefs or propositions are the most important kind. Consciousness is a combined factory and repair shop which fashions new propositions and sends them below, or calls up the old ones for reconditioning. But it is not a mass-production factory. It can only handle propositions one at a time. The deeper level of unconsciously held propositions, on the other hand, is a vast storehouse of beliefs. We know very little concerning it. Like the atom, we only know about it from what comes out of it. The Freudian psychologists have accidentally stumbled upon this storehouse, but they are only interested in the building and not in its contents. They are fascinated by its maladjustments and powers of concealment but beyond a certain point they do not care anything about what it reveals of normal functioning. Which is another way of saying that they are interested only from the point of view of abnormal psychology. This is a limitation on their part which warps even psychology, so that the valuable thing they have discovered does the world less good than it could. But we must forgive them, for they know not always what they do.

I am only insisting upon this point because of the little known fact that before we can discover the true philosophy, we must discover our own philosophy. The order in which we attempt to direct ourselves toward the truth is very important.

Several years ago I was sitting upon a beach in California when one of those retired old business men who had heard about death but did not believe in it, and who had come out to California to live pleasantly, drew his chair near to mine. He had heard that I was a philosopher, and wanted a confirmation of the rumour. Not knowing how to reply to what I thought must be a charge, I tried hard to make my admission of its accuracy sound like an avowal of its merit. I confessed that I was a philosopher. He was satisfied, and so presented the next question which he had been preparing for me.

'In a word,' he said, 'what is your philosophy?'

That was about five years ago. The glorified tourist camp which calls itself a hotel has never stopped sending me folders advertising the wonders which I know, and which it knows I know, it does not possess. And I have never stopped trying to answer satisfactorily to myself the question first proposed by the old man on the beach. I have run on ahead and tried to verify some of the things I believe, but I have not succeeded in finding out just what all these things mean. And the chances are that I probably never shall. And so if I am ever found, sitting in a living room with people who would like to be almost anywhere else, and, as I light one cigarette on the end of another in evidence of my permanent lack of self-assurance, informing them of the truth—the *truth*, note—of certain pro-

S

positions of philosophy, permission is hereby granted in the interests of plain dealing, for the exposure of the whole fraud and the release of the poor people. Because the truth will be that I know only a little about what I really believe, and will be uncertain concerning the verification of even that little.

The practical nature of philosophy consists in the fact that whether we recognize it or not, it is philosophy which guides our actions. If we are to act truly, we must learn first what is the philosophy, hidden in the depths of our belief, from which our own particular action springs; then we must seek to correct that philosophy in terms of what we can learn about the truth. For there can be only one true philosophy that is all-inclusive. The result of following it should be valid action. It seems unnecessary to add that the true philosophy is never altogether known, and that perfectly valid action is only an ideal. But to pursue the proper ideal even indirectly represents the utmost in practicality of action.

If my understanding of philosophy is correct, then philosophy holds us more than we hold philosophy. An entire volume would be required to set forth even the slightest hint concerning the most important of the philosophical problems, yet already we can see what their importance is to us. We do not know what we believe, but we do know that what we believe constitutes a philosophy. That should be enough to make us want to know whether the philosophy which we have is, or is not, the true philosophy. In some respects, certainly, it is surely not, and this will be the case, no matter who we are. And so, to everyone, an interest in philosophy must be a matter of the utmost concern.

Philosophy is indifferent to us in a way in which we cannot afford to be indifferent to philosophy. It exists at a level at which it cannot be hurt. Certain things can happen or not happen; certain beliefs may be held or not held. But in neither case can it make any difference to the propositions involved. The real core of the famous statement that the truth shall prevail lies in the fact that it cannot be harmed by not prevailing but will live to become a possibility again. This is only another way of saying that the truth is indifferent to its accidents, while we who seek the truth also have the accidents. Whether I know that running my automobile into a tree may cause all three of us: the automobile, the tree, and me, grave injury—I say, whether I know this or not can only make a difference to the parties concerned. It cannot possibly make a difference to the truth of the situation, which in this case, let us assume, is a particular instance of the general proposition that conflict is actual contradiction. So the proposition has nothing to worry about. It cannot be harmed, and it cannot go out of the possibility of existence; it will be as applicable in a thousand years as it is today. It does not have to worry about anything no matter how we carry on. But we do; and so it is not for the furtherance of philosophy of any sort, either consciously in the minds of philosophers, or deeply imbedded in the nature of things, that I plead for a better understanding of philosophy.

What I have in mind is rather the furtherance of humanity. The sea does not have to worry about the drowning man, but the drowning man does. And if he has not taken the trouble to learn how to swim, why that is of no concern to the sea. But I should think it would be of very much concern to him. Plato was by no means the first to blame the greater part of the human predicament and its evils upon ignorance, and we today will not be the last. For the predicament is compounded of avoidable as well as of unavoidable difficulties, and it is only the former that can be blamed upon ignorance. That this situation is partly recognized is attested by the swarm of scientists who today attempt to reduce the sum of human ignorance without any wish for benefits to accrue to themselves. Yet science is not enough. We have seen that philosophy which draws upon science has been called the queen of the sciences, but even this title is not sufficiently broad. For once again it can be seen that philosophy calls upon a great deal more than science and goes beyond it.

The truth that resides in philosophy is something like happiness, or like that human dignity to which all of us aspire. It cannot be pursued for its usefulness. Philosophy in its root-meaning is the love of wisdom, and if we love wisdom enough and follow it with sufficient integrity, there will always be practical applications which will result as a consequence of our not seeking them directly. For philosophy is of the utmost practicality, but in its nature is highly abstract. Those who would find an easy road to the understanding of philosophy might as well be looking for the square root of minus blue or for two and two to equal five. The nature of things itself has decreed otherwise. But to give something to philosophy is to get something from it in the same ratio. For it will then prove to be not half so foreign to the amateur as those who were fearful of its mysteries may once have thought.

The renaissance story concerning the middle ages makes the philosopher an alchemist and credits him with the search for a stone which will upon touch yield all required wisdom. Later centuries, those living in the nineteenth century supposed, had ceased to look for wisdom in a stone and begun to look for it within the brain. They reduced all philosophy to psychology, physics to epistemology, and logic to the 'laws of thought'. The mental sciences replaced the philosophical sciences. The way things were known preëmpted knowledge itself. Everybody was on his way toward the inside of the human skull.

But now in the twentieth century, the picture is changing again, this time back to the Greek view of life. Men have begun to see the absurdity of supposing that a chair's existence depends upon someone's knowing it. Human values, like natural relations, have begun to seem also to require an objective basis, and the emotions reveal themselves as reactions to values which stand independent of their apprehension by human beings. With this picture, we may return to the old image of the philosopher's stone, and once more see wisdom in it, not as an alchemist but rather as a philosopher: in the light of the wisdom we have acquired through our investigations of the theory of how knowledge is possible. We can understand now that a man is an entity, like anything else, and even though he is higher in organization than, say, a stone, he is still only higher and not a different sort of thing, at least *not altogether*. Thus arises the useful philosophical maxim that anything which can be said about a man is valid only when it can also be said in less degree about a stone.

When you read a modern philosophical work, look out for the examples; they are often very revealing. Whitehead frequently stops to exemplify some abstract point by saying, 'e.g., a stone'. This is the true philosopher's touchstone, and not the old one of the alchemist, nor the nineteenth century one of the skull. Alas, poor Yorick, his skull has been abandoned for the simplest object in the field, which shares its universality with the stars as well as with the skull, and does not require the terrific stresses and strains that the human brain must have in order to remain alive. Merely to live is to exist for the skull, but the stone settles for less, and can be one with the universe at that level where being and existence are not so very far apart, not because so much perfection is claimed but rather because so little is attempted. There is no final goal in all this, it is true, but there is a philosophical touchstone and so a little truth, at least. The stone can be counted on, which is to say, it can be counted. The ambition of the nineteenth century may well be reversed. We shall be fortunate if we can discover some way in which the mental relations of the brain can live up to the simple accomplishments of the stone. When once we can discover the amount of beauty in a work of art in the same way in which we can now take the cubic contents of a stone, we shall be able to look down upon the stone as something quite humble indeed. But we cannot do that now, and until we can we shall have to continue to regard ourselves as being to some extent at least still in the stone age.

In the light of this last remark it is interesting to note why philosophy has fallen into disrepute.

It has fallen into disrepute chiefly, I think, because it has been outconjured. The time was when the magic of philosophy showed itself in the wisdom of the philosopher. Wrapt aloft in the dignity of his profession, he could utter sage, and to most persons unintelligible, words unearthed from the sanctity of old books. He had theories of the nature of the universe;

he knew the secret of how knowledge itself was acquired; he offered advice concerning the conduct of life. He very definitely occupied a peak from the vantage point of which he was practically unassailable except by the aid of those in his own profession who could boast an eminence similar to his own.

Now all this has changed. The authority has not only been removed from him: it has been divided. The physical scientist is in charge of the secrets of the nature of the universe, which to the ordinary man remain secrets even after they have been explained, for except in rare cases the equations and texts of mathematical physics appear almost as unintelligible as were the profundities of the mystical unknown. The psychologist has taken over the explanation of the process of knowledge-gathering, but since he has done so in words rather than in mathematical symbols, the ordinary man finds more that he can use, and so psychology despite its failure to make appreciable advances has become very popular. As for the conduct of life, there is simply believed to be no hope for any rational analysis of its problems, and so it has been left in the hands of the philosophers, who, incidentally, share the popular distrust.

I have been describing how philosophy lost its professional authority to the empirical sciences. To the ordinary man, there are other and more concrete reasons for looking elsewhere. The ordinary man understands little of physical science but he can and indeed does appreciate very much the miracles of physical technology, the by-product of science. Against the very superior but still human authority of the wisdom of the philosopher, there came to the popular arena the man who could *do* things, the master of the practical inventory. Jesus has said that 'except ye see signs and wonders, ye will not believe,' and the signs and wonders came in a profusion which caughs them tumbling over one another. The light of philosophy hat been replaced by the electric light globe. Sewing- and washing-machines, radios, telephones, phonographs and automobiles, sent mere words of wisdom off the stage altogether.

I am not trying to suggest that these things are bad; quite the contrary. They make it much more possible for us to do what we wish to do; they are incomparable means, and we should keep them for what they are worth. But what is it that we wish to do? Where are we going? Technology has never answered these questions and neither has physical science. They have only given the lie to some wrong answers; but since innumerable answers are possible, the questions still remain open ones.

So the search for the answers to our questions will go on, must go on, in fact, in terms of the only method with which we are familiar, which is the method of philosophy. There is no way to stop inquiry so long as the desire to learn what it is all about remains a need of the human being second only to the needs for feeding and breeding. Inquiry cannot be stopped; but it can be helped. Scientific discoveries have only come in great number in those countries where there is a wholesale devotion to science. Philosophy will only be greatly advanced where there is both immense respect for it and interest in it. Respect and interest cannot be artificially stimulated; we have them or we do not have them. We can acquire them only by becoming convinced of their importance. And we can become convinced of their importance only by looking into philosophy thoroughly; examining its claims and judging of their validity in the light of all the knowledge that we can acquire.

There is no hope for human beings in the world apart from their search for truth. If any proposition can be defended, it is that the infinite being upon whom all the finite beings depend intended that we should try to help ourselves, for why else would we have the power of reasoning? Philosophy can never die, it can only suffer a sea-change. We must learn to recognize it whenever and wherever it reappears, and this means that we must learn to call the new thing by its old name.

Those who from long association with business expect a quick return on their investments must entertain a low opinion of philosophy. Presumably they would have to think the same about some business enterprises. Date trees do not bear fruit until many years after they have been planted for that purpose, and work elephants are not only slow to mate but to produce

[273]

young. Certainly the sooner an enterprise can show profits the better. But as we see that in the endeavours of groups of practical men there are some which require careful nurturing through a long period of waiting, so it is worse for even larger groups and bigger enterprises.

Society as a whole and without collective foresight or conscious planning makes certain long range investments to insure its progress. These investments consist in the life careers of certain individuals: pure scientists, mathematicians, artists, philosophers, even technologists. The outlay is small, and ought to be amortized over a long period. The stakes are high and the speculative possibilities are large: perhaps much will come of the gamble, perhaps little or nothing. Who can tell? The chances are very well worth taking, since what is needed is such a small fraction of the total capital of the society. The scientists sometimes require a pretty sum for laboratory equipment but not always. The amount needed by the mathematicians and artists is pitifully small. The philosophers require almost nothing. One fair-sized publishing house and half a dozen technical journals added to the salaries of the teaching positions in the universities would take care of all the possible needs of a whole rebirth of philosophy.

The whole enterprise and endeavour of philosophy is pitched toward the future. It will not have an effect upon the world of affairs until it has permeated down from the learned societies to the illiterate members of society. Aristotle's writings have had an effect in countless ways upon those who have not even heard his name, and Peirce's will probably prove equally powerful. The process cannot be hurried, and by the same token it cannot be stopped. The artist whose work is not understood at first, if he be truly a great artist with a fresh vision, will in the end teach his society new perceptions; he will furnish them with new eyes in painting and new ears in music if they but wait and be patient with him. The scientist will do the same for abstract understanding. And the philosopher will add to these by taking their sum plus what he is able to contribute himself in the way of the organization of the knowledge of the world as a whole, and construct with them a new comprehension and a new way of life.

But in the meanwhile we are impatient. It is a curious level of achievement that we in America have chosen for adulation. There are many stages in the application of a theory, from the discovery of the hypothesis and the demonstration of the theory to the actual construction of the finished product. Take the automobile, for example. Of course, somebody had to devise the internal combustion engine, another man was responsible for the belt system of manufacture, and still others for the present model. At the moment, a factory turns them out by mass production; and responsible for this is a vast hierarchy of executives, superimposed upon a base of manual labour, from the chairman of the board to the shop foreman.

Now, of course, the financial benefactor of the system is the inner circle which controls the corporation, which is generally the board of directors but may also be the operating executives. In a lesser degree it may even be extended somewhat to include the stockholders. But none of these men are the ones who receive the estimation of an admiring public. The chairman of the board does not deal in physical things but only in calculations on paper; his subject-matter is too nebulous to earn him the admiration of practical-minded people. At the other extreme, however, labour has never been a favourite, either, with the American public; sheer physical power undirected has not seemed to be the carrier of the real.

The heart of the modern industrial system, at least in the opinion of most persons, is the engineer, the shop foreman, the man who rolls up his shirtsleeves and gets things done. Now it is not the man with white piping on his vest nor the man in overalls who can roll up his shirtsleeves. It is the middle man, the construction supervisor, the contractor, the operator, who is in our opinion superlatively responsible for the success of the system. The man who can get plans from someone, money from someone else, and labour from still another source, and produce out of this miracle of raw material a going concern manufacturing thousands of copies of some complicated mechanism, like an automobile, a refrigerator, a radio, or a tank, is held up as the man of genius.

What does this do to philosophy? Obviously philosophy is speculative and theoretical; it, too, starts with marks on paper, but even worse, seems to end there. It does not seem to call forth the best energies of construction engineers; indeed it does not seem to call for action at all. Hence it appears to be quite superfluous. The philosophers in America, with one exception, have agreed with this judgment, and have sought to retain some semblance of philosophy using the judgment as a basis. They have developed an anti-philosophical philosophy, on the one hand, and a philosophy 'of experience' on the other. The anti-philosophical philosophy forgets that it, too, is dealing in philosophy, since a deliberate concern with the eradication of a thing is evidence of some kind of a preoccupation with it. And the philosophy of experience, which stresses only the fact of inquiry, of raw experience, and of learning by doing, forgets that it makes its own static conception of dynamics an exception to its own programme. To learn about the importance of experience from a book about experience is not to have any particularly vivid actual experience in the sense intended. Moreover, if everything is relative, finite, limited and subject to change, as the philosophy of experience tells us it is, then what about the philosophy of change and experience itself? Is it not subject to change into something more stable, abstract, formal and static, according to its own proclamations?

Philosophy cannot be its own middle man. The important thing to remember is that there are many levels of existence, each indispensable. If there were no theory, there would be no practice; if there were no practice, theory would be worse than useless. But the unity of theory and practice can only be purchased at the expense of the separate and independent existence of both theory and practice. Certainly to have a philosophy without any prospects of applying it is the same as not to have a philosophy at all. But on the other hand to proceed along practical grounds without any special theory or plan is the same as not to have any practice at all. For a country under

[276]

construction, the shop foreman is the important individual. For a country which is to take the leadership in cultural advance, the philosopher is the important individual. We have constructed our country; we have the material part sufficiently completed to make it possible to turn our attention to other phases, at least for a while. Those who invest no attention in theory will have nothing to practice later on. Thus philosophy looms as a vital necessity for the planning which America must do for the future.

Let us then not forget the special place which the philosopher has in any civilization. He is the speculator who plans the future. He is the man who belongs to at least one conception of things as they ought to be. We have had such a man; his name is Charles S. Peirce. He has been neglected in favour of James and Dewey. But if I am right that the country has passed through its James-Dewey phase, then it is high time to start the hue and cry of 'Back to Peirce.' James and Dewey are the philosophers of pragmatism, of experience and practical aspects. Peirce, who paradoxically started the whole conception of pragmatism, saw it in terms of a pure theory. He has never been properly recognized either by his own profession or by the general public; but the future belongs to him in a way which the past has not. He will lead us out of the limitation of doing into the greater freedom of thinking before doing. There we will find our leadership and our glory.

It is odd but true that in philosophy a time of low ebb should be chosen for a tidal wave. Never has the general opinion of the worth of philosophy sunk to a lower point than that it has reached in these latter days. Logic, the last of the philosophical topics to be a required course, is so no longer; the departments of philosophy, persistently carried on by despairing and discouraged men, are gradually being reduced in number and influence; and the echoes of abstract knowledge which reverberate from the halls of higher learning to the daily press and the radio and motion pictures, carry a message that philosophy is so moribund it is no longer sufficiently strong even to deserve ridicule. And there is no sadness, for philosophy is presumed to have reached that great age where its death must be greeted with welcome relief.

This is the atmosphere in which a philosophical renaissance has chosen to take place. The Greeks had supposed that reality lay in the vast external world in which man lived but which he had no share in creating. The Church of the Middle Ages accepted this view but insisted that the relation of man to his creator was the only vital point, and oriented everything else in knowledge toward that central idea. Science revived the Greek interest in the external world but did so under the guise of knowledge seeking. Hence in the Renaissance centuries the revolt against inert theology had issued in the name of humanism. The recent discovery that science is consistent with the detached and disinterested Greek view, has led to the discarding of the emphasis upon mind and the kind of external world it creates, and to an emphasis once more upon the external world and its effect upon us.

The philosophers who have been in the vanguard of this revival of realism have been chiefly the Scotch and English school from Thomas Reid to G. E. Moore and the early Bertrand Russell; Samuel Alexander, the Australian in England; the American, Charles S. Peirce; and the Englishman, Alfred North Whitehead. Of these, perhaps the most important are Alexander, Peirce and Whitehead, since it is these three who have constructed philosophical systems. As soon as these systems have their effect, which they will have by permeating through textbooks to the students in universities, and through them to the arts and sciences, and through these to the vast avenues of the public dissemination of knowledge, such as the popular magazines and digests, the motion pictures and the radio, the change brought about in the common view of life, its pattern and purpose, is bound to be immense.

Meanwhile, there have been giants walking the earth and we have not seen them; supermen in the good sense of benefactors, and we have been impervious to their presence. But if we have ignored them, can we continue to do likewise with their works? The man who makes suggestions is easily forgotten even by those who closely follow his lead. But the man who is responsible for the erection of great structures, great architectural systems of ideas, has left something behind him which we can hardly manage to overlook. The great power projects of the last two decades, dams whose physical presence itself is awe-inspiring, the great bridges of San Francisco and New York; Rockefeller Centre; the towering systems of philosophy erected by Peirce and Whitehead: these are the engineering marvels of the day. That all are not equally visible is more of a commentary on our eyesight than on the worth of what we do or do not clearly see. For philosophical systems exist on paper as blueprints for an indefinite future of action based on the constitution of the universe.

The plans are drawn on a grand scale, magnificent in ambition and superb in accomplishment. They are plans for a building intended to survive the disintegrating influence of time. From what we have seen of such attempts in the past, it is safe to guess that they will not survive in all their detail and with all their perfection. Here and there the structure will begin to reveal that it was not all we had thought it; imperfections will begin to show, flaws and cracks will reveal themselves as the framework settles and its weaknesses are made apparent. The marble will chip and the colours will fade. The edifice will be put not to its originally intended purpose but to nefarious uses, and on the whole a great deal of damage will be done to it for which the blueprints and materials, the architects and builders, can hardly be blamed. Yet with all this, the loss will never be absolute. Across the city from newer temples, something will still stand; a wall here, a column there, enough at any rate to suggest what the completed pattern might have been, enough, that is, to have an effect which continues. So that the Eternal Building which the poor fallen ruins had been meant to represent is represented always, handed down from unsuccessful endeavour to unsuccessful endeavour, in a continuity of endeavour which does not ultimately fail.

Much has been restored to philosophy already, in at least two of its branches: ontology or the theory of being, and symbolic logic. But much remains to be done, and meanwhile the reputation of the field of philosophy itself languishes under a cloud held over it in the popular opinion by the common acceptance of the wrong philosophy—one which denigrates and which would disintegrate philosophy itself. Surely the bird that fouls its own nest is not the one to emulate in flight. Yet there are signs even now that a thundering renaissance in philosophy is just over the horizon. The giants really are beginning to appear, and they are no less large because our eyes are cast too near the ground. The dimensions of Whitehead and Peirce are hard for the untrained vision to estimate. Their work is like music, immense architectural structures towering up beyond sight, vast in extent, but lying brick upon premised brick in a tight system of invisible but at the same time irrefrangible deductions. Some day not we but those who come after us will suddenly see what noble dwellings have been erected to house their spirits, and will thank our generations. For what has been made of such lasting materials that it cannot be destroyed is almost sure to be appreciated sooner or later. The world of ideas is impervious to the shellfire by which a culture endeavours to end its own existence. It can neither be betrayed by the appeasement of aggressors nor destroyed in war. It cannot even be sold out in the peace which follows the war. And it will make itself known, and by being known exercise an effect which is greater than the effect of anything unknown.

CHAPTER SIX

To Have Life More Abundantly

T H E first view an individual has of his world is a subjectively-centred one. This is the world of the infant, in which everything is constructed around his needs and requirements, a world that exists only for him and to the extent of his efforts. The second view the individual has of his world is an objectively-centred one. This is the world of the young adult, in which everything is constructed around impersonal forces many of which oppose him and with which he must struggle to obtain what he wants and to do what he has been taught is right. The third and final view the individual has of his world is an independently- centred one, depending neither upon subject nor object. This is the world of the full adult, in which everything exemplifies values and forces which are only partly exercised at any given time, a world which contains favourable as well as unfavourable elements, in which he recognizes he must struggle for things which cannot eventually fail even though they are not likely in finite time completely to succeed. In the first view, all is gained; in the second, something is gained or lost; and in the third, something may or may not be gained but nothing is ever lost. This successive widening of the horizon may be dignified by the overall designation of the dialectic of personality development. I had come at last, I supposed, to the third view. It gave me a certain quiet self-assurance which I had always lacked. Behind my shield of gross egotism I could now afford to cultivate true feelings of humbleness, of hope and even of some slight achievement.

Whenever I walk down Canal Street, which is the main business street of New Orleans I meet or am passed by an old professional acquaintance of my father's. The chances are that I went to school with his son. All the boys who were in my class in elementary school, at least all those of a comparable economic and social status, which is to say, the sons of business men, decided to become shadows of their fathers by engaging in the occupation which waited ready-made for them. Then they married and prepared to raise shadows of themselves in the same fashion. Yet they did not feel like ghosts.

The friends of my father entertain no high opinion of me. Leopold's boy did not turn out so well. Nora as well as Leopold spoiled him. He is rumoured to be vain as well as lazy. Not only does he refuse to do an honest day's work but he is said to devote all his day to writing, which anybody could do who had time on his hands and no inclination for more serious occupations. The sons echo this opinion but add a little puzzlement of their own.

They judge me as an individual but I am critical of them only as examples of a common type. When manifestations of the brotherhood of man are limited to contract bridge with friends, a stipulated *per annum* charity for strangers, and an immodest effort to make the proper 'contacts', the ideals of human life seem fairly remote. I think they have failed to take full advantage of their opportunities, and they think the same of me.

Thus again, there is the whole question of success, which has to be seriously overhauled. I know that if my books brought me money and immediate fame, I would rise in the local estimation. The man engaged in practice—let us say the business man—always supposes that the man engaged in theory—let us say the philosopher—is one who does not have the ability to engage in practice. But on the other hand I must bear in mind that the man of practice either develops a genuine scorn for the man of theory or tenders him a secret envy. Most of the errors of estimation committed by theorists and practitioners stem from a lack of the proper distinction between the relative, and equally necessary, roles of both kinds of specialists. I can only rise in the local scale of values by doing something practical; great theorists are never believed to exist in one's home town. The home town boys are classified as successes and failures of the practical life and failures of the theoretical. In some measure, the practical successes themselves are failures, and the fact that they do not know it only makes things worse, for they are apt to discover it too late.

It is impossible to contemplate the failures in life without some sympathy. They are wanting in understanding; they are also wanting to some extent in ability. Yet the successful ones of this world carry with them an awful responsibility: behind them there stand the nameless shadows of countless failures.

In a way, all men fall into two broad classes. Those in the first class think (and often say): 'I am just an average man and therefore the thoughts which pass through my mind should be interesting to the general public. Now you are a writer; why don't you set them down?' Those in the second class say (and often think): 'I am entirely confident that my books will be famous all over the world five hundred years from now.' My wife, Dorothy, says that there are only these two classes.

What I really sometimes want to do is to go up to one of my old schoolmates, and explain to him that I am one on whom philosophy has taken hold, a dedicated and a public man, and that this is so whether the public takes cognizance of this fact or not.

Here we are, then. I am already the author of one book of poems, six volumes of philosophy and some short stories, all published. I have written altogether three volumes of poems, a volume of short stories, and eight volumes of philosophy. I have planned many, many more, and I intend to write them provided external circumstances do not arise to prevent me.

Were I more self-centred, it is possible that I should be exceedingly bitter by now. I had hoped at one time to contribute to the pages of the French philosophical journal, the *Révue de Métaphysique et de Morale*. It shone like a beacon in the far horizon of old-world culture. The question was whether I was to exist long enough to have my work accepted in France. Shortly after I wrote an article on the work of Charles S. Peirce, the classical American philosopher, and it was accepted and published in the *Révue*, that learned journal, together with the France in which it was a landmark, ceased to exist. It was an eventuality I had not even envisaged.

[283]

T

The social world, the whole culture in which we have been immersed and out of which we have come, has been torn loose from its foundations and has been reeling crazily about. Where it will end we cannot tell. It vexes me that with all my philosophical pretensions I can as yet detect no signs of a direction. The war did upset everything. For all my knowledge of the perspectives of history, for all my familiarity with the abstract principles of ontology which govern existence, I am still as blind as the next man. This somehow would seem to be a severe indictment of philosophy, but I can only defend it by insisting that it is an indictment only of my own powers of observation and ratiocination, not of the whole of philosophy.

Can I retreat from the world upheaval and seek consolation in the library, devoting myself to the search for ideas which are independent of events? Hardly now, when all of us who are able-bodied are likely to be thrown once again into the field of violent action. It is a test, perhaps, to see how much suspense we can endure while still asserting that the possibility of a good life in the future is as firm as ever. Nothing could be more exciting for the philosopher than to find all the old conclusions abandoned in favour of a period of desperate struggle. Why did men who were middle-aged and beyond go to war so willingly? The struggle for existence in this connection can surely have meant nothing personal. Those who were approaching the last period of their lives could hardly have regarded a continued existence as anything feasible, since death in any case is certain and approaches swiftly. Evidently the struggle was not for personal existence but rather for the existence of certain values which are held to be worthy. It is not even clear what these values were. Russia, for example, with its new social order, its revaluation of all values, fought side by side with the capitalist democracies whose aim thus far at least, had been to maintain the *status quo ante*. All of us fought against a people whose values were limited quite frankly to themselves and were not intended for the common consumption. Perhaps this very statement of the situation reveals the values which were involved. I do not know. I do not know at all that such an easy distinction is analytical enough. We must be more specific.

But I do understand, and feel deeply, that, whatever happens to me the next time, I shall feel it intensely in terms not of myself alone but of the world as a whole. I do not mean that I am important to the world; obviously this is not true. I mean that there has been a gradually increasing preëmption of myself by the world. The world has become more and more important and even precious to me. I do not wish to miss a bit of it. I have no urge to retire from its endless conflicts and confusions to a tidy, virtuous and good environment in which certain of my pet values are visibly preserved. I wish to participate in everything. It gives me a pang that I cannot *feel* the joy of the professionalism of all the various activities. I would like to feel as well as to know what the bickerings of the priests among themselves are about; I would like to experience the world of the theatre from the inside; I would adore to be able to talk about interesting cases of disease with doctors; I wish to argue for clients in the courts; to lay a clean and level wall of bricks; to pilot a tramp steamer; to participate in the mazes of crooked politics. The colour and smell and texture of life should not be lost in our journey toward the good; for variety and novelty and mixedupedness have values of their own which cannot be gainsaid. The world is carrying me backward slowly, so that perhaps I shall end up with no necessity for writing about existence but merely be happy to be alive and fully in the possession of my faculties. Certainly except in cases of extremest pain or disease, life is more than worth living.

Philosophy like human beings has its youth, its middle age and its old age. In its youth, it poses questions, in middle age it attempts to answer them, and in old age it discovers that the answer is not yet to be had. I will learn more about this last phase in later years; at the moment it is a guess. Just now, anyway, I am unwilling to admit that I am no longer young, and still I know that in some ways I have not a firm grasp on my youth. There is something middle-aged about philosophy; a maturity busily engaged in finding that some of the answers to the questions which youth had put are closer to home than youth had thought.

In my childhood I can remember sitting in the living room of my parents' home, sighing for greater worlds to conquer: I thought that these lay outside. But I understand now that what is in the room is challenge enough, or even the room itself—any room will do. Let us suppose that someone walks across the floor in front of me; formerly it was my father, now it is my son. Appearances are not deceitful, they do not contradict the true meaning of events. But they lie along the surface of them. In the way of common sense, I see exactly what is happening and exactly what is happening is all that I see. What does the movement convey? To common sense very little; the event is insignificant, on the whole. But look a little deeper. What can be seen? If one is a philosopher it is something of a miracle. The plain fact of motion has troubled the philosophical mind for many centuries. How is it possible to be and not to be at a given place at a given time? The man of common sense is a true believer; to him there is no miracle, only the ordinary happenings of everyday life. The philosophical sceptic, on the other hand, goes to the other extreme, and refuses to accept the existence of any such thing as motion; it is impossible, he says. The true philosopher is one who questions, like the sceptic, but also one who accepts the evidence of his senses, like the man of common sense. He does not want to circumvent the plain and obvious fact of motion; he merely wants to understand it better, to penetrate it to deeper levels of analysis. He believes that what presents itself to him as a surface offers no contradiction to that which lies farther down.

What I have acquired through growing older is a keener sense of the things about me, the ordinary things. Once we were spending the summer on Cape Cod. I went out to the beach with a painter who was our guest. 'The sky is blue after the clouds of yesterday,' I observed.

He corrected me. 'No, it is white with blue in it. The clouds have not gone away, they have merely dispersed. You are not

[286]

looking at the blue sky directly but at the sky through a thin haze. Look again and you will notice.'

He was right. Why did I not observe it for myself? The study of appearances is called phenomenology. I am supposed to know about these things; as a philosopher I must be able at least to see what is in front of my eyes. Yet it is not so simple as all that. We cannot see without tremendous effort, without concentration or long practice. There the painter has it on us; he has a superior sense, and he is not the only one. The musician has hearing on us, the sculptor holds over us his sense of shapes. My respect for the artist increases by leaps and bounds. It is no easy thing, this matter of taking off from nature. The scientist does it in quite another fashion.

Looked at factually, of course, it is all a matter of education. The men of the future will see better because of the painter, they will hear better because of the musician, they will know better because of the scientist. They will adore better because of the saint, perhaps. And because of the philosopher, they will be able to put everything together and to catch a glimpse of the nature of the whole. We have a task to perform, an obligation to the indefinite future to fulfil, we men of the arts and the sciences and philosophy.

To think about this is enough to make me young again, to allow me to recapture all the tirelessness of youth, to plan, to dream, to get to work. So much remains to be done. There is no middle age, really, no growing old. There is only the widening and deepening of interests. All the ultimate questions are unanswerable, I suppose; and yet that is their fascination and their grip upon us. We seem to have been put on earth in order to seek the answers to questions which were put on earth to elude us forever. Yet each time we search something is gained. We find the fragment of an answer, a clue, a hint here and there. And the realization of all this is not merely marking time; it is an answer of a sort. It is a way-station where we are glad to have arrived but from which we must soon carry on.

The range of interests can have no limit, for we know of no limit to being. Beyond humanity there is the world, and I can find no trace of a gap between humanity and the world. People may be the most wonderful things on earth but they are not the only things on earth that are wonderful. Non-human nature, which I so much neglected to consider in my youth, now begins to mean more and more. Often I go fishing in the swamps. We have anchored our shrimp trawler at one end of Grande Isle, opposite Fort Livingston. There is not much left of the Fort except some brick walls, but we can see it from the boat as we ride up and down over the waves. We are in a current, the passage between the island and the Fort not being more than half a mile wide, if that, and the water rushes under us dragging at our anchor. The fishing here is erratic: either you catch thirty pound channel bass—bull reds, we call them in this part of the country—or you catch nothing. The wonderful part of it is that almost anything might be under your boat, you never know. One one occasion, I had been sitting, holding a line with cotton gloves, leaning against the cabin, waiting for hours while crabs ate my bait. Then I decided to light a cigarette, which necessitated removing the gloves. As I did so, something struck my hook, I did not know what. It pulled hard and started down the length of my boat; I let out line, and then when it whipped around I was almost pulled into the water. It passed me in the air, a giant fish, and then headed out to sea at a fixed speed. Nothing that I could do had any effect. I found a place on the boat to tie the line, but then it broke. The experience was like trying to hold on to the end of an express train.

The attraction is the mystery and the possibilities. Anything can come up out of the sea. In the meanwhile, if nothing does come, I have the smell of the marsh behind me, and the infinite open sea in front. I have the sky above me and many birds; in the winter I have duck and geese and in the summer pelicans. Fishing boats pass once in a while, shrimp trawlers, with their nets draped over them like veils on attractive women. I have cigarettes and maybe coffee, and I certainly have plenty of time and nothing to do. I can feel the sun beating down on me, and so I do not have to think very much; I can just vegetate.

It is worth while to remember, however, that there are processes going on whether we happen to be aware of them or not. That is the tremendous and in one sense the tragic thing. It sends me back to the city to do some quiet wrestling with my thoughts indoors.

But just now I am on the boat, half reclining, and riding up and down. I do not have a hat because the sun does not hurt me. I do not think that in this latitude I can be hurt by the sun. It is hot but I do not blister; I only tan and grow darker, and my skin fairly glows with a shine that gets through to my whole disposition. I am by nature a sun worshipper. I look around, squinting because of the strong light. Who am I? It is so difficult for the human being to gain a perspective in which he can see the world steadily and as a whole, with himself or even the whole human race as merely an infinitesimal part of it. We might at this point more advantageously survey the situation of some other animal, say a turtle. Let us, then, consider the turtle and the turtle's world.

Our turtle, let us imagine, is a species of *reptilia*; he could be a member of the *testudinidæ* or of the *chelonidæ* but in my part of the world, the Mississippi basin and the fresh-water swamps near the Gulf of Mexico, he is more likely to be a member of the *chelydridæ* or snapping turtle, *Macrochelys Temminckii*. Let us choose some particular one, say the one which last winter suddenly popped up near the boat from which I was fishing, had a good look at me, and was gone.

There are three things, then, that we have got to describe. These are: the turtle, the particular part of the world with which the turtle comes into immediate contact, and the remainder of the world with which he does not.

Let us not bother with the turtle himself: you can find out all about him in a book about turtles. But I might say this; that including the organization of the turtle's organism, there is nothing inside the turtle that was not outside first. The turtle cannot be understood except as a certain reaction with the environment; he is a limited power devised to affect the environment in a limited way and to be affected by it in a certain way. He is composed of elements which would on analysis prove to be the same as the elements of the world around him; there is nothing, so to speak, peculiarly turtlish about the turtle—except turtle.

So much for the turtle himself. Now about his world, the world with which he comes into immediate contact; it is itself subdivided into two parts. There is the part which the turtle knows about and the part which he does not. For instance, he knows about the water in which he swims, the air that he breathes; he knows about the dangers which lurk about him in the water: the sharks from whom he must withdraw into his shell. But he does not know as he looks at us that we are thinking general thoughts about him, that he is related directly to tortoises but only indirectly to torts, that he has a brother in an aquarium which I may have visited last year, and so on. Nevertheless, these are things with which he is immediately related and his not knowing about them does not make them any the less true. We might say that the world which is in immediate relation with him is part of the world which he directly affects and is affected by. It is a world of powers but it can be analyzed into one of relations. The turtle in the aquarium may not be his brother, for instance, it may be his uncle. This word, uncle, indicates a certain series of relationships according to which one thing has affected another.

Now let us reach out in our fancy and have a look at most of the mediated powers and relationships in which the turtle, all unknown to himself, participates. Every time he moves a flipper he disturbs to some extent the atoms in Aldebaran; it may be only to an infinitesimally small amount, but it does have an effect. Everything in the actual world, no matter how remote or how large or how small, is in action and reaction with everything else. He is indeed a very lucky turtle, for if we carry the investigation far enough we shall comprehend that this turtle is reacting with everything actual and is related to everything possible with which it does not have reactions. Where it does not have positive action-reactions, it has negative relations, at least. Thus the turtle is a turtle by virtue of the fact that there is a sandy shore in which it can deposit its eggs. But it is also a turtle in virtue of the fact that all other things are not turtle. If this chair and that house and these books were all turtle, and if there were nothing that was not turtle, then this turtle would not be the turtle that he is. But since this turtle being what he is depends to some extent upon other things being what they are, they are in a sense responsible for him. Thus we might say that our turtle is nothing more or less than the whole world striving to be a turtle.

What is true of the turtle would be equally true of anything else. A thing, anything: this chair, that man, the tree in the yard, the goose overhead, the wish which is father to the thought, the plankton helpless in the sea, and the stitch which in time saves nine—each is what it is in virtue of other things being what they are. We live in a world community of things on which we are helplessly dependent. There are things which might bring about our death, and other things which might hurt us in lesser ways. This has led us to distinguish in the actual world between friends and enemies. Such a distinction has got to be made, for it represents the true facts. But this situation does not alter the larger one, namely, that were it not for the whole situation we should not be able to persist for a moment. We should be gone in the flash of a second, or, worse still, we should never have existed to begin with.

I am sitting on the gunwales of the shrimp boat. The turtle comes up from the depths for a moment. He looks at me suspiciously, unable to distinguish me from the boat since I do not move in relation to the boat half so fast as the boat moves in relation to the water, and then he is gone under the waves again. He must not have approved of what he saw. Wise turtle; it is my kind which eats his kind or keeps it alive in zoos and goldfish bowls. We are brothers not only just under the skin but also way under the skin; we are brothers in the protein and the atom and we are brothers in the energy-emission. We are brothers under Casseopeia and under the sun and the blue sky.

Does he know of his other family relations? Can he sense those turtles which are dead and those which are as yet unborn?

He belongs with them as much as he does with living turtles. He, and they, exemplify separately and together the idea of *turtle*, which is not merely an idea in somebody's human brain but still another kind of exemplification, the possibility of there being such things as turtles. This is, in a way, the most inclusive kind of turtle.

Now the turtle is gone and the fish begin to bite. What an abundance of life there is here! And yet in a way how limited it is. We wish to have life and to have it, as Jesus said, more abundantly. But there are different ways of gaining the same objective. No matter how many turtles there would be, for instance, the sum of them would still be turtle. To be more abundant in value, in one dimension, means to be more complex. One man may apprehend more values than a million turtles. Yet where would man be without the turtle? It is a lesson we learn late in life: nothing can be omitted, and those things which are higher than others depend on the lower. The turtle is something we might never have suspected; he has his own precious place in the world.

Everything, including turtles, is a fit subject for love, and there are times, at least, when I love everything. I have the soul of a whore but not of an ordinary whore. Perhaps I ought to say it is the soul of a temple prostitute, and then perhaps I ought to add it is the kind of soul a temple prostitute ought to have. I like everybody and everything. God, I am sure, is above good and evil; man cannot be, and there is nothing either divine or human in man which would allow him for instance to remain a pacifist in the face of the prospect of Hitler ruling the world. But there are moments nevertheless, moments in the life of a man, when he can give himself to whatever exists. This is what I mean by having the soul of a whore. He gives himself, however, with the thought, and what is more important the feeling, that that which he is giving himself to at the moment is very, very holy; and that is what I mean by adding that I am a temple prostitute. Everything has more than one capacity, and the capacity in which the temple prostitute serves is always inclusive of the worshipful.

We may at this point remember the branch of philosophy which has been dignified with the name of phenomenology. Technically it is the study of appearances, but I should further describe it as the business of taking appearances with the seriousness which they demand. Things are always to some extent what they appear to be, quite regardless of how they came to be what they are by inheritance from the past and what they aim to become by direction toward the future. This wall, let us say, is tan; it is, then, a tan wall without any other pretensions. It tells us what it is quite simply and frankly. Now, let us forget that it is a *wall*; let us remember only that it is a tan, a feeling of tan which we get from contemplating something outside us, something which is tan. We can, if we will only let ourselves, love this tan; we can give ourselves to the feeling of tan, and the more often we do this kind of indiscriminate loving the more easily we shall find that we are able to do it.

Those who have listened to the pronouncement by the mystics on their experiences can only pause and wonder. It may be so; what they have felt and known may be as they say, but what good does it do us so long as they cannot communicate it? I confess to a prejudice against the unqualified acceptance of the experience of the mystic communicated as the bare propositional recital of fact. Aside from the good faith of the mystic, who may, however, be fooling himself just as much as us, there seems to be no valid reason to believe what he says. The attitude of scepticism in this regard is the healthy one which is brought on by exposure to empiricism.

But there is also such a thing as overexposure: differences become too black and too white. The world in which we live is not simple. There are signs all about us which would tell us, if we only had the patience and the contemplation to read them, that the feelings point to something objective which corresponds to them. The feelings which are aroused in us are instigated by something independent of ourselves. In the case of the feeling of tan, it is the tanness of the wall. It is tan for us, and, while we have no way to be absolutely sure of what

[293]

it is apart from us, it is a safe guess from corroborative evidence that, aside from those who are colour-blind, it is also tan in the same way for other persons.

Some philosophers, it is true, would argue on principle that we have no proof that the wall remains tan when no one is looking at it. This may be so; yet our common sense, and even our sanity, depends upon its being false. The eye, someone has observed, is no part of the visual field, and we can no more go around with tan walls in our eyes than we can with green trees, blue skies, or any of the innumerable qualities of nature. We must in order to apprehend qualities stand in a certain perspective. For instance, we can only see the tan wall of my study when we are inside the house or standing outside near a window. But the perspective only enables us to apprehend what is already there.

For my part I enjoy the tan colour of the wall with something which I imagine approaches the mystic's experience, but in far less degree. What happens to me in sheer contemplation of the qualities of nature, also happens to many others. I have no special capacities and I perceive nothing that is hidden from my fellow men. Many of them perhaps miss the bald assertiveness which is present in every quality. For it is the ordinary things of life which conceal the mysteries. It is not necessary to pull a rabbit out of a hat to discover in the rabbit or in the hat all sorts of extraordinary things: colours, tactile properties, geometrical designs, and life with all the complexities that living connotes. But what others miss they need only concentrate to obtain; that is one of the contributions of philosophy, and it is there for all of us.

I return to the temple prostitute, the aware temple prostitute, and the adoration of phenomena, the love of whatever appears. There is a reward for those who can give, and it consists in what they receive. It is a world, the world in which we exist and experience phenomena barely, that knows no deceits, no illusions. Whatever appears is real. The mirage in the desert appears as a well of water to the vision which has been stimulated by thirst. It is the real image of a well of water. To those who can see beyond, there is no well from which water can be drawn but only more hot sand. But still the well of water remains as a real image and the mirage as a real mirage. Things are what they are and not anything else. There is joy in the realization of the sheer participation in existence for those who in this mood wish nothing more.

The path to the understanding of humanity lies, as we have seen, in descending from the whole of nature toward its benevolent parts. But this is something difficult since we are accustomed through being men to look at the relationship the other way. Just as it is not possible in every case (as it was in mine) to reconcile an absolute filial devotion with the brotherhood of man, so it is sometimes difficult to reconcile the brotherhood of man with an interest in the cosmos. Does the world exist for the sake of human beings or do human beings exist for the sake of the world? This is an alternative which has agitated philosophers for many centuries without the discovery of any adequate solution. Perhaps I should say that both alternatives are continually being accepted, one after the other, and each contributes something to civilization. The difficulty seems to be that no solution is adopted which includes and reconciles them both.

At first glance, the former alternative seems to be the obviously correct one. Man ranges over the whole surface of the earth and takes advantage of as much of it as his wits enable him to. This is considerable. Now he even leaves the surface, and brings up advantages from the first layer beneath its crust, and flies above it in search of others. The animals are subordinated to his will and plainly have come to exist for him, as lower forms of life exist for them. Is he not, then, the lord and master for whom everything was created? Was it not God's purpose to make him the aim of existence?

Possibly so, if it were not for the fact that more affects him than he is able to affect. If we could confine the influences which are exerted upon him to those which exist on the surface of the earth together with those regions just below and above it, then he might appear more important than he does. But, the fact remains, even the surface of the earth is a very small place, literally an infinitesimally small place, in the cosmical universe. We have only to consider the endless reaches of the metagalaxy and the extent of the temporal sequence backward and forward to comprehend that even the generations of human beings occupy a tiny position in space and time.

Such is the lesson which recent physical science has taught us; but there is more. We have learned from biology to support our old belief in the supremacy of the human being: as an organization his organism is the most complex thing we have discovered; it constitutes a dynamic system whose intricacies seem unlimited. But again we may ask, what is it for? Plainly a mechanism so delicate was not designed merely to continue the manufacture of other mechanisms resembling itself, however important a subordinate function that might be.

We have to take into account the endless future and what could happen. So much more is always possible than ever exists at any particular date and place. These people that I know as my own kind, I must devote myself to them, but only in so far as they represent the same cogs in the wheel as myself in a movement that has as its goal an end which none of us has ever been allowed to contemplate. We can feel the final end but we cannot see it; and the name we have for this is religion.

Plainly, the world is more than we are, and if it does not overwhelm us, as it so easily could do in a thousand ways, the reason can only be that in the interstices of probability there dwells an ultimate cause which has designed even the cosmical universe so that we shall have a place in it. There is a sense in which everything exists for itself and another sense in which nothing does. Important as each thing may be, there is always something more important; and both these facts must be borne in mind whenever we consider the phenomena of a sheer humanity clinging desperately by the soles of its feet to the surface of a cooling planet, there to react in every tissue to values, such as truth and goodness and beauty and holiness, which are intangible but which yet have a cataclysmic effect upon everyone who is made aware of their existence. The hope remains that we can pull ourselves up by these values to a position from which we can fulfil our part in the purpose of the cosmos. It is a great duty and an even greater privilege.

The importance of the brotherhood of man can never be superseded so long as we recognize in our neighbours the true fellow-travellers of a common humanity. But mankind whatever its powers will always be something less than the universe. These truths mean that the only humanism that counts is a cosmic humanism. A cosmic humanism will have to consider not only that part of the universe which is useful to man but also man and his mission in the universe and the independent greatness of the universe itself, man or no man. For man has to take the cosmos into account in a way in which the cosmos does not have to take man into account. We fancy ourselves the most important things to ourselves but it may prove to be not so at all. For the distinction between man and the world in which he lives is not anything more than arbitrary, meant only for the convenience of practical treatment. Theoretically, it has no standing. There is no opposition between the world and us; we do not live despite the world but because of it. Cosmic humanism strives to take this fact into account. That is why when forces beyond our control (and these include a great many human social events, such as wars) act adversely to our welfare, we have no recourse except to say with Jesus, 'Thy will be done.'

Somehow involved in saving the world is the necessity for the abolition of false dignity, of pretence, and of hypocrisy. We are presented here, of course, with an almost insuperable task. I know this to be true but I cannot help it. The institutions through which we reach our various levels of worldly achievement, the universities and corporations and hospitals and law courts and other organizations, seem to have been designed especially for the convenience of the stuffed shirts, the men of stiff front, the bureaucrats and office-holders, the rubber-stampers and yes-men. These are the breeds which have discovered how conformity can make up for the absence of talent, how hewing to the line can substitute for originality and daring, and how, in short, the fact that the world is not led by them can be successfully covered up.

During the nineteen-twenties we had a curiously dual situation. The success of American business methods disguised all the shortcomings, and it was believed on the outside, at least, that the efficiency of modern American business organizations went clicking along like the smooth mechanism of a well-oiled machine. The people on the inside did not say a word; for the most part they really were hypnotized. Business made money hand over fist and nearly everybody believed the legends. But the collapse of 1929 and its subsequent effects have been tremendous in realms far beyond the economic. Nobody believes in anything any more, except brute, blind force; for force cannot be denied by any who have felt its destructive power.

On what, then, are we to base our hopes? All of us are frightened because it is so obvious that man cannot live by force alone. We must have some *con*struction, for without it even the destroyers of the future will have nothing to tear down. How can we build? The stuffed shirts are the most frightened of all, for it is in times like these that pretence is threatened and what we really are made of stands naked to exposure. Great strength is needed now, and honesty with ourselves; we must be prepared to face not only what we have but what we have lacked. Our philosophy must be based upon inquiry and the necessity for a constantly revised system of belief. We must at all times keep the accounts up to date; we must understand how everything that we know about is fitted together. But we must not ever regard our knowledge of anything as finally settled. We must be prepared to throw overboard whatever we believe, when confronted with the broader truths of later findings. The respect due to the spirit of inquiry requires that we shall exchange an interest in ourselves for an interest in our work. No matter how worthy we are, we shall die shortly; but our work, if it is any good, has a chance to live after us and to benefit further generations. We must do everything that we can do for the sake of pure inquiry and nothing for ourselves. We must write for the unborn perfect audience, which could exist even if it never does. In this fashion, men of true concern will take the place of office-holders, and we may hope to find in our universities men who do not find today and the truth irreconcilable. *'L'ésprit m'emmerde'* exclaimed Cézanne, who was at the same time an assiduous student of the Kantian metaphysics.

Forgive me if in my eyes autobiography is sin. My flesh creeps when in print I discover the presence of the awful first person pronoun. Of course, the custom is an old one, and many famous people have attempted to record their adventures. What is wrong with it?

Perhaps nothing, for the literary man, the politician, the actor, although even here I have my doubts. But for the philosopher, autobiography is fatal, and this for two reasons.

In the first place, to be a philosopher in any real sense of the term means to have a certain burning interest in an objective thing called philosophy. Since I am a philosopher, I want to find out about this objective thing without *me*. I want to lose myself in the mazes of philosophy, not philosophy in the mazes of myself. It is interesting to recall in this connection that the outcome of eventual importance seems to hang upon a similar evaluation. Philosophers are famous just in proportion to the extent to which their personal histories are forgotten. We know little about the personal life of Plato beyond his failure at Syracuse, less about the market-place existence of Socrates, and still less about Pythagoras and his golden thigh. What remains is chiefly the ideas, which are, after all, the essential parts, of the philosophers. The ideas account for the fact that men are philosophers and not something else. By not writing about oneself if one is a philosopher, one saves posterity the trouble of concealing the details, of losing the book in which one may have written them down, of forgetting so much that is unnecessary and irrelevant. For biography is a burden to posterity, which, in retaining its wealth of artistic and scientific works, must also carry the extraneous details of the lives of those who were originally responsible for such things. In other words, personal oblivion, when coupled with good works, is a short

[299]

U

cut to posterity. I was tempted to take it until I saw that by so doing certain information which ought to be rightfully in the possession of posterity would be lacking, and this put me back where I started. Destiny is even harder to anticipate than chance.

The second reason (I promised two) is that in writing about oneself one would be writing about nothing, literally that. The self is nothing except a network of reactions to and relations with things in the outside world, a world which of course includes also the human body. Take away these reactions and relations and there is nothing to describe. Even one's most private and inward thoughts are at least thoughts about something, and that something even if it happens to be other thoughts, must eventually refer outside to its correlates in the external world. Concentration upon the self as upon nothing, then, is futile. It denies the world and affirms only itself; it is barren, sterile, and wholly undesirable. So nothing entirely subjective is really worth while. The self taken by itself is evil Eastern mysticism has a corner on the self-contemplative commodity; let us leave to it the entire output.

Please remember, then, that whenever I have used the pronoun, I, or referred to myself in any way, I did so in general, never meaning less than one instance of a relationship of which the other end is the most important. I wanted to connect up some things in the modern world—and some other things which are not dependent upon the modern world—and I found that I could best do this by bringing in a connective and then hoping that it could be slipped out and only the connection kept. I have said: 'thus and so happened to me', but I wish remembered only that 'thus and so happened', or, better still 'thus and so could happen'. Do I dare to hope that it will be translated in memory, 'thus and so ought (or ought not) to happen'? An autobiography of this sort is not intended to be about a person but about his times. The abstract ideas which find their way into notebooks in this fashion get themselves on permanent record.

In this book I had hoped to take the reader inside a philosopher's mind. My purpose was not to show how it works, because I am not sure a philosopher's mind works differently from that of any other person. To believe that anything could be examined all by itself and without reference to the part of the world with which it interacts would require a prior belief in the kind of philosophy I do not happen to hold. My purpose was rather to take the reader inside a philosopher's mind in order to see how the world looks from that perspective. We are all to a large extent products of what lies about us; and it is not so much a question of what we are as of where we look from, since we ourselves stand in certain points of view or perspectives. I for instance am the view from James Feibleman; I am to a large extent the peculiar way in which I happen to see the external world. Since James Feibleman happens to be a philosopher, it should be (whether it is or not) helpful to those who are not philosophers to catch a flying glimpse of how such an occupation eventually forces a man to view the world in which he lives.

Philosophers are not exactly common in these times, if indeed they ever were. We do not incline toward them; we do not place much hope in the products of their labours. Rather do we put our faith in the findings of the natural sciences, in men whose method promises to produce some concrete results; and we tend to regard philosophers either as holdovers from the theological middle ages when they had a certain important position as the servants of religion, or as disappointed men of action who had adopted a strange means of consoling themselves for their failure.

Before we proceed any further I had better insist again upon an important distinction. The one I have had in mind is that between a man and his work. Most artists will not agree with the distinction; most scientists will. It seems to me, however, to be a clear one. A man may be a philosopher; let us say that he writes some volumes of philosophy. The question, then, is, are the books to be identified with the man? Obviously not, since the books are books and the man is a human being. Is the philosophy contained in the books to be identified with·

the man? Equally not, for although the books and the man may overlap in that both may hold the same philosophy, they are not the same thing. Both man and books are in this connection simply receptacles, so that the books hold only the philosophy while the man may hold many other things. If he has written the books some while past, he may, or he may not, continue to hold the philosophy; he may come to regard the books almost as though they had been the work of a stranger. We must in all cases reckon with the fact that a man is many things. However consistent he may strive to be, and this is one of the primary aims of the philosopher, he is still a walking mass of contradictions implicitly or explicitly held. If his work is consistent, he cannot be entirely identified with it, since he is not so himself. He will have many things in his mind, in his memory, and even in his character, which may be alien to this work and his point of view. It is possible and even quite common for the moral man to have many immoral desires. Such facts require and indeed demand a distinction between the man and his work.

In the case of the philosopher, we must distinguish between the man and the philosopher. It is the *philosopher* who sees a metaphysical proposition in the simplest thing, say a lighted match. It is the æsthetician who sees in a film tragedy an acceptance of the nature of things. But it is the *man* in his other aspects who cuts himself shaving, who loves to see his name in print, who turns around to watch a pretty girl, who ties his shoelaces in the morning. What the man does may be viewed objectively by the philosopher where both man and philosopher occupy the same actual and physical person. Conversely what the philosopher does may be viewed objectively, and endorsed or condemned by the man. In this book, I hope I have taken you a little way inside the philosopher's mind and shown you how the view looks from there. I hope that you have noticed that it is a tall tower you were in, and that the philosopher himself was out at the moment—although it would hardly do for me to call your attention too obviously to these things.

I have a friend who is a photographer. Like most artists who are extremely worried about the necessity for keeping up with the latest fashions in art, he is extremely serious and has no sense of humour. Like most inferior artists, he identifies himself with his work rather than with its audience and so wishes to give the latter the benefit of his intimacy with the pictures he has taken. The result is that a lecture goes with each photograph as he shows it. The photographs are quite good; the talk, as you may imagine, is very bad. He refuses to distinguish between himself and what he has done. He wishes to maintain the connection; this is the Pygmalion error.

I tried to explain to him that in the light of his own aims and ambitions he was making a serious mistake. He wishes his photographs, or works of art as he prefers to call them, to be immortal. Now, clearly he himself is not destined to live for ever, for as it has been bruited about, all men are mortal. This means that sooner or later his pictures will have to lead a life of their own if they are to get on in the world, for he cannot always be with them. I tried to explain to him that his method would be very satisfactory provided he could sell a copy of himself with each picture that he sold; but he does not understand this. The lectures and exegesis continue. They do not hurt the intrinsic merit of the pictures, of course; but they make one hope that the work is better than the man, for if it is not it will share Socrates' mortality with him.

Artists in general are afraid that what they have done is not unique. They wish to believe that their work is as extremely original as anything could possibly be, and that if they had not done it nobody else could have. This is possibly true, but not exactly admirable. The scientists feel otherwise. They truly believe (if they are true scientists) that what they have done would have been accomplished by someone else if they had not come along to do it. This is not only proper modesty; it is also proper egotism, since it identifies the man with the nature of things rather than merely with his own work. It means he believes that nature, and not merely his own genius, has called him to his appointed task. The artist is thus thinking only of himself and his position is unwittingly modest, while the scientist in thinking only of his work is unwittingly vain. That is why I prefer the point of view of the scientist.

The American philosopher, Charles S. Peirce, remarked that philosophy must be dull to be deep. I hope that in this book I have avoided both qualities, which ought to be saved for my technical works. Here I wanted to be as deep as I could without being dull—let me put it that way. I hope that I can interest the reader in philosophy. For the whole work has in a sense been shop talk. That was the plan, anyway. For I know that in the course of it, I have been unable to avoid a great deal of auto-biography and a little philosophy. I wanted to show you what it means to be a philosopher in our times and I knew that this would have been quite impossible unless I were willing to show from my own life how I came to be a philosopher and from my own ideas what kind of thing a philosopher is likely to develop into nowadays. But at the finish of these pages it should be remembered once more that the introduction of autobiographi-cal details was always done with an ulterior motive. The details of my life are relevant only in so far as they serve to illustrate a point I think ought to be made concerning the development of a philosopher. Likewise, the introduction here of philosophy itself has an ulterior motive. It is the only chance I have had to present my philosophical point of view and to show its practical relevance without having to lose myself in difficult arguments and proofs.

In my more technical works I am talking to professionals whether they are listening at the moment or not. In this work I have been talking to anyone who will listen whether anyone is listening or not. Consequently I can plead the efficacy of my philosophy with more emotion and breadth of view simply because I am not under the necessity, as I always am in pro-fessional books, of clinging to the minutiæ of argument. Here I trust we can see the wood for the trees without proving anything. For I have preferred to take my holiday from technical philosophy in explaining my trade as a philosopher. The success of this venture will depend upon the extent to

which the reader will be entertained, and while being entertained, acquire consciously or unconsciously not only a little
respect for what philosophy could be but also a little philosophy.

Plato was correct in thinking that the philosopher is a leader.
Leadership among true Christians consists in the ability to
make self-effacement prominent. We must learn to cherish our
own unimportance as a treasure, and to regard the utmost
disaster as a proof that God is in his heaven. And above all we
must learn to do this without undue concentration upon the
self. At the same time, we must exercise a firm and strong hold
upon our own being if not upon our own existence.

We have been fooled to the top of our bent by the inference
contained in the Socrates syllogism, so often quoted in the
textbooks of logic and intended only as an example of the
syllogism in Barbara. 'All men are mortal; Socrates is a man;
therefore Socrates is mortal.' We are all apt to fancy ourselves
little Socrateses. If Socrates was mortal, then no doubt so am I,
even though this conclusion rests upon nothing stronger than
the inferred mortality of all men. For the mortality of Socrates
rests upon the mortality of all men which is by no means
proved; there is only a high probability in its favour.

Perhaps it would be much better to go upon the assumption
that we *may* be able to live for ever. The attitude of hope produces a more constructive kind of life, and perhaps will lead to
someone's immortality if not to our own. The assumption that
all of us must die is not only depressing but shuts doors to
investigation—always a dangerous thing to do. We will never
discover in our investigations what we do not imagine even to
exist. Until the inevitability of death can be logically demonstrated, it is a preferable arrangement, at least for the purposes
of inquiry, to assume the opposite as our hypothesis.

We should start, then, from the proposition that no living
men have been logically disproved immortal. As for me, I have
every intention of living for ever, and if I do not do so, it shall
be because of forces which lie beyond my control. If I do not
live so long, at least it will not be through any shortsightedness
in my intentions. The only thing to do, for a rational creature

who wishes to keep his head in the air as well as his feet on the ground, is to walk hopefully toward the infinite future.

Armed with such resolution I face the prospect of war. The man of peace, the conscientious objector, is in most cases a very intelligent person who despite the sincerity of his conviction holds his own life to be dearer than that of his fellow man. He does not understand that to go to war does not mean to love fighting or even to be devoted to hate. It means in most cases a very superior kind of love. That is why in war time so many people, at least all those on the same side, find out how much they love each other. Then again, life is cheap, even one's own life. Logic and our hidden premises make certain demands upon us. We find that we can die for things we could not live for. We are quite willing to sacrifice our precious lives for causes to which we would be quite unable to devote years of vigorous peaceful effort.

This appears to be a paradox but it has perfectly good reasons. Those of us who live best or who die best do so on instinct. It is not possible to act from logic directly—nor, for that matter, to escape from the logical consequences of our actions. The persons who have earned for logic a bad name are those who fancy that having arrived at a logical conclusion they have only to act upon it. But action should be from feeling rather than from reason; the feeling itself is based upon anterior reasons. The reasons *behind* feelings are sounder and more profound than those which we hold consciously. We may have long ago forgotten the reasons for our feelings, but they are there none the less. Lucky is the man who is perfectly familiar with his own beliefs, if indeed he exist.

But wiser is the man who says, 'I know this thing is to be done, but do not ask me why.' The conscientious objector is a superficial reasoner whose deductions are taken from insufficient premises. He is a species of the genus rationalist, the truly irrational person. We know his kind and find him duller than most. He is accustomed to planning his life in rigid ways far beyond the normal. He is committed to the programme of everything in proportion but nothing in excess—except perhaps regularity.

We all know in a vague way what it is we want out of life, and this vagueness can itself be an exaggeration, though not necessarily so. The vague is not only the ambiguous; it is also the general. Values will not be pinned down; when they are, they are not values any more but relations. Logic is not built entirely upon relations; and that is why, in the logical thinking of those whose premises are insufficient, they appear to be the most illogical. It is a pity that logic must pay the price in the popular estimation that is earned for it by those who use it badly. No matter how rigorous one's deductive steps, if the premises from which one starts are not sufficiently wide, the conclusion will be absurd. And to follow absurd conclusions simply because they are conclusions and despite their absurdity may seem logical but actually is not. Most men are men of good will and must be left to follow out their own intuitions. The saying that a little learning is a dangerous thing can be given a narrower and more strict interpretation by adding that we can only successfully follow the rules of logic when we know them so well that we can for all practical purposes forget that we have ever learned them. The fear of certainty is also the beginning of wisdom.

The young man, I suppose, is always a dogmatist. One of the best criticisms I have ever heard was made to me after an argument of words in which toward the end my adversary had become genuinely angry. A friend who had been present but silent said to me later that my difficulty was that I had been right.

'It is not good,' he said, 'to be always right.'

In this, as I realized afterwards though perhaps not at the time, he had shown his own wisdom. Logic has got to be approached circumspectly and with feeling. It cannot be approached with any very matter of fact and literal point of view. For only half of life is logic; the other half is value. Being was defined by Plato as the power to affect or to be affected. It is this kind of value to which I am referring. Plato had in mind of course more than merely physical power. But it is power that yields logic by means of analysis. Logic can only give us the relations of power and can in no wise substitute for it.

I remember at the outbreak of the last world war having felt that when a man is asked to soldier for his country and so perhaps to die for it, there is no time for cool and collected consideration; there is merely time for action. We know that wars are wrong, that human differences ought to be reconcilable by mediation and persuasion. We know equally well that nobody wins a war, that wars are lost but never won; yet we do not wish our country to lose. It is a thing that we feel we want to do, to fight for our country. Somehow, there is no contradiction here between what we know and what we feel. And so we plunged in, gladly, willingly, understanding that although wars mark an interruption of normal pursuits, a break in philosophical discovery, yet somehow, despite the fact that we ourselves may have died, philosophy would be continued, possibly even because of our efforts; so that in dying we may have been serving the best interests of philosophy. Who knows? These things are as yet hidden, since we have our feelings and nothing else to rely on. If we have been given the proper kind of education and development through the years, then perhaps our feelings will rest on sound reasonings and will lead us aright. In the meantime, it must be as it will be; we can only move ahead.

We have reached today, or the end, of our story. Neither is finished, and if our hopes are to come true they never will be brought to a close. What does it mean to say that time will not stop? Nothing that we can picture surely, yet something very dear to our hearts. For we know that only in an infinite future can the mistakes and shortcomings of the present be rectified and perfection attained. My purpose in writing this book has been to show how out of a practical America and its immediate problems philosophy could emerge as naturally and unforced as day follows night. That is why I have gone through a personal tale with all its details, conventional and apparently insignificant. It is important just now—it would be important in any period—to illustrate how the philosopher, like the artist and the pure scientist, can be and inevitably will be a native product of these United States, as much so as Indian corn and baseball, as undeniable as the droughts of the middle west, the sunshine and fogs of California, the heat of the south and the cold of the north. I was born in New Orleans, and my philosophy, like myself, emerged from influences of the Louisiana environment as so many muskrats do every year. The farmer, the regional novelist, the poet, the philosopher, can no longer be considered in a maturing country to be alien freaks. They must be recognized for what they are: inevitable products of a rich and abundant soil. We can no longer afford to believe that only those things which remain close to the soil have legitimately sprung from the soil. Other things which manage in time to rise above it also sprang from it and retain their ties with it, like captive balloons which allow a far vision but depend for what stability they have upon the slender cable which connects them with the surface of the earth.

If this book has a moral, it is that a part of America's coming of age will mean becoming accustomed to having its share of artists and theoretical scientists and philosophers. The United States is an adult country now, which implies that, in addition to feeding and breeding, its citizens have set aside some of themselves for the express purpose of inquiring, so that the total population will have not only food and shelter and children but also their share of discovering what their world is all about. The search for reality motivates us all, though many of us never realized it and some will not admit it. But what we are is quite independent of what we know; self-knowledge is such a problem with many that no further goal is even envisaged. Then again, the problem of mere existence, of earning a living and finding a mate, usurps a great proportion of our waking time. Fortunately, what is important may not be judged by the number of hours it does or does not consume. What we wish is never represented adequately, and frequently not at all, by what we do. So that it remains for

[309]

others to tell us what we are really after, even though they interrupt us in the midst of our search to do so.

Life is a very complex affair; we understood its magnitude readily, but education and advancing years slowly make us acquainted with the enormous degree of its intensity. It is the terrible intensity, the very burning, of existence, that turns the most febrile of us away from the affairs of the everyday world, and toward an attempt to steel ourselves to be strong enough for the strain of even standing in the presence of that awful power. Look what has happened to the scientists; analysis has led them down and still further down, into the presence of unbelievably infinitesimal units of matter and energy; or they have looked up toward the impossibly large extension of the physical universe. Everywhere there is a receding background to be explored, a yawning cavern of endless inquiry where once possibilities had been thought to be rigorously circumscribed.

In America there is tremendous power; let us apply it where it will accomplish the most: to building a culture with a base line higher than anyone has ever before envisaged. The material means will insure that no one goes hungry or unclothed and homeless, and from there we shall start, not end; we shall go on toward new discoveries of laws that science will find, and new values that æsthetics will uncover. We shall have music that vibrates in other dimensions, broader and more complex and at once simpler than what we have today. We shall have imaginative motion pictures, with scripts that read like *Faust* or the *Divine Comedy*. We shall have poets whose writings seem hardly to require language at all, so keenly do their rhythms and meanings stretch and strain beyond it. We shall have philosophers whose architecture of ideas towers above all other enterprises in an invisible and silent miracle of construction. And that is not half of what we shall have.

I feel within myself an endless force and a gigantic future. There will be books, books which are entirely planned and merely require to be written. Only, let it be known that these books and this force are not mine. They did not originate within me or through any conscious initiation of my own. I am merely the passive agent, used by the ethos to inscribe itself in the customary forms. I do not intend by this interpretation anything mystical, secret or strange. Quite the contrary; nothing could be more matter of fact and usual. I am after all a function of the world about me; my books like myself issue from New Orleans, which is in Louisiana which is in the United States which is in North America which is in the Western Hemisphere which is on the surface of the earth which is part of a dead planet which is a satellite of the sun which is in the nebula of the Milky Way which is part of a constellation which is part of the astronomical universe which is part of the actual world which is part of the possible world which is the sum total of dependent being which owes its existence to an independent being, of which we can know nothing except the necessity for assuming its being. This is the series of dependencies upon which myself and my work rely. Should I not be humble rather than proud? Must I not feel some hope in my attainment, when I know that it pours itself out in such fashion after having been brought to bear in such a way? On the other hand, there is much abundance in the universe and many dust clouds and dark nebulæ appear to be thrown off just for the greater glory of chance happenings. All that can be said in the end is that we were constructed to suppose only what is supportable in the way of beliefs, and the proportion that anything comes into existence for no purpose at all will never find its way among those other propositions which make up the sum of human beliefs. We are alien to the neglect of anything. But if it is so, or if it is not, we can only bow our heads silently, or look up and laugh gladly, and think that it is well.

What kind of a world are we going to look for, what is it fair to expect? Viewed narrowly from a matter of ethics (and no social event can be said to have only one kind of occasion), the war produced the social breakdown which was inevitable from such a multiplication of false relations. Dishonesty in order to be viable must always depend upon a larger background of honesty. If everyone were to engage in stealing what everyone else had, the result would be to put us back to our original position. The matter is well illustrated in certain correspondence courses—how to have a magnetic personality, for instance. Suppose that there were such a thing as a 'magnetic personality' and that it could be acquired in this way. Then if everyone acquired a magnetic personality, we would be exactly where we were at the start: there would be nobody to magnetize. No, a magnetic personality to be successful requires a number of unmagnetic personalities upon which to work. It is an affair of simple arithmetic involving a limited series.

In international relations, we seem to have reached the same impasse. The war, regarded from this point of view only, seems to have been the logical outcome of political double-dealing. I am not suggesting, however, that this is the only way to look at it; many other factors were involved. But the point does have a bearing on the social world we wish to construct now. Nothing could be established through hate and conflict, although these are necessary enough in order to clear the ground for the establishment of something better. But what that better shall be is still a problem. The philosopher does not have the task of describing it in detail; probably he could not. What he can do without the likelihood of error is to set forth some of its broader requirements. He can state safely, for instance, that it will have to be founded on love. He can say that it will have to involve ideal and remote goals, goals which ought to be striven toward; he can say that it will have need of ideal ends and aims.

There is no man who has actually fulfilled all his potentialities and this statement holds for nations as well as for individuals. America is young or old; that does not matter. What lies before us is what counts. We have the land, the energy, and the people, to do great things, to help not only ourselves but the rest of the world; by example but not only by example: by concrete actions as well. The problem is large and constitutes a challenge; we are not afraid of it. We are not finished because we have not yet begun. We will see if we watch and if we wait what we can do. The past of the world is long, but not as long as the future which stretches into illimitable time before us. Watch us, watch for the values which we shall actualize. The world will outlive us as it has outlived everything else; nothing is as long-lived as the world. But we will live out our life, and we will outlive our cold wars We will find room for a love that will exceed anything that has ever gone before and that will be remembered and emulated in times to come. That is the role of which we are capable; it is also our destiny.

It is ended. War and the death of many men raised an endless question. I return to the theme of my childhood through the prospect of little children innocently standing by in a world at war. The question which reads, what is it almost all about? fades into the background for the time being, although it is still there. In its place there is the question, what ought we to do?

The answer is not so easily forthcoming. In a total war cold or hot most of us on both sides will be told what to do. Yet somehow that does not answer the question. It is more fundamental than that. We shall of course do exactly what we are told to do by our government. But since not all things can be pursued directly, the feelings we shall have about it, over and above what is normally to be expected, are hard to predict. All art, philosophy and even pure science, emerged from a superabundance of life. They are what we have left over after we have discharged our duties as citizens, fathers, sons, doctors, lawyers and taxpayers. In a time of crisis, the same problems remain. As citizens we are called on for violent actions and we willingly comply. But what are we to think and how are we to feel about existence as a whole? This complicated question is not solved by the immanent presence of intense life and intenser death.

There is perhaps no final answer yet discovered. It can be stated, however, that there are certain indications. In the brotherhood of man we owe enormous loyalties. We owe allegiance in the first place to everything in the world. Then on top of that and resting on it we owe allegiance to our fellow men and what they stand for. We fight against some of them for the greater good of most. For it is the sum of living men that we must bear in mind.

But is that all? Are there no other loyalties? Indeed there are; for the majority of mankind is comprised in the great company of the dead and perhaps in the even greater multitude of the as-yet unborn. We owe a fealty to them also. Are not men brothers despite the fact that they may not inhabit the same generation? Do we not, for instance, often feel closer to an historical figure than to living persons? There are so many more of our fellows out of the world than there are in it. We travel with a goodly company, albeit a small one: some several billions at the most. But what are they in number compared to those who have already gone out of the world and those who are waiting to come into it? In deference to the absentees, we should do nothing wrong. Leave your hotel room clean for the next guest. Turn your key in at the desk before you depart. It is a courtesy that we can extend to others.

Meanwhile there are the little children. They play, blissfully ignorant, as they should be, of the world. What are we building for them? How can we explain to them the kind of world in which we had hoped they would come to adulthood? Fortunately, they are not the last of an effort but the first. They are the vanguard of an army which shall recapture peace and culture and all the good things for which we, too, had striven but failed to hold. Perhaps they will in the end be wiser than those who can only work now and wait. All will be well.

We are faced with a divided world, and there is nothing to do now except admit it. We may want one world but that is not what we have, nor do we seem to know how to get it. Politics, as the Marxists would readily admit, is an extension of war in the direction of economics; but is that what it ought to be? Where are the values for which the artist, the scientist and the philosopher have endeavoured to stand? Their disappearance at the moment is the occasion for the despair of my generation. Many of my contemporaries are willing to fight because they feel that less will be lost if we win than if we lose, but they believe that, either way, most will be lost. I cannot think their thoughts nor feel as they do. Nothing of what they hold most dear can be lost because, as they mean it, nothing could ever be saved. We cannot fairly look to the recent past for comparison with our own times, any more than we can look to some golden age in the remote past. The present does not exist for the past but for the future. What if there is some difficulty now, it will not remain. Bad periods, like good ones, cannot exist for ever, and the things for which we fight, even if they vanish temporarily, must return.

We are taught by the philosopher to reverence the being of love and to regard hate as merely a shortcoming of actual existence. The same, we are told, is true for good and evil. Yet those of us who are caught up in the thick of things find that we must be preoccupied with hatred and evil, with opposition rather than affirmation, with conflict rather than concord. Where, then, is the superior reality of the positive values?

The answer is that they cannot be directly pursued, except in hostility to what contradicts them, and that they stand behind every action we take. Why do we challenge evil directly, if not so that we can clear the ground for the good and thus accomplish the good indirectly? We wish to eliminate what we hate only in order to make way for what we love. We plunge into the conflict boldly so that afterwards there may be harmony. And as we make our fight actively against the objects of our hatred, love is our silent partner, the thing for which we fight. The invisible force of love standing at our elbow is still the most powerful of all the powers that be. It is not hate that we fight against but love that we fight for, and love will survive everything else in the world.

Love is so vital that it makes even hopeless struggles worthwhile. The struggle where victory is possible is a struggle for triumph; but there is also the struggle for survival. The actual continuity of the things for which we care may be desirable but it is not absolutely necessary. To disappear from existence does not mean to melt out of being. And what has being may

[315]

return into existence again. The struggle against hopeless odds is something contributed to the glory of the values which cannot be utterly destroyed. Thus a fight which is worth making is worth making no matter what the odds. Things which are good and beautiful and true are so no matter what we do or fail to do; they are what they are in themselves. But the situation of their independence of actuality paradoxically lends a note of practicality to those actions of ours which are oriented toward them, in as much as they can be returned to existence wherever they have departed from it. Thus what we do for the values counts ideally where they fail to return but also practically since they always may return. There are lost struggles but there are no lost causes. This is the optimism inherent in the world at its worst. We look toward a world of the future which is always capable of being better than in the past it has ever been.

★

Index

Parthenon, 215
Pascal, 172
Pearl Harbour, 160
Peirce, Charles S., 16, 58, 80, 126, 147, 148, 229, 250, 257, 262, 277, 278, 304
people and ideas, 175
Percy, William Alexander, 37
permanence, 157, 160
personality, 193-195, 207, 281
perspective, 289
phenomenology, 287, 293
philosophers, their peculiarities, 241, 242
   popular idea of, 255, 256, 261
   making of, 257, 258
   their standing today, 262
   American, 276
   the men and their work, 299-302
philosophy, definitions of, 27, 232, 233, 236, 264 ; its aims, 237 ; its divisions, 237, 238 ; its influence, 245, 246, 274, 278 ; its history, 249, 270-272 ; temporal nature of, 250 ; need for study, 234, 245 ; unintelligibility of, 231, 242 ; and science, 142, 145, 235, 272 ; and religion, 236, 237 ; and philosophers, 230, 231, 240, 260 ; popular conception of, 256, 261 ; sources of its knowledge, 258 ; its standing today, 261, 262, 271, 272, 277 ; its inconclusiveness, 267, 287 ; return to Greek view of, 270 ; and action, 268 ; in America, 276, 277, 308, 319 ; its renaissance, 278-280
Philosophy, The Story of, 198
physics, 141-143, 248
pioneers, 50
   and pedants, 250-255
Planck, 6, 229
Plato, 8, 26, 107, 120, 247, 305
platonism, 65
Platonism and the Spiritual Life, 83
Plotinus, 65
Poe, E. A., 71

poetry, 8, 10, 41, 60, 61
poets in the world, 58-61
Pontchartrain, Lake, 188
popular books, 198-201
   lectures, 200, 202
   writers, 200-203
Positive Democracy, 150
post-war period, 68-70
Principia Mathematica, 245
Proust, 74
psychology, 248
publishers, 84, 85
Pygmalion error, the, 303

quantum theory, 6

racial differences, 38
Ramsey, Frank Plumpton, 257
realism, axiological, 149
Reid, Thomas, 278
relativity, 6, 249
religion and philosophy, 236, 237
revolt against science, 79
Révue de Metaphysique et de Morale, 283
riding, 138
Richmond, 48
Russell, Bertrand, 242, 245, 260, 278
Russian ballet, 54, 147
Ruelzheim, 4

sailing, 187-191
Santayana, 83, 94
Saviour in New York, A, 97
scepticism, 206
Scepticism and Animal Faith, 83
scholars, 251-255
science, and artists, 24, 303 ; as a source of knowledge, 141, 258 ; as today's religion, 235 ; history of, 248 ; and the Church, 249 ; and philosophy, 145, 272
Science and the Modern World, 199
Science and the Spirit of Man, 143, 144, 146
Sears Roebuck & Company, 119, 122, 123

GEORGE ALLEN & UNWIN LTD
London: 40 Museum Street, W.C.1
Cape Town: 58–60 Long Street
Sydney, N.S.W.: 55 York Street
Toronto: 91 Wellington Street West
Calcutta: 17 Central Ave., P.O. Dharamtala
Bombay: 15 Graham Road, Ballard Estate
Wellington, N.Z.: 8 Kings Crescent, Lower Hutt